THE KAYAKING BOOK

Revised Edition

THE KAYAKING BOOK

Revised Edition

Eric Evans

Former Olympic Kayaker

and

Jay Evans

Former U.S. Olympic Coach

A PLUME BOOK

PLUME
Published by the Penguin Group
Penguin Books USA Inc., 375 Hudson Street,
New York, New York 10014, U.S.A.
Penguin Books Ltd, 27 Wrights Lane,
London W8 5TZ, England
Penguin Books Australia Ltd, Ringwood,
Victoria, Australia
Penguin Books Canada Ltd, 10 Alcorn Avenue,
Toronto, Ontario, Canada M4V 3B2
Penguin Books (N.Z.) Ltd, 182–190 Wairau Road,
Auckland 10, New Zealand

Penguin Books Ltd, Registered Offices:
Harmondsworth, Middlesex, England

Published by Plume, an imprint of New American Library, a division of Penguin
Books USA Inc. This revised edition published in 1988 by The Stephen Greene
Press, Inc. It was published simultaneously in Canada and distributed by Viking
Penguin Inc.

First Plume Printing, April, 1993
10 9 8 7 6 5 4 3

Portions of this book were originally published in *Kayaking: The New Whitewater
Sport for Everybody* by Jay Evans and Robert R. Anderson. Copyright © Robert Jay
Evans and Robert R. Anderson, 1975.

 REGISTERED TRADEMARK—MARCA REGISTRADA

Library of Congress Cataloging-in-Publication Data
Evans, Jay, 1925–
  The kayaking book / by Jay Evans and Eric Evans.—Rev. ed.
    p.   cm.
  Bibliography: p. 239
  Includes index.
  ISBN 0-452-26941-5
  1. Canoes and canoeing. 2. White-water canoeing. I. Evans, Eric.
II. Title.
GV783.E938 1988
797.1'22—dc19   87-30254
                                                                      CIP

Printed in the United States of America

Set in Optima and Palatino by Maryland Composition. Produced by Unicorn
Production Services, Inc.

Contents

Acknowledgments

The following people helped me locate photos for this revised edition: Barb McKee, Stan Wass, Bob Woodward, Colleen Laffey, Ciro Pena, Slim Ray, Fletcher Anderson, and Dave Getchell. I could not have done the job without their help.

I am especially grateful for the help provided in the equipment section by Charlie Walbridge and in the sea kayaking section by Lee Moyer.

Introduction

THE LURE OF OPEN WATER

Water is a fascinating thing. Next to the air we breathe, it is probably the most significant thing on this planet. Certainly there is more of it around than any other material, for three-fourths of the earth's surface is covered with it, and over 80 percent of the human body consists of it. It is the universal fluid: we drink it plain, or we doctor it up by adding color, flavor, and gas to it. We use it to create power and light for growing food, washing our clothes, mining for rare metals, and transporting goods from here to there.

Of all the substances on earth, water has some of the most interesting characteristics. First of all, it is wet and slippery. It slithers around unless penned up, and it works tirelessly to escape its bonds so it can rush downhill until it eventually joins the ocean. If dammed up, it will quietly bide its time and then descend as rain somewhere else on earth in its relentless journey to the sea.

Fresh water is quite heavy, weighing about 62 pounds per cubic foot. This means it can create a lot of force. The kayaker discovers this when he tries to dislodge his boat from a rock in the rapids: water can exert 8 to 10 tons of force against a boat hung up in a fast-moving current.

Water also has personality. It appears alive. It can sparkle; it can look ominous. Its gentle sound can lull you to sleep, its boisterousness can tingle your nerves, or its forbidding roar can fill your heart with apprehension.

Water is incredibly versatile. As a liquid, it is most common, but as a solid, it can cool you off on a hot day or store itself up for the spring runoff. As a crystal, it gives birth to the world of skiing, tobogganing, snowshoeing, and snowmobiling. As a solid, it can be skated upon.

Water as a liquid is dynamic. It can form the tiniest ripple from a trout nibbling on the surface of a quiet pond, or it can become a 50-foot tidal wave roaring across the wide expanse of the Pacific Ocean.

One of the greatest moments in the history of mankind must have been when man first discovered that he could move in water either by swimming himself or by riding on a log. Together with the invention of the wheel and the uses of fire and metal, man's ability to propel himself in water marked a major breakthrough in the development of civilization. Down through history, no craft propelled man as simply and effectively as the Eskimo kayak. It was the quintessential utilitarian watercraft: light, strong, and nimbly versatile.

But as man mastered water, he also learned to play in it; the utilitarian yielded part of its domain to the aesthetic. And it didn't take long to realize that the boat so perfectly suited for work was ideal for play. More personal than other craft, the kayak is an extension of one's body; kayakers feel a part of the water they are exploring. No other boat acts as such a subtle, thin conduit between man and water.

There are only two ingredients necessary to enjoy kayaking: an ability to swim reasonably well with confidence, and an appreciation of and fondness for water in all its various modes and moods. If you enjoy the smell and touch of water, are fascinated by the power of moving current in a river or ocean, are calmed by the placid feeling of a quiet pond, or are thrilled at the sight of rapids, then perhaps kayaking is for you.

In general, people of all ages enjoy kayaking. Children just barely big enough to see over the cockpit and strong enough to lift a paddle have been seen kayaking merrily around millponds and gentle streams. The Eskimos began to teach their children the Eskimo roll as soon as the children had reached the age of 12.

Experience has shown that youngsters of 8 and 9 often have a remarkable sense of balance and movement and can handle themselves smartly in the water. Of course the fact that these little folk probably weigh only 60 pounds or less certainly gives them an advantage, for with so little weight in the boat, it rests as lightly on the water as a leaf and seems able to turn at a mere suggestion.

During the later adolescent years and in the twenties, those who enjoy kayaking will often wish to expand their horizons and will turn more serious about the sport. They will work to hone their skills and train their bodies in order to paddle wilderness waterways with safety. Many schools, colleges, and youth groups are embracing kayaking as an ideal environmental sport. Still others will be drawn to the rewards of competitive kayaking, which takes many forms on flat and moving water.

Perhaps the golden years of kayaking extend from 30 to 60. The lure of distant waterways remains strong, but many find that, ironically, there are just as many opportunities for exploration and fun close to home. Maturity also brings a greater appreciation for the actual act of paddling itself. The intrinsic movements of kayaking become less a means to an end or destination than ends in themselves.

Older people should not shy away from kayaking either. Steering your own little craft around the coves or inlets of a wilderness or nearby pond, in search of fish or wildfowl or even an elusive view of a sunset, can be a rewarding experience. If, gliding along silently, you round a bend and suddenly come upon a deer—or better yet, a moose or an elk—the day will long be remembered.

A well-known set of rapids that has given you many good times in past years will always welcome you again as a long-lost friend. And what can be more satisfying than introducing a young paddler for the first time to one of your favorite whitewater runs?

As therapy kayaking is unmatched in its ability to wash away the pressures of a too highly charged modern society. A weekend trip, or even a Sunday afternoon paddle, can rejuvenate your spirits for a taxing week ahead.

Thoreau was right: rivers are a constant lure to the adventurous instinct in mankind. If Henry were alive today, he would pursue that lure with the modern recreational kayak.

PART I.
BOATS, EQUIPMENT, AND SAFETY

1. Kayaks

From Sealskin to Plastics

The Eskimos

Over the centuries, the earliest known inhabitants of the Arctic regions of North America developed a remarkable craft for traveling over icy bays, inlets, and even open ocean. These light and fast-moving skin boats were designed primarily for hunting and fishing. Called "kayaks" by the Eskimos, they were masterpieces of primitive engineering. Made of driftwood and the skins and sinews of animals, the ancient Eskimo kayak was a remarkably resilient and durable craft, both light to handle and swift in the water.

There were no official dimensions—it depended upon the materials available—but many were about 18 feet long and less than 2 feet wide. Sharply pointed at each end and streamlined, they were not only easy to paddle but also quite seaworthy even in the wildest water. Sealskin was stretched tightly over a frame made of bone and driftwood carved to fit. Seal sinew lashed the frame together. The deck, particularly in the stern, was often quite flat to accommodate an inflated bladder and line attached to a hunting spear. The bow deck sometimes held a spare hunting tool or paddle.

Eskimos sat in their kayaks, rather than kneeling, in a small cockpit built into the midpoint of the deck. An Eskimo could sit in this cockpit, chaise longue style, and fasten his waterproof parka around the rim of the cockpit to make his craft watertight even when the largest of waves broke over him.

Since rarely could Eskimos find driftwood wide enough to provide efficient paddle blades, many of their paddle blades were less than half as wide as the ones used today. Nevertheless they used both single- and double-bladed paddles of various lengths.

1

Two Eskimos in a skin kayak were photographed near Nunivak Island, Alaska, in the early 1900s. The hole in the bow is a built-in grabloop. Note the unusual single-bladed paddle. Most tribes used double-bladed paddles with the blades in the same plane, unlike modern paddles with blades set at right angles. (U.S. National Museum)

Aside from the remarkable engineering feat of the kayak design itself, the Eskimos also provided today's kayaker with other inspirational legacies:

1. *Grabloops.* Carrying kayaks overland or fastening them down in a storm could be tricky, so a waterproof hole was made near the tip of the bow (and sometimes at the stern as well) to provide a place to grab the kayak or tie it to a tent stake, post, or rock. Most modern kayaks are made with a short line looped through the bow and stern that serves the same purpose. We call them grabloops.

2. *The Eskimo Roll.* Since the Eskimos designed their kayaks for speed, the craft had to be quite narrow. A slender boat is unstable and is in danger of capsizing. A tip into the freezing waters of the Arctic can be lethal. The Eskimos cleverly developed a maneuver employing the paddle to bring a capsized kayak back into an upright position again without getting out of the boat. Since their parkas fitted tightly around the cockpit, by using their paddles effectively, they could roll back up without taking in water. This remarkable centuries-old technique has been handed down through the years and is now known as the Eskimo roll. It is considered a basic self-rescue technique for all people wishing to learn the art of kayaking. It will be covered in Chapter 6.

3. *Light-Materials Technology.* The Eskimos also set a standard for lightness and flexibility that today's science has been hard-pressed to match.

Dried sealskins, sinew, and driftwood are very light materials. Many Eskimo kayaks weighed less than 26 pounds. Even with modern technology in plastics and chemistry, only highly specialized racing kayaks weigh less than this.

Kayaking as a Sport

As early as the sixteenth century, English explorers in the northern seas saw Eskimos using kayaks to travel and hunt on water. In 1865 Londoner John MacGregor built the famous *Rob Roy* kayak and toured many of Europe's rivers in it. Later he founded the Royal Canoe Club of Great Britain. (The English refer to kayaks as "canoes.") The club held kayak races on flatwater in 1867. Annual competitions were held beginning in 1874, and by 1885 kayak races were held on the Continent.

Before World War I, people in southern Germany looked longingly at the fast streams flooding down the mountain slopes of the Alps. The traditional open canoe, although known in Europe, was simply not maneuverable enough for safe navigation in whitewater, and without a deck cover, it tended to fill with water from the splashing waves. The Eskimo kayak, though far more maneuverable and with a covered cockpit, also presented a problem. Its length made it awkward to transport from place to place—especially by train, the way many Europeans traveled in those days.

The ingenious Germans devised a collapsible kayak, one that would fold and could be carried like two large suitcases. One package contained the folded wooden frame, the other a rubberized fabric outer skin. Called a *Faltboot,* it could be quickly assembled on the river bank by inserting the erected wooden frame into the fabric. After a day's boating, the *Faltboot* was easily disassembled and packed away for the trip home. Thus the collapsible kayak became the first major technological breakthrough since those of the Eskimos, and it ushered in new possibilities of adventure and sport.

Other refinements were also taking place. Those interested in racing kayaks in flatwater soon discovered that while the old Eskimo design was fast, by making a few subtle changes here and there, the kayak could be made to go even faster. To aid in turning such boats, rudders were affixed to the stern and controlled by wires connected to pedals in the cockpit. It is generally believed that Hans Edi Pawlata in Vienna made popular the so-called Eskimo roll to right a capsized kayak in 1927. Much of his technique, of course, was borrowed from the Eskimos.

Racing down the rapids from a starting point to a finish line became popular as early as the 1920s in Europe. It was called *Wildwasser* or wildwater racing. In 1936 the Summer Olympic Games were held in Germany, and flatwater kayak racing became an Olympic event.

In the early 1940s, a National Championship wildwater race was held on a 6-mile stretch of the remote Rapid River on the border between New Hampshire and Maine. On the Rhone River in Geneva, Switzerland, the first World Championships in whitewater slalom were held in 1949. Over 80 competitors from seven nations came to test their skills on a 12-gate course located where the Rhone flows through the heart of the city. Ten years later, the first World Championships in wildwater were held on the Vesere River in France. In the United States, the first slalom sponsored by the American Canoe Association was held on Delaware's Brandywine River in 1952. In the early 1950s, more races were conducted on some of the fine whitewater streams in Colorado. During these years, touring and exploring rivers and lakes by kayak continued to grow in popularity.

In the past decade, sea touring by kayak has rekindled an interest in the Eskimos and their oceangoing craft. In a sense, then, we have come full circle.

The Advent of Plastic

In the 1950s, kayaking took another major technological leap forward. Just as foldboats were an advance over the ancient skin-and-driftwood boats, plastic emerged as an exciting new material that could be adapted to the construction of kayaks. Fiberglass-reinforced resins made it possible to construct a kayak without interior framing for the first time. These boats were light, flexible, and durable, requiring little upkeep. To this day, the finest in lightweight, high-strength kayaks for whitewater racing are made from this material. In addition this new material allowed damage to be easily and permanently repaired on the riverside with only the simplest of tools. In 1960 Jay bought what is believed to be the first all-fiberglass kayak sold in the United States, by the Hans Klepper Corporation, but it wasn't until a few years later that the amazing "fixability" of this new material was brought home graphically to us. In 1966, on the Rapid River in Maine, Eric's fiberglass kayak was split completely in two. After an afternoon of resin, cloth, and a warm sun, the kayak was repaired and Eric was paddling that early evening.

Fiberglass (or, as the English prefer, "glass-fiber") created a minor revolution in kayak building. It increased the availability of inexpensive kayaks as well as their ability to take unusual punishment. The new, easy-to-work material encouraged backyard design experimentation. This, in turn, promoted the development of new techniques and the running of rivers formerly considered unrunnable. Kayaks became more responsive to the paddler's touch, and fierce rapids no longer restricted the boater who now knew that he had a very durable craft under him.

Fiberglass construction is still preferred for touring and racing kayaks, but the average rock-bashing river runner needed something tougher. In the early 1970s, roto-molding revolutionized kayak construction. Although heavier than fiberglass, roto-molded polyethylene is an incredibly tough and durable material. Many of the new, difficult whitewater runs, which are a breeze in a roto-molded plastic kayak, would destroy a fiberglass boat.

The Modern Kayak

Even in its various forms, the modern kayak is still an extremely simple and functional craft. It consists of a deck and a hull and a seating arrangement for one or more paddlers. Kayaks range in length from the short junior models or those used for surfing or kayak polo—between 7 and 11 feet long—to racing kayaks and oceangoing craft that may be 15 feet or more in length. (In metric the range is from about 2 to 4½ meters.) They are all about 2 feet (61 centimeters) wide, and their height amidships is rarely more than 18 inches (45 centimeters). Some kayaks weighing only 10 pounds have been built, although most modern kayaks tip the scales at 30 to 40 pounds (or from 11 to 15 kilograms).

Let's take a look at each of the major parts of a modern kayak.

The Hull

The subtle shape of the hull is the major factor in determining how the kayak performs in water. Long, narrow, sleek hulls are fast, but less maneuverable. Those that are wider and flatter provide better turning capacity but are not as fast in the water. Slalom racing kayaks are flatter, wildwater racing kayaks narrower; cruising kayaks strike a happy medium between the two extremes.

The Deck

A kayak's covered deck has two basic purposes: to help keep water out of the craft and to define the place for the paddler to sit. Decks are customarily less ruggedly built than hulls because they are less likely to come in contact with the river bottom.

The Cockpit

This is where the paddler sits (in the middle of the boat) and controls the craft. It consists of the seat itself, a *coaming* (the convex lip around the outside of the cockpit), and part of the bracing system that supports the paddler's hips and back. The seat usually rests not more than an inch or so above the bottom of the hull, and attached to the seat are adjustable hip pads and backbraces that provide a comfortable and snug fit. These braces permit the paddler to feel as if he were wearing the kayak, not just sitting in it. Seats in some kayaks can be adjusted forward

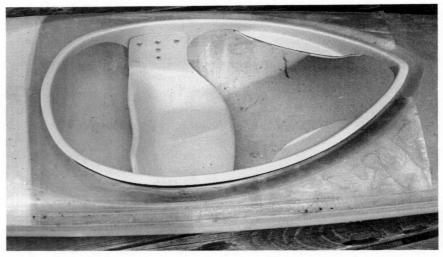

A kayak cockpit where the seat and braces are made of the same material as the hull and deck. (Eric Evans)

A cockpit where the seat is made of foam. (Eric Evans)

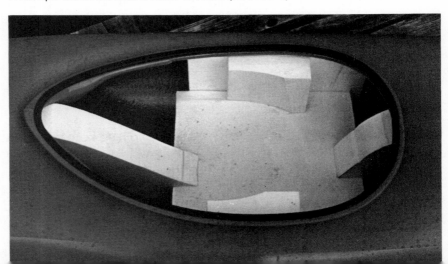

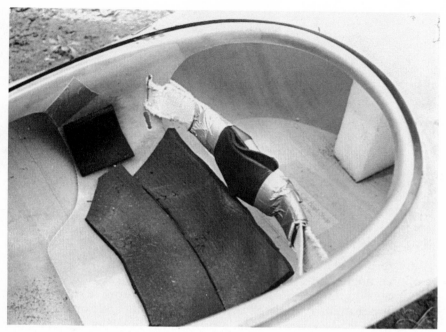

A backstrap and padding add comfort and support. (Eric Evans)

and back to compensate for changing gear loads and wind and water conditions. Hipbraces prevent the paddler from sliding around in the seat. The backbrace—usually an adjustable strap across the back of the seat—provides a firm support for the lower spine.

The coaming acts as a ledge under which a spray cover (also called a spray skirt) is fitted. The spray cover prevents water from entering the kayak.

Footbraces

Most kayaks have adjustable footbraces attached to the inside wall of the hull forward of the cockpit. With the backbrace and thigh braces, the paddler, by pressing his feet firmly against the footbraces, gains the excellent longitudinal support essential to good paddling. Footbraces should be adjustable to accommodate paddlers of varying heights.

The complete bracing system of a kayak includes footbraces, kneebraces, and hip-braces. (Old Town Canoe Company)

Knee/Thigh Braces

Flatwater racing kayaks do not normally need kneebraces, since lateral motion is not required to propel the boat forward. But sea touring, white-water, surfing, and polo kayaks should have a firm, comfortable set of kneebraces. Situated directly under the coaming and sometimes part of the underdeck, kneebraces help provide the marvelous stability to a kayak in rough water or to one that needs to be turned quickly.

Grabloops

Modern kayaks are designed with some means of grabbing or tying them at the bow and stern. Not many boats use the old Eskimo-type hole; instead a line is looped through and attached to the end of the kayak. Such a grabloop offers an essential grip for retrieving a kayak in the water, for lifting a kayak, or for fastening it to the top of a car.

Types of Kayaks

From a distance, most kayaks simply look like long plastic tubes with a hole in the middle for a paddler. Yet, closer inspection shows, even subtle differences in contours make a big difference, not only in handling characteristics but also in how the boats can be used.

There are many basic types of kayaks today to choose from. In a real sense, kayaking—like many other sports—has become specialized. No longer can a paddler take a comfortable cruise on a river on Saturday and then, on Sunday, win a slalom race using the same boat.

The most common form of kayak in use today is the recreational white-water boat. It is a single-seater with reasonably high volume. It is fairly fast, maneuverable, and comfortable. The serious slalom racer, however, must use an extremely low volume and highly maneuverable craft. A wildwater or marathon racer needs a superfast model, maneuverability not being quite so important. This type of boat, of course, tends to be quite tippy—a characteristic not suitable for the weekend tripper.

Today's outdoor adventurer has a wealth of types from which to choose. Specialized recreational kayaks have evolved for riding the ocean's surf, for playing kayak polo, and for long-distance paddling at sea. For flatwater racing, single-, double-, and four-seater kayaks are available. Demand still exists for folding boats and for those that are partly or totally inflatable and for others to which a modest sail can be attached.

The Recreational Whitewater Kayak

Quite often a beginner will be attracted to a stable single-seater that is easy to handle. Usually it's a kayak designed along the lines of the slalom kayaks of the sixties and early seventies. It will have enough interior room for comfort and to store a limited amount of duffel. Manufacturers refer to these as "general purpose" or "touring" boats. These are excellent craft and are suitable for a modest weekend trip on a river; they can also be used if you wish to try your luck in an informal wildwater race. But don't expect to take first place using this kind of kayak—it is not designed for it. Older, secondhand slalom models can also be perfectly suitable for the beginner, and they sometimes can be purchased quite inexpensively. These recreational whitewater kayaks are good starter boats for beginners.

Recreational *short boats* are also popular. These kayaks are about a foot (31 centimeters) shorter and a little wider than the approved slalom boat,

The recreational whitewater kayak.

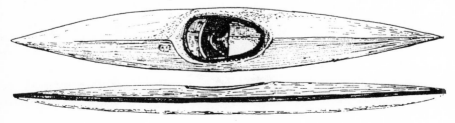

whose dimensions are governed by international racing rules. Originally they were simply reconditioned slalom boats with the ends chopped off and recapped. Now they are built a little wider at the cockpit to provide greater stability and maintain adequate volume. They are extremely maneuverable in whitewater and remarkably stable. The short boat is an ideal craft for those not interested in slalom racing or long expeditions but who prefer short whitewater trips and playing in the rapids.

Some manufacturers build junior kayaks for young children. The craft is similar to a slalom kayak except it is likely to be as much as 2 feet (61 centimeters) shorter and have good volume and stability. For young people weighing less than 110 pounds (41 kilograms), these smaller kayaks are easier to manage. Children big enough to hold and control a double-bladed paddle will enjoy such a boat, but they must be very competent swimmers and learn all the basic safety techniques for handling a kayak.

The Slalom Kayak

These are kayaks that are a bit more streamlined and maneuverable. To meet international racing regulations, they must be not less than 13 feet 2 inches (4 meters) in length or narrower than 23¾ inches (60 centimeters). A slalom racing kayak is extremely light, some weighing less than 25 pounds (9.3 kilograms). A pronounced upward-sweeping curvature of the hull at either end provides great maneuverability. The bottom section of the hull is quite broad and flat. Recent trends dictate that the boat be low volume—that is, with little room to spare between deck and hull, and with sharp sides. (In contrast, touring kayaks have high volume, meaning greater fullness throughout their length with more rounded sides and less of the slalom kayak's pumpkin-seed appearance.) What this low volume means is that paddlers literally have to "shoehorn" themselves into these kayaks, and the resultant wedging is uncomfortable for any length of time. For large, tall paddlers with big

The low-volume slalom kayak.

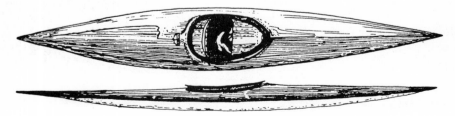

Austria's Norbert Sattler races his low-volume slalom kayak on the Nantahala River in North Carolina. (Slim Ray)

feet, the modern slalom kayak is a cramped nightmare. Slalom kayaks have seats and braces that fit very snugly so the paddler can maintain full control of the boat at all times.

The Wildwater Kayak

According to international rules, a kayak designed for racing in wild-water must be no more than 14 feet 8 inches (4.5 meters) long and at least 23¾ inches (60 centimeters) wide. Speed is essential here, ma-neuverability secondary. The long, narrow, V-shaped hull cleaves the water cleanly but sacrifices some stability and turning ability. The hull does not turn up much at either end, just enough to slice through the waves and slide over submerged rocks. The bow and stern are extremely sharp, and the deck is designed to part the waves. Its widest point is behind the cockpit. This makes the wedge-shaped hull on either side and in front of the paddler a straight line, facilitating a more powerful and efficient forward stroke.

Like a speedboat or a racing car, the rakish wildwater kayak looks fast. When efficiently paddled, it is by far the swiftest boat in the rapids.

Hank Thorburn's wildwater kayak knifes through the waves on the Millers River in Massachusetts. (Eric Evans)

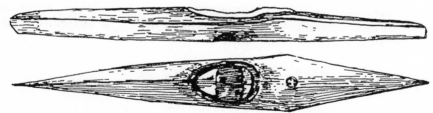

The wildwater kayak.

The Touring Kayak

These kayaks are most popular on lakes and quiet rivers—wherever a good compromise between straight-ahead speed, stability, and gear carrying is demanded. They do not turn as well as a recreational whitewater boat, nor are they as fast as wildwater racing craft or many sea touring kayaks. But for long-distance quiet-water tours, these touring kayaks with their larger cockpits are a comfortable, efficient means of putting miles under your hull while catching the scenery.

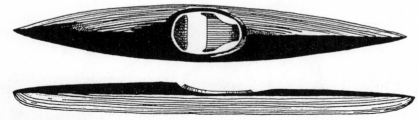

The touring kayak.

The Flatwater and Marathon Racing Kayaks

Flatwater racing has been an Olympic sport since 1936. It is a highly specialized, competitive activity requiring great technique, bursts of power, and endurance. The types of craft include a single-seat kayak (K-1), a two-seater (K-2), and a four-seater (K-4). All flatwater racing kayaks are remarkably sleek and narrow, requiring precision paddling especially in the two- and four-paddler boats. Some flatwater racing kayaks are made of fiberglass, others of molded plywood. They have steering rudders. Sometimes they do not have spray covers; kneebraces similar to those in whitewater kayaks are not needed.

Marathon racing in kayaks, after years of popularity in Europe and England, is now catching on in the United States, where marathon racing in canoes has long been a well-established sport. Marathon racing kayaks are either speedier versions of wildwater racing kayaks with a rudder or outright flatwater racing kayaks.

The Folding Kayak

The fiberglass revolution in kayak construction did not spell the doom of *das Faltboot* (folding kayak). This unique portable craft that can be stored in two bags still appeals. Its knockdown feature can be a distinct advantage, since it permits the apartment dweller the pleasure of owning a boat without having to find major storage space. Once at the river,

Two flatwater touring kayakers let the wind work for them. (Wayne Marsula)

its tubular framework is erected, fitted into a rubberized canvas skin, and held rigid with a snap-lock fitting.

Folding kayaks come in many models and sizes. Their chief use, however, is for flatwater cruising and camping. They tend to be larger, more spacious, and quite stable. Moderate whitewater streams can be run in folding kayaks. These boats find favor with family groups. Often a sail can be attached complete with a mast, rudder, and leeboards; small outboard motors have also been attached to folding kayaks. The cockpits in folding kayaks are generous in size and often have backrests. Spray covers are not generally used except in rough water.

The Touring K-2

Two-person kayaks are manufactured primarily for the noncompetitive touring market; they are not used for racing. One paddler sits directly behind the other. In some K-2s, one large open cockpit suffices for both people. In other K-2s, separate cockpits are provided. Although positioned close to each other toward the center of the boat, the cockpits allow ample legroom between paddlers.

The K-2 is used pimarily for touring and camping. The Scandinavians design two-seater kayaks for extensive travel along the seacoast and fjords.

Kayaks for Surfing

Kayaks built for surfing in the ocean, often called *wave skis*, may be the sportiest boats of all. They are short (usually around 10 feet or 3 meters long), with a very flat hull and a broad, upturned bow shaped like a duck's bill. The cockpit is located a little behind the midpoint and contains the customary bracing of a slalom kayak. More extreme design eliminates the deck entirely. The paddler sits in a customized shallow

The touring K-2.

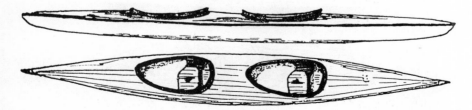

seat with two indented places forward for his feet. This deckless kayak has a hull thick enough to provide for sufficient flotation, and the top of the hull is shaped so that it does not ship much water.

Slalom kayaks have been used for surfing, but their pointed noses cause the boats to dive forward into the sand lying just under the breaking surf. Wildwater kayaks are unfit for surfing; they knife through the waves rather than riding over them.

If surfing appeals to you, it is better to stay with the craft that has been so ingeniously designed for it. Advantages of a surf kayak over a surfboard include the fact that you can enjoy surfing from a comfortable chaise longue position rather than balancing precariously on a slippery board. Also, with the aid of the double-bladed paddle, you can turn your craft around, head back out, and get in many more runs in an afternoon. (More about surfing kayaks and wave skis can be found in Chapter 12.)

The Bat Boat for Kayak Polo

Kayaks suited for playing polo are hard to find. Most of them are made in England. If you take a slalom boat with its unusually good maneuverability, chop the bow and stern back about a foot (31 centimeters) or so, and patch the holes with rounded tips, you'll have a perfectly adequate "bat boat." Kayak polo, in which players use their paddles as mallets to hit a water-polo ball toward the opponent's goal, is a popular sport in indoor swimming pools during the cold winter months when the rivers and lakes are frozen.

The sharp point of most kayaks precludes their use in pools for kayak polo: they might damage the side of the pool or an opponent's boat. Thus the distinguishing feature of the bat boat is the blunted bow and stern. Like slalom kayaks, bat boats need a good seat and firm braces to facilitate quick maneuvering.

The bat boat.

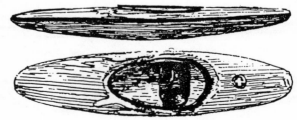

The Sea Touring Kayak

It may be hard to believe, but in the 1950s, a German physician paddled alone in a kayak across the entire Atlantic Ocean. In 1977 kayaks rounded dreaded Cape Horn at the southern tip of South America. Many more people in the past few years have enjoyed just poking around the coastline on both coasts.

Single-seat kayaks for ocean travel are truly the Rolls-Royces of boating design. Regal and stylish, their long, graceful bows and sterns allow them to ride smoothly over the largest ocean swells.

Since maneuverability is of secondary importance, oceangoing kayaks tend to be quite long—some are 16 to 19 feet (about 5 to 5¾ meters) in length. In addition to the customary braces, many models have waterproof hatches in the bow and stern decks to make it easy to get at stored gear. Common accessories include a compass and light, a sliding seat, a pump, a horn or whistle, a rudder, and deck fixtures to hold your paddle or to store a spare paddle. (Chapter 11 provides further information on these craft.)

The sea kayak.

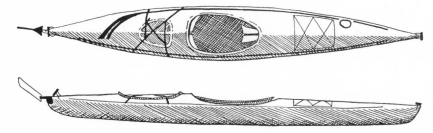

Sea kayakers nearing shore. (Stan Wass)

The inflatable kayak.

The Inflatable Kayak

A leading manufacturer of airships (dirigibles) in the late 1890s created the first modern inflatable boat in 1936. Inflatable kayaks now come in one- and two-person models. The single-seaters are usually a little longer than a slalom kayak, while the two-seaters can be as long as 17 feet (nearly 5¼ meters). These boats (often referred to as "duckies," short for "rubber ducks") are extremely popular for running mild whitewater. They are maneuverable, stable, and extremely forgiving for beginners. Self-bailing models used by western outfitters allow very difficult drops to be run without swamping.

The Kayakamaran and Kayacht

The kayak version of the traditional two-hulled catamaran, the kayakamaran consists of two large-volume touring-class kayaks fastened together side by side complete with a rudder assembly, a 17-foot (5¼-meter) mast, a 59-square-foot (5½-square-meter) mainsail, and a 31-square-foot (nearly a 3-square-meter) jib. It seats two people easily and could carry four in a pinch. The kayacht is simply a single-hull version of the kayakamaran with a lateen sail, seating one person only.

Kayakamarans and kayachts are available commercially, either in kit form or already assembled. They can be transported on car tops and are ideal for lake cruising, coastal marshes, and bays, as well as for the ocean itself.

Building Your Own Kayak

(The following section is not meant to provide you with detailed, step-by-step instructions on how to fabricate your own kayak. Rather it purports simply to give you a general picture of how it can be done. As

The kayakamaran.
(Kayakamaran)

this book goes to press, the most authoritative book available on the subject is Charlie Walbridge's *Boat Builder's Manual*, which gives comprehensive treatment of all phases of kayak building and repair.)

Three common ways suggest themselves to most people when they think of building their own kayaks. The easiest is to put together a kit. The kit, of course, is much cheaper than a finished boat. It usually consists of a deck, hull, seat, and some kind of bracing materials. It's your job to seam the hull and the deck together, install the seat, and fit the braces to your specifications. If you're a handy person, experienced in handling fiberglass and resin, and follow the manufacturer's instructions, you can realize substantial savings. For those inexperienced in fiberglass work, there are a few manufacturers who sell wood-and-canvas kits.

The second—and less popular—method for building a kayak is to design one of your own using wood or aluminum and rubberized or waterproof cloth construction. Here, of course, the sky's the limit in creative design. The technique is similar (on a much larger scale) to constructing a model airplane.

By far the most popular method of building a kayak is to do it by hand, using a mold and fiberglass. But first, three important points must be stressed:

1. *Ethics.* Home builders rarely have the time or talent to build a mold from scratch. The temptation is to pull a mold from a commercially manufactured boat. This is not only morally wrong, but it is illegal and can involve patent violations. Before such a mold is made, you must have the written permission of the manufacturer—for your protection.

2. *Health.* Some people are allergic to fiberglass. The inhalation of the fumes of many chemicals is harmful, and skin contact with them can be irritating. **The toxic effects of fiberglass and resin are cumulative.** Therefore, if you're indoors, it is absolutely essential to provide excellent ventilation at all times. The use of face masks and gloves is also highly recommended.

3. *Partnership.* Although working with fiberglass is very easy and safe once you get the hang of it, the very best way to learn is to make friends with someone who has done it before. Get a partner. It is much better when two people work simultaneously on a boat, anyway. The work goes more smoothly, and there are two more hands available when needed. One of the best ways to find a partner is to join a kayak or canoe club. And, if possible, serve an apprenticeship by helping an experienced paddler build his kayak before starting your own.

Boat Materials

Boat designers (and everybody else) want a material that's strong, has high impact resistance, and is somewhat flexible, yet durable. It must be light, easy to form and repair, and still be inexpensive. Sound like a tall order? True, but in space-age plastics, such materials are available. Applied to the construction of kayaks, the resiliency and versatility of these materials have encouraged design innovations that have brought about many new and exciting paddling techniques.

The chemistry of these new materials is highly complex. But, like electricity, we don't have to understand it perfectly to harness it to our needs. There are only three main components: resin, fiberglass cloth, and a catalytic agent or hardener to bond the cloth and the resin together. When all three components are mixed in proper ratio, a chemical process takes place that cannot be reversed. The new product formed in the desired shape is ready for use.

A well-ventilated boat shed and the materials for building a kayak: rolls of fiberglass cloth, a barrel of resin lying on its side, a hipbrace and seat/coaming mold on the wall, and molds for the hull and deck. (Robert F. George)

Types of Cloth

Fiberglass cloth comes in a variety of weights and weaves. Quite common for kayaks are 6-ounce and 10-ounce (per square yard) cloth woven into basket-weave designs. Chopped-strand mat (without a weave) comes in a variety of weights and thicknesses and is used mostly as stiffening reinforcement, since it lacks the flexibility of woven fiberglass cloth. If you wish to get exotic, you can purchase teakwood-print cloth to make your kayak look like a teakwood boat.

Nylon, aramid, polypropylene, S Glass and Kevlar fabrics resist tearing yet are extremely light, flexible, and durable. (Some are used in making bulletproof vests.) Often a combination of these fabrics molded together will provide the ideal material for your kayak. Improvements and new designs in fabrics continue to be made.

Types of Resin

The liquid medium in fiberglass kayak construction varies in texture from the color and viscosity (but not the aroma) of molasses to a very heavy jellylike substance. When chemically bonded, resins can be either soft and flexible or hard and brittle according to need. Some chemical firms blend these characteristics to achieve the balance they wish.

Two common kinds of resin used in the construction of kayaks are epoxy and polyester. Epoxy resin is stronger than polyester but is also more difficult to handle, more toxic, and much more expensive. Polyester is quite easy to handle and is generally suitable for most kayak construction. Polyester resin is also toxic, but less so than epoxy. Any kind of resin work should be done in a well-ventilated area.

Other plastics are used in making boats with great success, but they require special techniques and special equipment. For the most part, these plastics are used by commercial manufacturers.

Interior Structural Support

Most kayaks are built to be light, but in so doing, there's the danger of building a craft whose deck or hull is so flimsy that it might be dented by heavy waves. There are several ingenious ways to counteract this and still have a lightweight kayak. One is to stuff a 3-foot section of 2-inch wide Ethafoam on edge into the bow and stern cavities of a kayak. (Styrofoam can also be used, but it is less desirable because it tends to chip away.) The Ethafoam fitted in vertically will help preserve the shape of the kayak in the roughest of water, prevent the hull or deck from denting, and help provide flotation at the same time.

Other means of stiffening the hull and deck include the bonding of inverted T-shaped pieces of fiberglass mat to the inside of the hull and deck, and bonding wooden or plastic rods covered with fiberglass tape where needed.

The Process Itself

Having secured a mold legally and properly, you then should decide what kind of a *lay-up* you wish. Here's where your imagination comes into the picture, and a wide variety of options are available. Choose whatever combination of cloths you think will do the trick (6- or 10-ounce cloth and mat, for example) and cut the material roughly to the dimensions of your hull and deck. Common lay-ups include three layers

Werner Furrer adds the final touches to his sea kayak plug. Later a mold will be taken from the plug. (Bart Jackson)

of fabric on the hull and two for the deck with reinforcements at bow, stern, and around the cockpit.

Next, prepare your mold with great care. It should be smooth with no traces of an earlier boat left. A mold release wax should be applied generously and carefully to the mold. Check to see that every square inch of the mold is covered by the release material. The smallest un-covered part will adhere to your boat, making its extraction from the mold difficult, with serious damage to the mold.

The layers of cloth are then placed in the mold and saturated with activated resin using paint brushes, paint rollers, and squeegees. Too much resin will make the kayak heavy and brittle. Too little resin will prevent proper bonding between the cloth and the resin, creating tiny pinholes that reduce strength and allow water to enter the boat.

As the cloth cures, the waste around the edges is trimmed off. The hull and deck molds are clamped together, and a seam of saturated fiberglass cloth is pressed out along the interior seams. Once everything is cured and the mold removed, added strength can be created by placing an outside seam where the hull and deck join along the gunwale.

The seat and coaming unit, which was probably molded while you were waiting for the hull and deck to cure, can now be attached to the deck and the foot- and kneebraces installed to fit as you like.

Grabloops are drawn through a hole near the deck ends and then tightly wrapped to prevent seepage. A cup of activated resin is poured down to the point while the kayak is tipped up to a vertical position.

After everything has cured, you should examine your kayak for pinholes, sand all the rough edges, and test both the deck and hull to see if you need any structural support. Finally, be sure to place flotation bags at either end of your kayak before you try it in the water.

Repairs

One of the attractive features of fiberglass kayak construction is that a fiberglass kayak is so easy to repair. Should a minor break occur in the hull or deck, it can be quickly and easily corrected—often from inside the kayak where it won't even show. For a more serious fracture, you may wish to consider putting patches both on the inside and on the outside of the boat.

The damaged area must be perfectly dry and well sanded. Usually two or more layers of cloth are used for a patch. Saturate the cloth and brush it on firmly over the affected area. If the crack goes all the way through, be sure to tape the back side to prevent the resin from draining through. After a couple of layers have been applied, thoroughly sand the cured patch for a smooth finish.

Having built a fiberglass kayak, you'll probably have cloth, resin, and activator left over. Bundle them up and you'll have a handy emergency repair kit for the future. Another handy tip: carry a roll of gray duct tape (available at any hardware store) with you on boating trips.

Purchasing a Kayak

Most kayakers today do not build their own boats. The time, money, and mess involved just aren't worth it for most people when you consider that fiberglass kayak manufacturers can do a much better job and that kayaks made of roto-molded polyethylene have a large share of the market. The latter are made in expensive, sophisticated machines that can't be duplicated by the home builder.

Although acquiring a kayak is not one of the major investments in a person's life, it still involves a commitment of approximately $300 to $800. So it's important to consider carefully what your needs might be. Here are a few tips.

An Inventory of Your Needs

If you're a beginner, you'll want a stable boat. If you plan to use your kayak for traveling distances on inland lakes and rivers, you'll want one that steers easily and has good speed. If you're thinking about overnight trips, you should look at kayaks that have a large volume so you can store your gear. Do you plan to paddle singly, or do you prefer a partner in the boat with you? Will more than one person in your family be using the craft, and each for different purposes? Spend some time asking yourself just what you might want to use your kayak for.

Kayaks, if cared for, can last a long time. But don't neglect to consider the trade-in value before you purchase one. There are many facets to the sport; once you've mastered lake cruising, for example, you may wish to sell your boat and buy a sea touring model or a surf kayak. A boat in good condition is a marketable asset and obviously will sell better than an old clunker.

Basic Boat Characteristics

Generally speaking, the most common and popular type of boat is loosely called the recreational whitewater kayak. It is relatively short, very stable, yet extremely maneuverable. Most beginners in the sport naturally gravitate toward this type of kayak.

In a sense, the recreational whitewater craft stands in the middle of the kayak spectrum. To the right of it, you find boats designed strictly for cruising and sea touring. They will be longer, have a little more volume for storage, and not be as maneuverable as the recreational whitewater types. Further to the right, you'll find the sleek, needle-nosed wildwater racing kayaks—fast, tippy, and hard to turn. At the extreme, you'll find the flatwater and marathon racing kayaks. These are fast as greased lightning, and unstable unless you are accustomed to them. They have no need for turning ability.

Toward the left of the spectrum from the recreational whitewater boat, you will find the forefront of slalom racing design. These are very low volume, extremely maneuverable, and often not very comfortable to sit in. Still further to the left, you'll find some specialty boats designed specifically for surfing, squirt boating, or kayak polo. Each is maneuverable in the extreme—not fast at all, but very stable.

Surely, with so many exciting designs to choose from, there will be a kayak just for you.

A sea kayaker checks the fit of his boat on the soft grass at a sea kayaking symposium in Maine. (Eric Evans)

Your Comfort

Being able to sit comfortably in your boat over reasonably long periods of time is a prerequisite for pleasure in recreational kayaking; therefore it's important to sit in the kayak before you buy it. Your hips should fit snugly, but not so tightly that circulation to your legs is cut off. If, on the other hand, you feel too loose in the seat, you can add pads to the hipbraces.

Special attention should be paid to the footbraces. They should be adjustable so that the ball of your foot rests comfortably against the surface of the footbrace. You shouldn't have to reach with your toes to touch them, neither should your feet be jammed up against them.

Kneebraces can be adjusted, if necessary, by taping an extra sponge-rubber pad over the regular brace. The backbrace should give you firm support at the lower spine.

In summary, you should fit into your boat in a comfortably snug manner—snug enough so that by rocking the kayak from side to side with your hips, you can tip the craft on its side, and comfortable enough so that your legs don't fall asleep as you sit there.

Renting

An excellent way to gain some information about the type of kayak you want is to rent a kayak a time or two before you make a purchase. There are many outfitters across the country who rent both canoes and kayaks. Contact the National Association of Canoe Liveries and Outfitters (NACLO) for a free directory of rental places nationwide. NACLO's address is located in Part V at the end of the book.

The Canoe/Kayak Specialty Store

Many outdoor stores and canoe/kayak specialty shops sell kayaks. Try to find a place with knowledgeable salespeople (folks who paddle themselves!) and a variety of kayaks on display. The very best stores will have a pond out back so that you can "try before you buy." You can contact the manufacturers and distributors listed in the back of this book and ask for the name of their closest dealer. A good salesman will ask you what activities you intend to pursue with your boat and will match your needs to a good design.

Attending a kayak event can be an excellent way of finding the boat you want. Kayaks are often for sale at races, at sea kayaking symposia, where people surf, and where clubs meet to go cruising on rivers.

Shopping Tips for Buying a Used Kayak

For the beginner, a secondhand kayak could be a logical choice. Specialty stores usually don't sell used kayaks, so you will be without the services of a knowledgeable salesperson when you go shopping for a used boat. Such a boat's structural condition can be easily ascertained simply by looking at it carefully both inside and out. Next you should sit in it. Don't be concerned about scratches on the hull, but carefully check any patches that you see. Most well-used fiberglass kayaks will have patches.

And, of course, float the craft in the water to see if it leaks.

Here's a handy checklist to take along.

- Check the footbraces to see if they're adjustable.
- Test the grabloops for strength.
- Find out if flotation (air bags) is included in the purchase price.
- Check the boat for comfort while sitting in it.
- Check the stiffness of the hull. (It should give a little but not be too flexible.)
- Check both the hull and deck carefully inside and outside for pinholes. (Pinholes leak.)
- Check the seams, particularly inside the kayak. (A rough edge will puncture an air bag.)
- Run your hands carefully over the coaming and kneebraces. (Sharp edges will scratch your skin.)
- Line the kayak up directly in front of you and examine carefully from both the bow and stern. (Is the boat warped?)
- Check the whole cockpit area for stiffness. (The coaming and seat should not be too flexible.)

2. Paddles, Lifejackets, and Helmets

The three most important accessories in kayaking are paddles, lifejackets, and helmets. Paddles are necessary for locomotion and boat control. Lifejackets are a necessity at sea, in the surf, in any kind of whitewater, and during cold weather. In fact you are now *required by law to have a lifejacket with you* when you are in the kayak. Helmets are essential in whitewater.

Paddles

In kayaking you use a double-bladed paddle (a blade at each end of the shaft) to propel and control the boat. It is the paddler's most important asset: not only is it the tool by which the kayak is propelled and steered, but it is also used to right the paddler in case of a capsize.

The four basic parts of a kayak paddle are:

The Shaft. About 4 inches (10 centimeters) in circumference, 1⅛ inches (nearly 3 centimeters) in diameter, and 4 to 6 feet (120 to 183 centimeters) long, the shaft is fully rounded at the midpoint, then gradually becomes oval shaped close to the paddle blade. The shaft must be strong, light, and not too flexible.

Take-down paddles are made in two pieces with a ferrule joint at the midpoint. This is for ease in storing but often makes for a weaker paddle. It is not, therefore, as popular with paddlers in heavy whitewater. The two-piece paddles are popular in the longer touring lengths, and a take-down is often used as a spare on long trips.

The Throat. The part of the paddle toward the end of the shaft as it joins the blade is called the throat. Some throats are perfectly round, but the better ones are oval shaped to give the paddler a better grip and to make orienting the blade easier.

The Blade. Attached to each end of the shaft at the throat, the blade is approximately 7 to 10 inches wide and 14 to 18 inches long (or, in metric, about 18 to 25 centimeters wide and 35 to 45 centimeters long). If the blade is too big—that is, if it presents too large a surface area to the water—it will quickly fatigue the paddler. One too small will not push enough water.

Most kayak paddles have *feathered* blades—blades set into the shaft at an angle to each other, somewhere between 75 and 90 degrees. This decreases wind resistance when the upper blade slices through the air

Kayak blades are feathered—set at an angle—and slightly curved for more power in stroking. (Ledyard Canoe Club)

prior to dipping into the water again. Nonfeathered paddles are not efficient in most situations where paddlers commonly encounter headwinds (river canyons). They are making a comeback, however, in long-distance touring on large bodies of water where sidewinds are a problem. The side of the blade that pushes against the water is called the *power side, power face,* or *face,* while the other side is called the *back.*

To increase the blade's effectiveness in the water, most blades are *spooned* (slightly concave on the power side). Spoon blades offset 90 degrees clockwise are for lefties, while right-handers use a paddle feathered at 90 degrees counterclockwise. Sometimes left-handers learn to use counterclockwise offset paddles and right-handers the clockwise.

For the sake of simplicity, throughout this book, we assume that the paddler *is using a right-hand-controlled paddle.* By "right-hand control" or "left-hand control," we mean the hand that maintains a constant grip on the shaft throughout the complete forward stroke. The other hand grips the shaft firmly as the blade digs into the water, then relaxes its hold to allow the shaft to twist a bit on the recovery stroke.

Feathered flat-bladed paddles may be used with either right-hand or left-hand control. Flat-bladed paddles, however, are considered not to be efficient.

The Tip. The extreme end of the blade, the tip often takes a lot of abuse and punishment. Therefore the tip must be of rugged construction.

Some tips are made of a very tough, hard piece of wood, others of fiberglass or metal. This cap at the extreme end of the paddle helps to prevent the blade from cracking and from absorbing water.

A tip flat across the bottom of the blade is preferred in slalom racing because it puts the maximum surface area into the water. This gives the racer the best grip in the water. A more rounded tip is preferred by cruisers and by some wildwater racers because the blade enters and leaves the water at the end of the stroke with minimum resistance.

Types of Kayak Paddles

The slalom racing paddle is fairly short and square tipped. It must be very strong to withstand the extreme demands made upon it. The wildwater racing paddle is somewhat longer and lighter, with more rounded tips, slanted to permit a clean entry into the water. Flatwater racing paddles are a further refinement of wildwater paddles. Sleek, smooth, incredibly light, they are designed to enter and exit from the water cleanly. General, all-purpose paddles fall between the two extremes.

All paddles should weigh 2 to 3 pounds (or 0.75 to 1.1 kilogram). Any paddle much under 2 pounds may not be strong enough. Those over 3 pounds can quickly tire the paddler's wrists and arms.

Take-down kayak paddles are not too common, but can be a welcome addition as a spare on a kayak trip. Pulled apart from an interlocking sleeve at the middle of the shaft, these paddles can be easily stored inside a kayak or taped to the outside deck for emergency use. Another interesting innovation in folding kayak paddles is the one that can be easily converted into two single-bladed canoe paddles. A T-grip fits into the hollow end of each shaft.

What Paddles Are Made Of

By far the nicest-looking paddles are made of wood. The ancient Eskimos would have appreciated fully the aesthetically pleasing appearance of an exquisitely laminated wooden paddle. Both shaft and blades are constructed of multiple laminations using different kinds of wood to assure the lightest yet strongest and most durable product. Knot-free maple, spruce, fir, cedar, basswood, and ash have all been used by paddle builders. Wooden paddles do, however, require an occasional touch-up if there are nicks in their varnished surfaces.

Kayak paddles are also made of fiberglass. The blades are fabricated with an intricate combination of fiberglass cloth and resin, then molded to the design, size, and weight desired. The blades can be affixed to shafts of a variety of materials: wood, tubular aluminum or another light alloy, or even tubular fiberglass. Further shaft refinements include a light composition filler for the shaft tube to prevent water infiltration and to help the paddle float. The outside of the tube is wrapped in a plastic or epoxy material to make it feel warmer and to give a better grip.

Ingenious combinations of wood, metal, and fiberglass can create very sturdy paddles light enough to float, but not easily broken. They can be pleasing to touch and handle and need very little maintenance. They rarely warp if left out in the sun.

Which Paddle for You?

There are several options. A finely crafted wooden paddle is a masterpiece of construction, but like a good piece of expensive furniture, it should receive loving care and attention. It feels warm to the touch. Thanks to modern laminating techniques, today's wooden paddle can be extremely strong and durable.

Combination paddles (those made from a combination of metal, fiberglass, and sometimes wood) are very serviceable and require practically no maintenance. They can be knocked around a bit and see heavy usage without much danger of damage.

Folding or take-apart paddles may be just what you need for the kind of kayaking you intend to do—especially if you are thinking of trips in the wilderness.

For the beginner, it really is not crucial to have a general, all-purpose paddle rather than one specifically for slalom or wildwater racing. Either of the latter two kinds is perfectly suitable for learning all the basic strokes. A paddle designed specifically for flatwater racing should probably not be used while you are learning the Eskimo roll. Junior paddles are shorter. They have smaller blade surfaces and are now available for preteen-agers.

Some manufacturers sell paddle kits. The shaft and blades are supplied. You attach the blades to the shaft according to the type of hand control you wish.

The *length* of your paddle is important. Listed below is a suggested guide for suitable length (please note that the wider your boat at the cockpit, the longer the paddle you will need):

Your Height	Whitewater Play or Slalom	River Touring or Wildwater	Sea Kayaking or Flatwater Racing
5'4"	78.8" (202 cm)	82.3" (211 cm)	85.0" (218 cm)
5'6"	79.1" (203 cm)	82.7" (212 cm)	85.4" (219 cm)
5'8"	79.5" (204 cm)	83.1" (213 cm)	85.8" (220 cm)
5'10"	88.3" (206 cm)	83.5" (214 cm)	86.2" (221 cm)
6'0"	81.1" (208 cm)	83.9" (215 cm)	86.6" (222 cm)
6'2"	82.0" (210 cm)	84.3" (216 cm)	87.0" (223 cm)

The chart should be used only as a general guide. Your effectiveness with the paddle (aside from your technique) may depend upon factors other than your height; for example, your body weight, how it is distributed, your arm length, and so forth. If you are 5 feet 8 inches tall, you might, for instance, wish at the start to try a paddle approximately 213 centimeters or 83 inches long for general cruising, using a slightly shorter paddle for slalom, or one a shade longer for wildwater or sea kayaking. With a little experience, you'll soon find out if you're comfortable and effective with that particular length. The trend over the past few years is toward shorter paddles for *all* phases of kayaking.

Lifejackets

Your lifejacket or PFD (personal flotation device) is your greatest friend and protector in the water. A proper lifejacket will not only help to keep you warm and cut the wind but will support you if you capsize and become separated from your boat in the water. That's its main function, of course, to keep you on the surface in a relatively upright position so you can breathe and not be obliged to tread water to stay afloat.

History of Lifejackets

Lifejackets manufactured before the turn of the century were made of cork and balsa wood. The next flotation used was kapok, a vegetable fiber found in tropical tree pods and resembling milkweed. Kapok fiber had a waxy coating that provided the necessary buoyancy, and the fiber was sealed in vinyl packets to prevent exposure to the water. Unfortunately these packets could be punctured, rendering the lifejackets useless. The use of kapok today is prohibited in most of Europe and in Canada.

In the 1960s, a very light, flexible, body-fitting lifejacket came out of

France. Called the *Flotherchoc*, it featured small air-filled vinyl packets placed inside nylon chambers. The *Flotherchoc* resembled a vest rather than the older, more traditional horse-collar variety. It was an instant favorite, but, over time, even its vinyl air packets could puncture, losing buoyancy.

Space-age plastics came to the rescue later in the decade, and now a closed cell foam encased in a nylon vestlike garment is used. Each tiny cell within the foam is a separate entity, unlike a sponge, which has channels joining its various chambers. These closed cell foam pads could be punctured over and over again without losing very much buoyancy. Some of the better closed cell foam pads will not deteriorate even when they are compressed. The vest drapes comfortably over the paddler's chest, shoulders, and back. It can then be snugged up tight with a drawstring or a zipper.

Lifejacket Approval

The United States Coast Guard (USCG) and the Underwriters Laboratories have been monitoring lifejackets for many years. Under regulations established in the early 1970s, you are required to have at least one USCG-approved lifejacket for each person in your recreational boat. The regulations themselves are somewhat technical, but all you need to remember is that you should wear your USCG-approved lifejacket in a kayak and that your lifejacket must be the right size for you and marked with an approved USCG number.

The USCG has approved five different types of lifejackets, only three of which concern us in kayaking. The first, Type I, is a big and bulky vest-type jacket with enormous buoyancy and ability to keep you afloat. It is designed to turn even an unconscious person in the water from a face-down position to a vertical or slightly head-back position. Type I is suitable anywhere, but because of its bulk, it is unusually appropriate for paddlers exploring heavy whitewater rivers such as the Colorado in the Grand Canyon. Type I was a favorite lifejacket of the late Dr. Walter Blackadar, who explored some of the greatest whitewater rivers in the world. Type I is less popular with racers and general recreational boaters because of its bulk.

Type II is designed to perform the same function as Type I except that it's smaller, has less buoyancy, and is more commonly shaped like a horse collar than a vest. Unfortunately the horse collar restricts a boater's twisting neck and head action and therefore is not very popular with most kayakers. The Type IIs are the least expensive of the approved types and can often be found at boat livery rental places.

A selection of Type III PFDs for kayaking. (Charles Walbridge)

Type III is designed to keep a conscious person in a vertical or slightly head-back position in the water. Type III comes in many styles, is the most comfortable of the three types, and therefore is a favorite with many paddlers. It's basically a nicely fitting closed-cell-foam-filled nylon vest. Short-length lifejackets are generally best for kayakers.

Other Considerations

If you're thinking about racing, there are some things you should know. First of all, flatwater racing kayaks, for some reason, are exempt from the USCG regulations—no lifejackets needed. Second, to be eligible for whitewater competition, a racer must wear a lifejacket with a minimum buoyancy of 13.2 pounds (4.9 kilograms). This may not seem like much protection, but it must be remembered that the weight of the human body in water is only a fraction of its weight on land. A lifejacket listed at 13.2 pounds of buoyancy will hold most people up easily. Incidentally, the Type III USCG-approved jacket satisfies this requirement nicely. Water-ski belts are unacceptable for use in kayaking.

Those adventuresome kayakers interested in cruising, camping, and exploring nature's waterways should consider a wilderness vest. It's a lifejacket with four pockets in front to store matches, compasses, and other wilderness necessities.

Choosing Your Lifejacket

Since there are well over a dozen manufacturers of Type III lifejackets, you will have a good variety to pick from whether you intend to go cruising, surfing, or racing. Keep in mind that USCG-approved life-jackets are available for children and infants, too.

Your best practical test for a lifejacket is to wear the top part of your paddling clothes into a store and try on Type IIIs while sitting in a kayak, if one is available at the store. Next put on the spray cover and see if the lifejacket tends to ride up around your neck; you wish to avoid this if possible. Make sure your arms can move in all directions freely without chafing. Does the lifejacket move with your body as you twist and turn? (It should.) Make sure the zippers or clasps work freely and easily. Often a plastic zipper will catch less sand and dirt and thus work more smoothly than a metal zipper.

Check to see that the lifejacket is labeled USCG-approved with proper wording and type number. Check the seams for strength. If it feels comfortable and has met all the above-mentioned conditions, buy it. But your responsibility does not end there. Even if you find that it doesn't fit right after you've worn it a few times, *do not alter it.* An altered life-jacket loses its USCG approval. Get one that does fit. Inspect your lifejacket from time to time to see that it is free of rips, tears, and holes, and that all the seams are firm. Never use your precious lifejacket as a boat fender, cushion, or kneeling pad.

Helmets

In a very real sense, the helmet is the lifejacket for the head. It has a similar set of functions. Its primary purpose, of course, is to protect you against sharp blows to the head from rocks lurking in the rapids. It also provides warmth, protection from the sun and insects, as well as from the rain.

When should you wear one? Always, in every kind of whitewater. Just as you need a paddle and a lifejacket, you should also automatically reach for your helmet whenever a whitewater trip is planned. Although fast-moving water creates cushions around rocks, you can still receive a stunning blow to the head if not protected. What's worse, especially in the rivers of the United States, people have used riverbeds as dumping grounds for old autos, refrigerators, and other large appliances. These create a hazard as well.

The weekend flatwater cruiser or oceangoing kayaker does not need a helmet to protect himself from rocks, but some kind of head covering is advisable to ward off insects and prevent sunstroke. Shade from a wide-brimmed hat feels mighty good on a sunny day, and such a hat makes kayaking much more pleasurable when the weather is inclement.

Some people wear helmets while surf kayaking, and it's a good idea. Occasionally beaches have rocks protruding from them, and there is always the danger of being hit on the head by another surf kayak or paddle.

In the early days, once people recognized the need for head protection, bicycle helmets, rock climbers' helmets, hockey helmets, and even motorcycle and football helmets were seen on the waterways. While these helmets were certainly better than nothing at all, fortunately manufacturers have now produced some interesting head-protecting devices uniquely suited to kayaking needs.

Characteristics of a Good Helmet

The whitewater boater has specific needs: the helmet should be light (preferably a pound or less); the inner hat band (cradle) should be adjustable to the contours of the head; it must fit snugly; visibility should be good; vision should not be obstructed by the brow of the helmet reaching too close to the eyes; peripheral vision should be good, but the temple area of the skull in front of the ears must also be protected; it should be reasonably waterproof yet have good drainage for what little water does seep in; the helmet must provide for good hearing because recognizing the sound of rapids ahead is critical to safe boating. The chin strap should fit snugly so that the helmet does not get ripped off if you take an unexpected plunge into the water or get hit by a large, forceful wave. The helmet should float, of course, if you lose it in the water.

Kinds of Helmets

Solid shell helmets are made from hand lay-up fiberglass using a specially formulated high-impact material. Although these helmets offer superb protection, they are somewhat heavier, weighing more than a pound (373 grams).

A good whitewater kayaking helmet should protect the sides of the head as well as the top. (Bob Woodward)

Perforated shell helmets—those with narrow drainage holes—are made of injection-molded high-impact polycarbons and polypropylene plastics. Some are also made of Kevlar—that extremely tough material used in the manufacture of bulletproof vests. These helmets are extremely light (under a pound) and are the favorites of racers. They will serve you well in most situations but are not designed for unusually severe impact.

There are a few rock-climbing helmets on the market today that can also be used safely in kayaking. They often have a thick molded plastic shell lined with a crushable foam for a snug fit around the head. These helmets weigh over a pound.

The interior fittings of a helmet are important. The inner cradle (hat band) should be adjustable and not absorb water. Adjustable sling suspensions are popular; others are built with closed cell foam padding. Still others come with a specially fitted, interchangeable inner padding for different head sizes. The chin straps should not chafe and should be easily adjusted. They should fasten so the helmet will not wobble when you turn your head quickly.

Whitewater helmets have rapidly become a mark of individuality. Helmets have been seen on the waterways with the person's name or club insignia on them, even national flags. Others sport a high-flying feather or are painted with a bright fluorescent color. Still others have bits of ribbon streaming behind them. To each his own. Kayaking is a sport that thrives on individuality.

3. Accessories for Kayaking

In this chapter, we cover the major accessories used by kayakers. They include items for the kayak itself, personal gear, and tips on how to transport your kayak to the river, lake, or ocean.

Americans have been accused of being crazy for gimmicks and gadgets. Those who find themselves interested in the exciting sport of kayaking will not be disappointed. Many innovations and ingeniously designed accessories are available to increase your paddling comfort.

Kayak Accessories

Flotation Bags

The most important kayak accessory is flotation to make the craft unsinkable. A kayak filled with water, sinking slowly to the bottom of a river, indicates a lack of foresight on the part of the owner and creates a potentially dangerous situation. Proper flotation keeps a swamped boat riding high in the water—decreasing the likelihood of collision with rocks as the boat is swept downstream—and facilitates rescue.

When fiberglass kayaks first became popular in Europe and in the United States, the need for flotation quickly became apparent. In plain words: fiberglass by itself doesn't float. Beach balls, inner tubes, and even lifejackets were stuffed into both ends to help keep a swamped kayak afloat. They had a way, however, of working free and popping out of the boat.

Eventually more sophisticated means of flotation evolved. *Float bags*—air-filled vinyl containers tapered to fit into the ends of a kayak—became popular. A smaller one was squeezed into the bow in front of the footbraces and a larger one stuffed into the stern directly behind the cockpit. A further refinement involved split bags to be fitted into each side of the interior of a kayak with a deck-supporting foam wall inside the boat. Easy-to-reach hoses for inflation by mouth, similar to those used in inflatable camping air mattresses, are attached to the bags.

Some kayakers rely solely on a vertical foam wall (commonly Ethafoam or Minicell) support system in the bow and stern of their kayaks. The foam gives rigidity to the deck and hull but provides a small measure of flotation as well. This arrangement is not recommended unless split bags are used on either side of the foam.

The more flotation your kayak has, the higher it will ride in the water, making it safer, less prone to damage, and a lot easier to rescue. No kayak should ever be launched in any kind of water anywhere until it has an adequate means of flotation in the interior of *both* ends of the boat.

Spray Covers

A second important accessory for a kayak is the *spray cover*. It serves a variety of purposes. In cold weather, a spray cover helps to keep your legs warm. It keeps waves from splashing into your cockpit on a windy lake, in the rapids, or in the ocean. In a capsize, it keeps the water out of your boat so you can execute the Eskimo roll. The spray cover is as important an accessory to your kayak as your paddle and flotation bags.

Spray covers have four basic parts: the tubular skirt that fits around the paddler's torso, the deck that flares out from the torso to stretch across and cover the cockpit, a special grabloop at the front of the cover for quick removal, and an elastic cord around the bottom of the cover to help seal it watertight under the coaming.

Spray covers are made either from a light rubberized waterproof cloth with elastic cords or from nylaprene or neoprene rubber. Cloth spray

The spray cover should fit snugly around the coaming and the paddler. (Bermudes)

covers are good for moderate whitewater and are very durable and less expensive. Suspenders can be attached to hold the skirt high up on the paddler's chest for greater protection against the waves.

Neoprene spray covers keep the water out better than cloth covers and keep you much warmer. Some neoprene rubber comes with a thin layer of nylon on one or both sides for added strength. Like the cloth spray cover, most neoprene ones use an elastic cord around the outer perimeter of the cover to seal it under the coaming. Nevertheless some spray covers use a prestretched nylaprene rim band as the tension member around the coaming, instead of an elastic cord. It is knot free and wrinkle free, therefore more watertight.

Although spray covers can be purchased commercially, anyone handy with a sewing machine and a pair of scissors and familiar with neoprene glue can fashion a personally fitted spray cover for himself. It is not a technically difficult procedure and can be done some winter evening before the boating season starts.

Miscellaneous Items

The fastidious flatwater boater may wish to wax and polish the hull the way he would a prized automobile. Fiberglass boat waxes are available; there are also a number of paste waxes that can help bring back the original color and shine of the boat, and these can add a measure of protection and waterproofing as well.

Kayakers exploring ocean waterways out of sight of land and those encountering fog should have a compass in a waterproof case fastened securely to the deck in front of the cockpit where it is easy to read. Sea travelers will also want flares, smoke canisters, and a waterproof flashlight. A ship-to-shore walkie-talkie or a VHF radio is not a bad idea either.

Expedition kayaks sometimes have footpedal-operated detachable rudders to help with steering over a long expanse of water.

Cold Water and Weather Protection

Nothing is more discouraging than sitting in a kayak cold, wet, and miserable. There really is no need for it. A judicious selection of clothing can bring you through the wildest waves, the highest surf, or the most inclement weather in comfort. As some of the old-timers at the Ledyard Canoe Club in New Hampshire used to say, "It's not too cold to go paddling—you're just not dressed warm enough!"

The Paddling Jacket

Let's start with the upper body, and the first line of defense against wind and water is the standard paddling jacket. These are usually made of lightweight uninsulated nylon, which sheds rain or the water splashed on you when cutting through waves. Although not completely waterproof, paddling jackets keep your wool sweater, pile, or wet suit worn underneath relatively dry for long periods of time. In addition, paddling jackets hold heat, acting as a vapor barrier to retain warm body moisture.

The jacket should be one size too large for you so there'll be no restriction of your arms and shoulders, even if you wear a sweater or wet-suit top underneath. A good paddling jacket has elasticized cuffs and a fully elasticized waistband to help keep out water and wind. It should fit snugly, but comfortably, around the neck. Velcro closures also work well for adjusting cuffs and neck openings.

Some nylon paddling jackets are lined with a thin layer of foam to help retain body heat, while still others have neoprene at the cuffs and neck for added warmth and protection against water. It is vitally important that the paddling jacket's collar and cuffs can be sealed tight. Paddling jackets for sea kayaking should have underarm zippers for ventilation and a zippered kangaroo pouch for daily necessities.

Paddling jackets are great by themselves on cool summer days. In the fall, you can wear them with pile or wool underneath, and in cold conditions, you can wear a paddling jacket over a wet suit and pile.

Pile or Polypropylene

For insulation underneath a paddling jacket or dry suit, pile and polypropylene have come to be recognized as the best by people who regularly get wet. In former years, we'd just grab any old wool sweater that was lying around the house, throw it on underneath our paddling jackets, and go paddling. Wool was warm but it had some disadvantages. First, it absorbed water and took a long time to dry out (and there's nothing worse than putting on wet paddling clothing in the morning!). Second, it stretched wildly out of shape. Finally, it would rot and fall apart under repeated use in the wet. Then along came pile with none of these drawbacks and all of the warmth benefits of wool.

There are several weights of pile and polypro available ranging from lightweight polypro at 3 ounces all the way through to heavy pile at 12 ounces. And polypro and pile can be used for other sports as well.

The Wet Suit

Any time the water is below 50 degrees Fahrenheit (10 degrees Celsius), a wet suit should be worn while boating. Thanks to research, kayakers now have an interesting variety of choices.

A wet suit acts like another layer of skin to retain body heat and prevent penetration by the cold. The little water that seeps through to your skin is trapped and quickly warmed. You will not be perfectly dry in a wet suit, but if it fits properly, you will be very comfortable. It's good protection from the rain, and it keeps you from being scratched by bushes along the river bank. It also helps prevent bruises from rocks.

Wet suits are made of neoprene rubber, which fits the contours of the body. They are now available in a variety of color combinations and often come with nylon skin on one or both sides for added strength. Three-eighths- and ¼-inch-thick neoprene is a little heavy unless you plan to kayak in the polar regions. One-eighth-inch-thick neoprene is popular because it can provide enough protection and warmth while affording excellent flexibility. One-sixteenth-inch-thick neoprene is a favorite with racers, since it is the lightest of all and is the most flexible. Glued seams don't leak, and they keep you warmer, but they cost more than sewn seams.

Wet suits come in a variety of styles:

The Farmer John. Sometimes called *Long John,* this wet suit covers the legs and torso but is sleeveless. Worn with a paddling jacket, this style is very popular because it affords unrestricted upper body movement. The ⅛-inch-thick Farmer John is a general, all-purpose favorite.

The Standard Wet Suit. Consisting of a long-sleeved jacket and pants, this suit covers the arms, legs, and torso for total protection. Upper body movement is very restricted depending upon which thickness you choose.

The Shorty. Cut off just above the knees and sleeveless, this wet suit keeps the torso warm and is popular with surf kayakers. Shorty or Farmer John wet suits combined with waterproof exterior rain pants provide even greater warmth. Rain pants, made from a light rubberized material, usually come equipped with a waist drawcord and a snap closure for the ankles.

The Wet-Suit Vest. This style is just what the name implies: it's simply a vest of neoprene. It's particularly effective at the start or end of the cold weather season.

The Combination Vest. A simple wet-suit vest with waterproof nylon sleeves attached, its sleeves have neoprene cuffs to keep the water out. This Combination Vest is the best of both worlds. It makes obsolete the

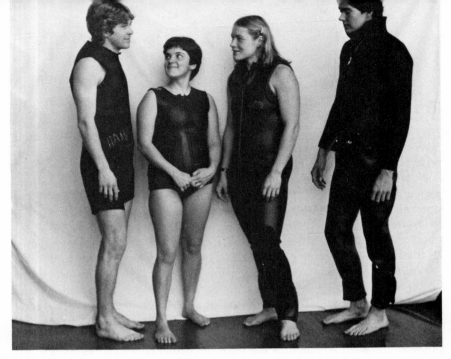

Wet suits. From left to right: Shorty, Vest, Farmer John, Standard. (Evans Associates)

old long-sleeved restrictive wet-suit jacket while providing more protection for the arms than the Farmer John or the Shorty. A full-length zipper down the front aids in ventilating your torso as it gets overheated while paddling.

Wet suits can extend your paddling season significantly. Wet suits also add a measure of buoyancy to a swimming paddler but should not be worn in place of a lifejacket.

The Dry Suit

The first dry suit we ever saw was worn by Colorado kayaker Roger Paris back in the late 1960s, but it has only been in the 1980s that dry suits have exploded in popularity among kayakers who get wet regularly. Aficionados claim that once you try a dry suit, you'll never go back to neoprene.

Dry suits seal the water out by using an entirely waterproof material, waterproof zipper entries, and very snug-fitting latex rubber seals at the neck, wrists, and ankles. They are intentionally loose-fitting garments to allow the paddler to wear pile or polypro underneath; the looseness also means no restrictions on paddling movements. The best dry suits are made from stretchy, breathable material, and you enter the one-piece suits through a zipper in the back, which means that someone must help you get in.

The latest in cold-weather protection: the dry suit. (Bermudes)

Most people wear nylon pants over their dry suits to protect them. The seals must be treated regularly with silicone to keep them from drying out, as salt water and perspiration are hard on the seals.

Dry suits are not cheap: most are in the $200-to-$400 range.

Foot Protection

Booties are available from ⅛-inch-thick neoprene reinforced by a molded hard rubber sole and heel. These can be worn with or without *wool* socks. The hard rubber sole has a tread that helps keep you from slipping on the rocks. In warm weather, a pair of old "holy" sneakers do a fine job of protecting your feet. Plastic river sandals that attach firmly to the foot also offer good protection. Loose moccasins, loafers, and ordinary sandals quickly come off in the water and are unsuitable.

One-sixteenth-inch-thick neoprene covered with nylon makes a good sock. You can wear these neoprene socks inside your old river sneakers or river sandals on the coldest day and remain comfortable.

Neoprene booties with a hard rubber sole. (Bermudes)

Pogie. (Jay Evans)

Hand Protection

In our view, the most underrated equipment breakthrough in kayaking was the Pogie. We had wet suits and we had paddling jackets, but for years, we searched for a way to keep our hands warm while at the same time maintaining a good feel for the paddle shaft. Rubber kitchen gloves were too cold, wet-suit gloves were too bulky, and leather gloves got soaked. Those of us who tried to "tough it out" bare-handed simply suffered, and not always in silence! Then, in the early 1970s, whitewater racer Bonnie Losick invented the Pogie, and it was such a simple device that we kicked ourselves for not having thought of it sooner.

A Pogie consists of a piece of ⅛-inch-thick neoprene/nylon that fits over the wrist like a sleeve. It is cut in such a way that, as you grip your paddle with your bare hand, the neoprene/nylon can be wrapped around your knuckles and fingers and be attached back to the sleeve with a Velcro fastener. The fastener will pull away easily and safely should you need to withdraw your hand from the paddle.

Miscellaneous Items

For kayakers paddling in cold conditions along the seacoast or on an open lake where a helmet is not required, a good all-wool hat is highly recommended. It will resist rain, and when pulled down over your ears, it can provide plenty of warmth.

For those of you who wear glasses, don't forget to outfit them with an elastic strap around the back of your head to prevent them from being knocked away by a saucy splash of a wave. A defogging compound rubbed onto your lenses can help keep your glasses clear.

Finally, a small first aid kit kept in a waterproof container can be a valuable asset to a kayak trip.

Protecting Your Gear

Storage Bags

Waterproof equipment storage bags come in many shapes, styles, and sizes. When purchasing a bag, look for lightness, waterproofness, and ease of access. The bag should be easy to open and close. A bag with shoulder straps comes in handy when you're carrying gear down to the river bank.

Net Bags

Some paddlers like to carry along net bags. Like onion sacks, these bags are perforated and make a handy receptacle for all your wet clothing. These bags breathe freely, allowing your clothes to ventilate and preventing mildew.

Small Bags and Pouches

Small, individual vinyl bags with Velcro or plastic-zipper closures are good for carrying small articles and your lunch or a snack. Waterproof pouches are important for other small items, such as matches and sunglasses.

Hard Shell Cases

We used to have army ammo boxes for storage of things that needed protection. Today there are light, handy boxes made from ABS plastic that are crushproof and waterproof.

Camera Bags

First of all, they must be waterproof, yet easy and quick to open in case a photographic possibility suddenly appears. Second, it's good to have a shoulder or neck strap on a camera bag. Third, some camera bags come with an inflatable chamber. This not only prevents your camera or binoculars from sinking to the bottom of the river in case of capsize, but it also cushions your equipment to prevent abrasions and damage from rough handling.

Boat and Paddle Covers

Whitewater kayakers have never been known to baby their paddles or boats—they get such rough usage in the rapids anyway. However, flat-water kayakers have always been extremely cautious in the care of their boats and paddles. A nick or scratch on the hull of a whitewater boat is little cause for concern. For the flatwater racer, it can mean the difference between winning and losing a race. Consequently, flatwater racers often keep their paddles (and sometimes their boats as well) in a protective cloth bag to prevent chafing during transport. The bag also protects the equipment from the elements and makes for handy storage.

Transporting Your Kayak

Owners of collapsible (folding) kayaks have it made. All they have to do is to pack their boats away in two duffellike carrying bags and toss them into the trunk of the car, and away they go.

Cartop Racks

Owners of rigid kayaks need a little more ingenuity. Die-cast aluminum brackets are available that grip the rain gutter of your car securely. When they're bolted to a two-by-four or support member, you'll have a multipurpose rack. There are also cartop carriers for automobiles without rain gutters.

A further refinement is sometimes called a *kayak stacker*. It's a vertically upright post fastened partway along the crossbar. This allows you to stack several kayaks on edge, thereby increasing the capacity of the cartop rack. Kayak paddles can be tied securely alongside each kayak.

Just as important as the cartop rack itself is the tie-down system you use. Interstate highway speeds of 65 miles per hour create considerable wind drag on kayaks stacked on top of your car, van, or camper. Therefore you must secure the kayak to the rack, preferably with a tight-fitting elasticized cord. Even more important, both bow and stern of the kayak must be securely fastened to the car's bumpers. This removes the risk of the kayak becoming airborne and flying off your car while you're cruising down the highway. Specially fitted tensioners and hooks can be used if you want to avoid having to knot your tie-down ropes. Plastic bumper hooks are handy because they simply fit over the edge of the bumper; but unless the tie-down rope remains very tight, the plastic hooks can slip loose. If this occurs at the rear of your car, you might not notice it right away. A safer system is to find some way of actually tying or fastening the rope around the bumper itself.

Always keep in mind that no rooftop car rack system for holding kayaks should ever be allowed to stand alone. The bow and stern of the kayak must be tied to the bumpers as well.

Trailers

Kayak trailers hauled behind a vehicle can carry up to two dozen boats if properly made. Trailers are ideal for college outing clubs and outfitters. The better ones are well balanced so that the trailer tongue can be lifted off the ground or unhooked from the trailer hitch even when the trailer is loaded. A storage area should be provided for paddles and other gear. A well-built kayak trailer should have good vertical stability (not tip over easily), a spare tire, complete wiring for lights, and a safety chain that attaches to the bumper or frame of the car.

Caution

All kayaks and other gear must be securely fastened to the trailer, and the driver of the vehicle towing the trailer must know how to back the trailer up without jackknifing it. When passing another vehicle on the road, the driver must remember to pull at least three car lengths ahead before swinging back into the regular driving lane. This will give plenty of clearance for the trailer. Be sure that the turn signals and taillights function properly on the trailer.

Trolleys

In Western Europe and England, small, folding, two-wheeled trolleys can be seen aiding in transporting kayaks, something like wheeled luggage carriers. These trolleys fit at the midpoint of the kayak, and you simply pull the kayak along by the grabloop at the bow or stern.

It can sometimes be a long walk with your kayak to the river's edge from where your vehicle is parked. One easy way to carry your kayak is to team up with a partner. Place your two kayaks side by side. One of you takes the two bows, the other the two sterns, lift them off, and away you go.

4. Safety

Kayaking looks more dangerous than it really is. Water is not, after all, man's natural medium, but statistically speaking, kayaking is one of the safest sports around. Perhaps this is so because those who have taken part in the past have put a high premium on safety. Unlike some sports, kayaking has had a tradition of attracting cautious, conservative people. Perhaps it is the potential for danger in a water sport that at once attracts the adventurous person but also makes him wary and careful.

The sport, however, is not without risks. Underlying your participation in the sport must be the understanding that *you* assume and control that risk. Control entails using appropriate equipment, acquiring good skills and physical condition, and exercising excellent judgment in matching equipment and skills to the demands of the environment.

Throughout this book, aspects of safety are stressed where appropriate. Nevertheless, safety in kayaking is so important to your enjoyment of the sport that it warrants a chapter of its own. A most thorough discussion of kayak safety can be found in *River Rescue* by Les Bechdel and Slim Ray (see the bibliography in Part V).

Equipment

Kayaks

Your kayak should be structurally sound, watertight, with grabloops and flotation at both ends. It should have a firm-fitting but easily detachable spray cover. If you have an inflatable kayak, it should have multiple air chambers.

You must be able to exit easily and quickly from your boat at all times. This means that flotation bags and foam support walls must not hinder the quick exit of your legs from inside the kayak. It is possible for a kayak to become wedged between a couple of rocks in the rapids. This can happen even to expert boaters. When a kayak is pinned, the water creates an enormous force on the boat—enough to jackknife or buckle the craft. When this happens, the paddler, sitting in the chaise longue position, is vulnerable to having his legs pinned by the deformation of the boat. Deformation can happen almost instantly, although sometimes it takes a minute or two for the deck or hull to collapse. The paddler should forget about trying to pry the boat loose or about doing an Eskimo roll. The paddler should get out of the boat *immediately* and swim to safety.

Fortunately manufacturers are beginning to recognize this potential hazard. In some kayaks, reinforcing around the cockpit has been discontinued, allowing the cockpit area to absorb stress only up to a point. After that it breaks rather than bends. Once the kayak splits open, pressure on the legs is relieved, and the paddler can quickly and safely exit.

The result is a broken but easily repairable kayak. More important it means that the paddler is able to extricate himself from a potential hazard. When you're buying a kayak, consider one that has a breakaway cockpit.

Lifejackets

According to ACA Safety Chairman Charlie Walbridge, 50 percent of all boating deaths could have been prevented with the use of an appropriate lifejacket. Make sure your lifejacket is in good condition and is secured snugly to your torso. Wear it at all times while kayaking.

Helmets

Helmets are required for whitewater paddling and are recommended for pounding surf, where your own loose boat or paddle may be your greatest enemy.

Cold Protection

In all outdoor travel away from shelter, a kayaker has a responsibility to his own body to make sure that it is warm and protected. Cold air, strong winds, and cold water will quickly lower your body temperature. This in turn reduces your ability to save yourself. It steals your strength and numbs your fingers, so that even with people nearby to help you, your ability to help yourself is lessened. What's worse, the lowering of your body temperature (hypothermia) affects your reasoning ability; unfortunately you will not realize that this is happening.

Dry suits or wet suits should be worn when the combined air and water temperature is below 100 degrees Fahrenheit (nearly 38 degrees Celsius). Windproof paddling jackets and pile, as previously explained, are also good safeguards. The sensible kayaker always has a complete change of dry clothes in a waterproof package in the kayak or stored in his car at the take-out point at the end of a day's trip.

Soaking-wet clothes lose about 90 percent of their insulating value; you lose heat from your body five times as fast in wet clothes as in dry clothes. If you cannot stay warm, then you must quickly get out of the wind or rain, go ashore, and get inside an automobile with the heater turned up to maximum. If no car is available, build a fire and make a secure, protected campsite. Never ignore shivering: your body is telling you to take whatever means are available to start restoring your body heat.

Removing wet clothes and getting into a dry sleeping bag or wrapping yourself in an insulated blanket can help. Contrary to myth, the consumption of alcoholic beverages is not helpful: hot tea or hot soup is much better. A bathtub filled with water as hot as you can stand is better than a hot shower.

Paddles

Your paddle must be structurally sound; check it before leaving for a trip. On isolated runs, you'd be wise to carry a spare: a C-1 paddle or a take-down kayak paddle fits best inside the boat.

Rescue Gear

The kayak itself is a handy piece of rescue equipment. In a rescue mission, paddle quickly over to a capsized boater and allow him to grab the point of your bow in order to right himself. An abandoned kayak floating downstream can be nudged over to shore by a kayaker pressing the bow firmly up against the side of the overturned boat.

On a large lake or at sea, several kayaks can *raft up* by coming alongside each other and extending their paddles over each other's decks. This provides a stable platform for the one kayak or person that needs assistance.

A throw-line rescue bag is a very useful piece of rescue equipment. It consists of about 60 to 70 feet of ⅜-inch nonkinking yellow or orange polypropylene line that floats. The line passes through a grommet at the bottom of a nylon bag that contains a foam disc for flotation. The line is tied outside the bottom of the bag to form a large grabloop. The remainder of the line is stuffed into the bag, with the free end sticking out.

To use it, hold the free end with one hand and, with the other hand, toss the bag containing the grabloop with an underhand motion. It is best to throw beyond the swimmer in the water rather than short of the swimmer. If thrown beyond the swimmer, the line can be quickly pulled back to where the swimmer can grab it. Aim slightly downstream of the swimmer if he's floating down the river. If the swimmer is perched on

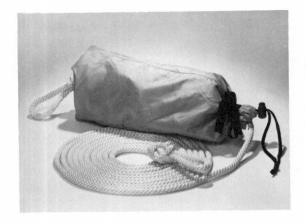

Throw-line rescue bag.
(Charles Walbridge)

a rock, aim slightly upstream so that the line will float to him. Once the swimmer has grabbed the line securely, make sure your feet are well braced with the line wrapped around your waist.

Throw-line rescue bags are small enough that they can fit into a kayak for ready use. When throw-line rescue bags are not available, ring buoys and heaving lines can be used, but these should not be stored inside the kayak.

Some experts prefer a 70-foot length of ½-inch twisted polypropylene rope without an attached bag. It's thrown underhand or sidearm. The rescuer throws part of the coil out over the water, while the remaining part pays out of the nonthrowing hand as the rope becomes fully extended.

Boaters should experiment thoroughly with both kinds of rescue ropes, decide which system they prefer, then perfect their throwing techniques.

Two spring-loaded carabiners are useful for rescues and handy for clipping rescue bags and loose items in to the boat. A first aid kit and matches stashed inside a waterproof container are also essential elements, particularly on isolated runs.

Skills

Being a good swimmer and comfortable in the water are prerequisites to developing your kayaking skills slowly and systematically. Start with the basic strokes on flatwater or in a pool. Learn the Eskimo roll (Chapter 6). As you improve, practice your maneuvers in easy whitewater and then *gradually* increase the difficulty of the rivers or the water you paddle.

Self-rescue is the quickest and best safety measure of all, and there are certain basic rescue skills that should be mastered right away. Train for capsizing. Practice exiting from your boat and swimming quickly to the bow or stern. Maintain the kayak's overturned position (this traps valuable air inside that helps buoyancy) and ferry it to shore. Remember always to remain on the upstream side of your overturned boat so you won't get wedged on a rock.

If you do wet exit in the rapids, swim or float on your back with your feet forward and high. Maintain an aggressive attitude about reaching shore with all your equipment, but release it if necessary. Once near shore, flip over onto your stomach and swim aggressively to the bank.

If you feel yourself about to broach a rock while paddling, lean into it and pull or claw your way around it.

Judgment

Judgment in kayaking means recognizing environmental hazards and, perhaps more significantly, recognizing your own skill limitations.

Hazards

Water reading and what to look for in rapids are discussed later in Chapter 9, but a few pointers here can be helpful. High water looks inviting to the adventurous, but higher than normal stream flow significantly raises the possibilities of danger on the water. As the flow rate increases, so does the difficulty of making a rescue. Generally speaking, one should not go kayaking on a river in a flood. Brush, fallen trees, and other obstructions can pin a kayak and trap its occupant.

Dams along a river sometimes cannot be seen until the last minute, and the water below a dam often curls back on itself and can trap the unwary boater. On smaller streams in agricultural areas, fences and barbed wire are sometimes stretched across for the benefit of the farmer by keeping his cattle in, but not to the benefit of boaters.

In remote wooded areas, logs and pulpwood are floated downstream. In cold weather, there is always the chance of ice accumulating along the river bank or on the surface of the water itself.

Beware of dam releases, which cause a sudden rise in water levels. When kayaking at high altitudes, bear in mind that on hot sunny days, snow melt from the mountain peaks can cause a significant rise in water levels.

One of the most insidious dangers in river travel is not what appears on the surface of the water, but what lies just under the water level. Sharp rocks, submerged logs, discarded autos, broken glass, and other

The arrows indicate a "horizon line"—an immediate signal to pull to shore and inspect the hidden dam or weir that undoubtedly lies just below the line. (Ledyard Canoe Club)

menacing things dumped into the river create ever-present possibilities for trouble. Never kayak in bare feet; always wear sneakers or light-weight protective footgear.

Never attempt a lake crossing if the waves are too high for you or if the wind is too strong. Chapter 11 looks more closely at the inherent risks in sea kayaking, but it can't be emphasized enough to be aware of the tide and the time of day and to make sure to have the tide work for you rather than against you. While ocean kayaking, avoid busy harbors, channels, and shipping lanes. Stay well away from large seagoing or high-speed craft.

Skill Limits

As the old saying goes—"An ounce of prevention is worth a pound of cure." In light of this, it is important to have a frank, unbiased assessment of your boating ability. Resist peer pressure if necessary; get out of your boat and walk down the river bank if you are unsure of your ability to navigate the rapids safely. If the surf is coming in too high, stay put on the beach. Everyone has limits. The expert who won't run a Class V rapids and the Class III cruiser who isn't comfortable in a Class IV rapids are exactly alike. Only *you* can be responsible for your safety, so *you* make the decision, not your peers or your ego.

Group Responsibilities

A minimum of three craft is necessary for all whitewater trips or trips away from land.

Be familiar with the stretch of water to be covered. Knowledge of the area at high tide and low tide (or at high or low water levels) is essential. Knowing the abilities and limitations of all members of your party is also important. Are there any weak swimmers in the group? Do any of them have a history of convulsions or fainting spells?

One defective paddle or leaky kayak can spoil a trip for everyone. Make sure all equipment is in good repair. First aid kits and repair kits should always be brought along.

Never encourage an inexperienced boater to try a stretch of the river beyond his ability. If the group is large (more than six kayaks), consider splitting into smaller groups. Each group should be of the same skill level; designate a leader and a *sweep*, an experienced boater who brings up the rear. On the water, boats must be spread out enough for maneuverability, but all boats in each group should stay within sight of each other.

If your trip is an extended expedition into the wilderness, a daily trip schedule should be filed with appropriate authorities. Checkpoints should be established along the way and preplanned exit routes selected in anticipation of an emergency.

Eric had an experience on the Upper Deerfield River in Massachusetts in the mid-1970s that serves as an example of the subtle pressures a leader can experience. He was leading an exploratory trip on the Deerfield, a river he had heard about for years but never paddled. His group included good boaters and novices (mistake No. 1: novices and exploratory trips don't mix). The put-in was reached after a long struggle down a very steep rock-strewn bank; hiking back up would have been a nightmare. At the start, the rapids looked hard—too hard for novices. At that moment, Eric had severe reservations about paddling the river. But the enthusiasm of the expert boaters, the hour-long drive to the river (during which anticipation about the run had been high), and the thought of hiking back up to the van overran his caution. Well, the trip was a fiasco, with boats and boaters being separated at every rapids. Hindsight said that Eric should have either sent the novices back to the van (to drive down to the take-out) or canceled the trip on the spot and had everyone hike back to the van.

PART II.
BASIC KAYAK TECHNIQUES

5. Getting Acquainted with Your Boat

Plan of Presentation

The purpose of this chapter is to present the basic kayaking procedures. These procedures are constant points of reference throughout the rest of the book, and any variations in method can be superimposed for special circumstances that are considered in later sections.

1. Throughout it will be assumed that the paddler is a competent swimmer and is ready to don sensible protective equipment after graduating from the shallow pool to deep and/or flowing water.

2. The sporty, ultramaneuverable recreational whitewater touring kayak is the "demonstration model" for the steps that follow. This choice is partly because it is the favorite all-purpose boat for whitewater or flatwater, and partly because it requires the widest range of paddling technique. Owing to hull design, the sleeker cruising or sea touring kayaks are much easier to track, and the wildwater racing or flatwater racing kayaks are hard to turn at all as the result of emphasis on forward speed. Therefore, if newcomers to the sport can learn how to control, stabilize, and propel the often tippy, mind-of-its-own recreational whitewater touring kayak, they can apply this acquired technique to managing less recalcitrant boats.

3. Since every good paddler becomes virtually ambidextrous in the course of getting into the water and practicing, the matter of handedness and master-sidedness does not enter into basic kayaking techniques. The procedures described *start from the right*.

Once upon a time, Nathaniel Hawthorne remarked that his friend Henry Thoreau had told him it was necessary only to *will* a boat to go in any direction, and the boat would immediately assume the desired course as if imbued with the spirit of its pilot. Perhaps Thoreau was simply being a good salesman for the joys of boating on Walden Pond or the Concord River; certainly he wasn't talking about any craft that resembles the modern sporty kayak.

Anatomy of a Kayak

Grabloops: you use these to lift and carry a kayak, to haul a capsized kayak to shore, and also to help tie down a kayak on a car rack.

Flotation bags: these are plastic bags filled with air to give a capsized kayak plenty of buoyancy.

Footbraces: adjustable for short or tall people; the balls of your feet should rest comfortably against them.

Coaming: the lip around the cockpit over which the spray cover fits to keep out water.

Kneebraces: foam pads or molded braces for your knees to rest comfortably against.

Seat and hipbraces: often molded together as one unit, it hangs from the coaming about one inch off the bottom of the kayak. Many seats are also contoured out of foam and secured to the bottom of the hull.

Backbrace: an adjustable strap located behind the hipbraces. Like seats, these also can consist of foam placed behind the seat.

Deck: the part of the kayak above water.

Hull: the bottom part of the kayak, most of which is underwater or rests on the water.

Gunwale: that point where the hull joins the deck; often a distinct seam around the kayak that joins the hull to the deck.

Jay's first kayak was named *Igluk* after the Eskimo god of mischief—and with good reason. One day during the early stages of his courtship with *Igluk* on a placid New Hampshire stream, a farmer haying close by noticed his predicament and called out: "You'll have to show 'er who's boss!"

So he was forced to learn kayaking technique. Which boils down to (1) knowing how to get in and out of your boat; (2) knowing how to right yourself when the kayak tips over; and (3) knowing how to paddle it so it will go precisely and effortlessly where you want it to go in any kind of water or weather—in circles, sideways, forward, and backward. And you'll find out how much your back, hips, abdomen, and legs contribute to control and propulsion.

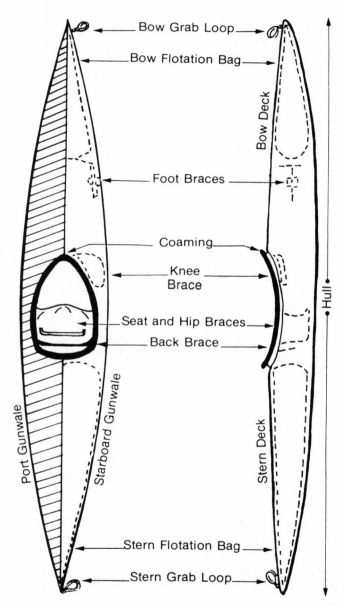

Bow Grab Loop

Bow Flotation Bag

Bow Deck

Foot Braces

Coaming

Knee
Brace

Seat and Hip Braces

Back Brace

Hull

Port Gunwale

Starboard Gunwale

Stern Deck

Stern Flotation Bag

Stern Grab Loop

Anatomy of a kayak.

Dry Run: Adjustments

If you're new to kayaking, you must shed the notion that you sit in a kayak: what you really do is *wear* it, because the kayak feels almost like an extension of your body. Then, ideally, it will respond to a command from your brain.

There are a few things, though, that you'll need to check out before you wear your kayak in the water, because if the fittings are too tight, your legs will soon fall asleep, and if the fittings are too loose, you'll rattle around inside the boat like a loose tie-rod.

For Legs, Back, and Knees

If you are tall, you may wish to move the footbraces forward toward the bow to be sure there'll be enough room for your legs to stretch out.

Some kayaks come equipped with a backbrace that can afford a measure of support to your lower back. This strap, which is often made of canvas webbing or rubber about 2 to 3 inches wide, stretches between the hipbraces just behind the seat. It can be adjusted to give you the firmness you need in order to feel comfortable yet snug in the seat.

Carefully run your fingers over the inside surface of the kneebraces, which are located just forward of the seat under the coaming. This is to make sure that there are no rough spots that might irritate your knees when you press them tightly against the braces. Any roughness should be smoothed out.

Now the Spray Cover

Because its purpose is to keep all water out of the kayak so your lower body will remain warm and dry when you're paddling, your spray cover must fit you and your boat snugly—*but not too tightly,* lest it constrict your movements.

Step into the spray cover (with the long part toward the front) and draw it up to your waist. Some spray covers have an adjustable drawstring at the waist, which is a handy feature. Neoprene spray covers seldom need adjustment at the waist, since they are so flexible. But if necessary, the waist opening can be made smaller by cutting out a 6-inch (15¼-centimeter) V at the waist and gluing the two sides back together with wet-suit cement (in sewing this would be called "making a dart"). Or if the waist is too small, simply cut a 6-inch (15¼-centimeter) slit at the waist, into which a slender, pie-shaped wedge of neoprene can then be cemented, enlarging the waist to the desired fit.

Once the waist is adjusted, you're ready to try the spray cover on the coaming. Still on dry land, step into the kayak—being sure to "hike up your cover" on the backside before you lower yourself into the seat (if it is caught under your derriere, it will be awkward to extricate after you're settled in the cockpit). Extend your legs forward until your feet touch the footbraces, and rest your knees against the kneebraces. If the seat and the foot-, hip-, and kneebraces all fit properly, you'll begin to feel what it means to "wear a kayak."

Using both hands, tuck the skirt part of the spray cover under the outside of the rolled edge of the coaming, *always starting from the rear* and working your way forward. Most spray covers are supplied with a release loop or some other safety device at the front end of the skirt that releases the cover immediately in case of emergency. If yours has such a loop, make sure the loop sticks out ready for use; then try it to insure that it will slip the spray cover off the coaming.

The spray cover should fit snugly enough around the coaming to be watertight. It should also have enough flexibility that it will slip off the coaming if you draw your knees up and push yourself up and away from the kayak. Try this a couple of times to satisfy yourself that the spray cover will come away from the coaming when necessary.

Stepping In/Out When It's Afloat

Once you've discovered what it's like to wear a kayak on dry land, your next move is to locate a quiet, shallow pond, lake, or pool and learn how to enter a kayak while it is resting on the water.

Bobbing gently at the water's edge, your little craft with its rounded bottom and 23-inch width offers a tiny cockpit that seems hardly big enough to get into.

As you look down at it, your first inclination might be to place your foot somewhere in the middle of that cockpit.

Your next move might be to put some weight on that foot.

Your next—and final—move will be to hold your nose quickly as the kayak skitters away and you fall headfirst into the drink. (Don't laugh: this actually happened years ago in the most polluted section of the Potomac River to a first-time kayaker who eventually became a National Champion.)

Stepping In

Here's what you *should* do. Place your kayak parallel to and against the bank or poolside in shallow water and hold your paddle behind you

Use your paddle as a brace to stabilize the kayak, and enter sideways, placing both feet in the cockpit before swinging your weight into the seat. (Ledyard Canoe Club)

with both hands. Squat down facing the bow. Reaching across the cockpit (assuming that you are entering the kayak from the *right*), hook the thumb of your left hand—which is still gripping the paddle shaft—under the coaming behind the seat. Next, place the right paddle blade so that it rests on the shore. Thus balanced by the paddle and crouched low next to the boat, step sideways into the boat, putting your left foot directly in front of the seat and slightly to the left of the centerline of the hull. Bring your right foot in next to the left foot, swing your fanny over the gunwale, and settle into the seat. Extend your legs forward until your feet touch the footbraces. Swing your paddle around in front of you, and you are ready for business.

Sometimes more experienced paddlers grip the coaming of the foredeck with their left thumb while holding the paddle in front of them (instead of holding the paddle and gripping the coaming behind them) as they enter, but this method is a little less stable and therefore takes a little more practice.

Stepping Out

To get out of your boat, first make sure that your spray cover is free of the coaming—if you had it on. Then draw both knees up toward your chest. Place the paddle behind you and—while holding it—grip the rear of the coaming with your left hand just as you did while entering the kayak. Your right hand should grip the shaft, providing you with a measure of stability as the right paddle blade rests along the shore. Carefully lift your right foot out of the boat and place it down on dry land next to the boat. Then do the same with your left foot and stand up.

You may want to practice your entry and exit several times to get them down pat before you try them with your spray cover on. And don't forget to hike up your cover in the back before you lower yourself into the cockpit.

The Wet Exit

As you begin to get the feel of what it's like to wear a kayak in the water, your first inclination may be to begin some forward strokes to see how neatly the little craft will skim across the pond. This would be like undertaking to drive on an ice-slick road without knowing how to keep from slewing out of control: you had better know the technique for getting out of a skid even though you hope no emergency will require you to use it.

Similarly, with a kayak, you should *learn first what to do if your boat capsizes.* This is one of those things that every paddler has in his repertoire, whether he's on a seemingly placid tour or is racing through whitewater on a slalom course. A good kayaker will rely on the Eskimo roll, which will be described step-by-step in Chapter 6.

But first things first. So push away from the shore until you are in waist-deep water. Place your hands on the gunwales—you're chicken if you reach for the spray cover instead—take a deep breath, then slowly capsize the kayak by leaning all the way over to your right.

Now you're upside down in the water, wearing a kayak. To prove that you don't feel uneasy about this new and unusual sensation, slowly slap the gunwales of the kayak three times before reaching for the coaming. Next release your knees from the kneebraces and draw your feet up as you detach the skirt from the coaming. Always keep in mind that you hold yourself in a kayak with muscle power and all you have to do is release tension (in no way is anyone tied into a kayak). *All this should be done in slow motion.* Push the boat gently away with your feet as you slip out of the cockpit. If you are not wearing a mask or nose plug, exhale slowly through your nostrils to keep water out of your nose until you have surfaced. Repeat the wet exit procedure until you are absolutely comfortable with it.

Later, practice the wet exit with a paddle, keeping in mind not to let your paddle get away from the kayak: catch it immediately as you swim toward the bow or stern grabloop. You can hold the paddle *and* grabloop in one hand as you use the other hand to help propel yourself and your boat toward shore.

Maintain Contact

Always maintain contact with your kayak.

The easiest way to do this is to keep one hand on the coaming as your head comes to the surface of the water, then swim quickly down to the bow or stern grabloop and begin to tow your boat to the nearest shore.

Keep It Upside Down

Always keep the kayak upside down when you're towing it to shore after a wet exit: it will ride higher in the water that way, because of the air trapped inside.

Stay Upstream Yourself

Always *stay upstream of your boat* when you're swimming with it in moving current, and you'll never be pinned on a rock or other obstruction.

If you keep this point in mind whenever you practice—even in the gentlest of currents—it can become an almost automatic reflex when you're obliged to exit in whitewater.

Solo Kayak Recovery

Your companions have slipped around the bend of the river, just barely out of sight, and suddenly you capsize. Not yet knowing the Eskimo roll, you do a wet exit, remembering to keep your kayak upside down as you head for the nearest shore. You also remember to keep your paddle at hand.

But help may be out of earshot, and you are on your own.

Now what?

First, while you stand in shallow water, run the bow or stern of the kayak as far as possible up on the shore, *still keeping the boat upside down.* Slowly lift the lower end of the boat—the end that is lying in the water— and allow all the remaining water to slosh toward the cockpit and drain out.

Quickly snap the kayak over, float it, and *presto!* you're ready to get

To empty the water from a capsized kayak, run the stern end up on shore or poolside while the boat is upside down, and lift the bow end to let the water drain out of the cockpit. (Ledyard Canoe Club)

in, catch up with your companions, and remind them that kayakers should always stick together.

The solo kayak recovery is also helpful when, more experienced, you are practicing maneuvers and are tipping over rather frequently.

The Critical Point

In learning to drive a car, you have to get the hang of what the gearing, brakes, and steering wheel do before you head out into rush-hour traffic. Likewise, in kayaking, you must get used to your boat, its reactions, and its controls before you point your bow toward open water and its currents.

Start with exploring the stability of your boat and determining the critical point of capsize. The critical point is the maximum number of degrees you can lean to either side before you actually lose control and tip over. You'll be surprised what an extreme angle it is.

To find your critical point, position your kayak close to land in about a foot (31 centimeters) of water and extend your paddle until the blade rests on the shore: you are now using the blade as a support when you lean too far. This support is a stabilizer, and it's a rudimentary form of the *paddle brace*—which will be discussed in the next chapter under "Preliminary Exercises" to the Eskimo roll and will be discussed in full in Chapter 7 under "Stabilizing Strokes."

Supporting yourself with an extended paddle brace, lean as far as possible to one side to determine the critical point of capsize—often an angle as great as 90 degrees. (Ledyard Canoe Club)

Now try first to lean at least 45 degrees without letting the boat slip out from under you. Then proceed to 90 degrees, where you wiggle back and forth with your hips just to show the kayak that you are in command. Recover and repeat several times, on alternate sides, until you develop a good feel for the craft.

This exercise has an added importance because it gives you a sense of hip action and the power that the muscles of your abdomen and legs can exert on the kayak to make it react properly under you. This controlling action is the *hip snap,* and it is one of the most important components of kayaking.

Three Basic Control Strokes

The Sweep

The sweep is a turning stroke. It is too early to go into the fine points of paddle handling. These will be discussed in the section dealing with the forward stroke (Chapter 7). For now it is enough simply to hold your paddle comfortably with both hands, keeping in mind that the scooped side—or face—is the business side of the paddle blade 99 percent of the time.

Try a sweep by placing the right blade in the water near the bow— at the 1 o'clock point—about 5 inches (13 centimeters) deep, then sweep out and around as far as you can without letting the blade sink deeper

To turn using a sweep stroke, bring the paddle around from 1 o'clock to 5 o'clock without letting the blade sink completely below the water's surface. (Robert F. George)

A really vigorous sweep stroke will lift your bow and sink your stern momentarily. (Eric Evans)

below the surface. One should be able to complete a round-the-clock turn in just three strong stokes.

Practice the sweep both to the right and to the left.

The Draw

The purpose of the draw stroke is to pull the kayak sideways in the water. What a great move this is to have in your bag of tricks when you're running the rapids and a rock suddenly looms in front of you!

To perform the draw, lean and reach out with the paddle to 3 o'clock. Lower the blade into the water as far as the throat, then pull the paddle steadily and evenly toward you, leaning strongly sideways toward the paddle to increase leverage and power. In order to secure the best purchase of the blade in the water, make sure that your top hand on the paddle shaft is as directly above the bottom hand as possible. If your top hand is too low (down near your chin), you will simply massage the surface of the water with the bottom blade, and the draw will lose much of its force.

Remove the blade from the water as it approaches the gunwale. Beware of having the draw stroke continue so that the blade starts going under the boat at the end of the stroke; often a capsize will result. With practice you will not have to remove the blade from the water at the

The draw stroke moves the kayak sideways. Insert the paddle as far as the throat on the side toward which you want to move, and pull steadily toward you. Lean toward the paddle to increase leverage. (Robert F. George)

end of the draw, but by simply rolling your wrists forward (thus changing the angle of the blade 90 degrees), you can slide or "feather" the blade back out to its original starting position.

It is also possible to draw while using your hips to hold the kayak on an absolutely even keel—that is, without leaning in the direction of the paddle.

Or, as an exercise to increase hip control, try holding a lean *away* from the direction of your paddle. You'll be surprised how easily the water slips under your kayak this way.

Practice drawing on either side for 50 yards (45 meters) at a stretch. At the Hampshire College pool, we sometimes hold draw stroke races from one side of the pool to the other. Relay races can also be held in this manner for practice.

During successive draw strokes, you will likely find that one end of the kayak will move ahead of the other; you won't be able to keep the kayak straight as you move steadily sideways. To correct this, try starting the draw stroke just a few inches more toward the end of the kayak that is lagging behind in order to bring it even with the faster end.

The Scull

Somtimes it is important to maintain a lean longer than a normal draw allows. This is where the scull stroke comes in.

Actually the scull is not much more than a multiple draw stroke wherein the blade never leaves the water. It cuts a slight arc through the water as it is pulled toward the gunwale, then slices its way out again away from the boat in a motion rather like forming a figure eight. It is a graceful maneuver and a very nice way of moving your kayak into a better position laterally.

If you are sculling to maintain a leaning position, then you should keep your top hand on the shaft (the hand farthest from the water) as low as possible. To provide more of a sideways movement à la the draw

The scull stroke enables you to maintain a lean or maneuver your kayak sideways. Move the paddle in a slow figure eight from bow to stern. (Robert F. George)

stroke, raise your top hand in order to secure more purchase for your blade in the water.

After a long hard paddle on a hot day, a good sculler can refresh himself by leaning far enough over while sculling to duck his head in the water.

Practice sculling on both the right and left sides for 50-yard (45-meter) intervals.

Summary

You have now learned the parts of a kayak and how to get in and out of one safely and easily. You have learned how to attach your spray cover to the kayak and that it helps keep the boat dry inside. You may have been surprised to find out how stable a kayak really is. After getting it to capsize, you discovered you weren't trapped in the boat after all. Releasing the spray cover from around the coaming and then gently pushing away with your feet slips you out of the cockpit smoothly. Once the kayak was emptied, you practiced the three basic control strokes: sweep, draw, and scull.

Don't be in a rush to go kayaking down the river or across the lake quite yet. May we urge you in the strongest possible terms to take time to master that exciting maneuver, the Eskimo roll (discussed in the next chapter), before you venture out on the water. Next to common sense, it's the best kayak safety insurance you can buy.

6. The Eskimo Roll

Eskimo kayaks first appeared in Western European annals on a map by a Danish cartographer, drawn perhaps as early as 1425. But it was not until 1767 that there appeared written information available to Europeans about the Eskimo roll. David Crantz, in his *History of Greenland,* describes 10 different methods Eskimos used to bring their fragile little skin boats back upright after tipping over. In 1927 the Austrian Hans Edi Pawlata learned to roll his kayak and began teaching others how to do it. This dramatic technique provided a springboard for the rise in popularity of kayaking in Europe. It stands as one of the major milestones in the history of modern kayaking.

After World War II, European kayakers such as Paul Bruhin and Erich Seidel brought their skills to North America. Some of the first Americans to learn the Eskimo roll were from Colorado. One of them, Ron Bohlender, came east in the mid-1950s to the West River in Vermont. In front of a large, admiring crowd at a place on the river called the Salmon Hole, he suddenly threw his paddle away and capsized. The crowd gasped. The kayak began to drift slowly downstream upside down. People ran down the river bank to rescue the boat. Suddenly a second paddle came out from under his boat, and with it, Bohlender completed an Eskimo roll. The crowd cheered. Bohlender had hidden a collapsible paddle under his deck. While head down, he had somehow drawn it out, fitted it together, and used it to roll.

Preparing for the Eskimo Roll

The Eskimo roll—the complete capsize followed by a self-recovery full circle to an upright position again—is one of the most dramatic maneuvers in kayaking. It's something that anyone can learn with a little patience. There are people who can perform the full Eskimo roll without using a paddle at all: of these, some can bring themselves back upright with only one bare hand; and a real stunt man can do it with only his clenched fist.

Formerly the roll was considered an advanced trick reserved for the expert. This attitude has undergone a change, though, and today the Eskimo roll is regarded as so essential to safety that the beginning kayaker must master it *before* he ventures out on a river or lake.

Mastery of the Eskimo roll not only assures an excellent margin of safety in most situations, but it also promotes psychological confidence and prepares the beginner for learning the other basics of handling a kayak. So what if you capsize? With a reliable roll, you can come back up immediately, ready for anything.

In our teaching of the Eskimo roll to literally thousands of paddlers over the past 30 years, we have seen astonishing successes and miserable failures. We both fell into the latter category while trying to learn this maneuver. Jay took an entire summer in the late 1950s trying to learn the Eskimo roll in a heated pool in South Hamilton, Massachusetts. Then again, he had no instruction and no book to guide him. In the early sixties, Jay tried to teach Eric how to roll, and the student made a common mistake day after day for almost a month: trying to muscle his way upright instead of using finesse and technique.

On the other hand, we have had students learn the maneuver in a half hour or less. One day, in the midseventies, someone from the kitchen staff at Hampshire College arrived at the pool during one of Eric's rolling sessions. He watched for about 15 minutes and then asked if he could try it. Whereupon Eric tried offering assistance. The newcomer refused, saying he could do it on his own. And by golly, he did! He is the only person we have ever seen do the Eskimo roll the first time without going through at least some of the preliminary steps. Eric, recalling his earlier efforts at mastering the roll, could only shrug and offer congratulations.

More than likely, however, you will have to be patient. But the roll, truly mastered, is like riding a bicycle: you never forget how to do it.

The following sequence for the roll has evolved over the years and is designed specifically for the average person who has no special athletic ability.

First—Observe

If possible watch an expert perform the roll several times in slow motion. Stand in shallow water and, with each of his revolutions, concentrate your attention on a different aspect of the maneuver: notice where and how he grips his paddle; note the sweeping motion of his arms, then the motion of his upper body; pay particular attention to the blade angle. Study him in action from the front, from both sides, from the rear. Next, take a pair of goggles and watch his roll from several underwater positions.

As you watch from all angles, this is what you see: a deliberate full capsize until he is completely upside down in the water; the placing of the paddle in the correct position, and then the arc of his stroke sideways just under the surface; a hip snap and a backward lean (*lay back*) of the upper torso—and he's brought himself upright again, on the side opposite from the one he went down on.

Preliminary Exercises

Now that you have the overall picture in mind, you're ready to get in your boat and perform in sequence the following exercises that build up to your own Eskimo roll.

Note: all the procedures described are accomplished in water *no more than 3 feet (92 centimeters) deep*—which will give ample clearance for even a tall person upside down in a kayak. The photographs to demonstrate the sequences were taken of paddlers in the shallow end of a regulation swimming pool, but the kayakers could just as easily have been practicing at the shallow edge of a pond if they had established that there were no obstructions underwater. Of course, in open or unfamiliar water, each would have been wearing a helmet, as every capable boater does.

Exercise No. 1: The Eskimo Rescue

This first exercise consists of a partial capsize and recovery back up on the same side, and it is designed to give the new kayaker confidence in his ability to control his boat and himself, and to demonstrate the value of the hip snap and the lay back in his recovery to an upright position.

Aside from your own boat, the only thing you need for the Eskimo rescue is another kayaker stationed at 3 o'clock, with the bow of his boat pointing directly at you only a foot (31 centimeters) or so away from your right elbow.

Reach over, grab his bow with both hands, and slowly lower yourself to your right into the water, allowing your kayak to capsize while you

In the Eskimo rescue, first allow your boat to capsize while you hold on to the bow of a friend's boat that is positioned perpendicular to yours. To right yourself, combine hip snap with a minimal pull on the rescue boat. (Jay Evans)

maintain your grip on the bow of the helping boat. Then, still hanging on to his bow, use a hip snap and lay back to see if you can get your kayak back upright again without having to chin yourself too much on the bow of the rescue boat. Exerting pressure on your kneebraces will help your hip snap immensely, so here you press your right knee strongly in against its brace to add power to your hip snap and force your kayak to slide back under you again.

The idea of this exercise is to rely chiefly on the hip snap, and to a lesser degree the lay back, and to use your arms and hands only to a minimum extent as you pull yourself upright.

Repeat, alternating the side you capsize on, until the procedure of recovery becomes second nature. Increase your lean as you practice so you can go over with confidence the full 180 degrees, until you and your kayak are completely upside down, before you come back up with the help of the other boat.

Now you're ready to go all the way over *without using the standby craft to help you tip over*.

Bend forward at the waist—any capsize is smoother if your trunk is positioned low—lean to the right, and ease yourself into the water as your hands rest lightly on the gunwales.

Pause there upside down for a moment to let things settle. Then slap your hands on your hull as it lies above water to draw your partner's attention. He will quickly bring his boat over to you until his bow nudges your near hand. Grab his bow with both hands, give a good hip snap to do most of the work, and bring yourself back up again.

The Eskimo rescue sure beats having to wet exit, tow your boat to shore, and bail it out before you can get going again. And the rescue is particularly useful when a bunch of beginners are together practicing or are training in an indoor pool.

Exercise No. 2: Assisted Recovery to the Opposite Side

This exercise is similar to what you did in the Eskimo rescue, except that here you make a 360-degree turnover, coming up on the *opposite* side in your recovery. You're getting closer to the actual Eskimo roll, even though you rely on a helper to recover.

In Exercise No. 1, you got the hang of a controlled capsize to the right without assistance. Now, though, you will use the same method, but you will *capsize to your left*. And the important part will be how you recover on the second half of the revolution—through the remaining 180 degrees—and come up on the right as before.

First have a helper stand in waist-deep water on your right side just behind your cockpit. There he will position your paddle steadily on the

This kayaker, practicing an assisted recovery to the opposite side, had capsized to his left side and is recovering on his right side, using a friend's paddle to help pull himself upright. His head and shoulders should emerge last. (Ledyard Canoe Club)

surface of the water parallel to your boat and about 6 inches (15¼ centimeters) away from it.

Then, when he is ready, you will capsize to your left.

After you complete the capsize, reach across your body until you grasp the paddle shaft that is being held for you (your helper must maintain firm control of the paddle, keeping it immovable).

Finally, pull yourself up toward the paddle and, at the same time, use your hips to make the kayak slide under you until you are completely upright again. However, *your head and shoulders must emerge from the water after the kayak has begun to assume an upright position.*

Try capsizing several times on either side until the recovery becomes a very natural and relaxed motion—and always with your head and shoulders coming up *last* and leaning backward toward the stern, for this point is highly important to a successful Eskimo roll. If you let your head and shoulders emerge first, your assistant can remind you by rapping his knuckles on your unsuspecting head as it comes up. A couple of sharp raps and you'll remember to keep your head down.

Exercise No. 3: The Little Fingers Technique

The necessity of a good hip snap in executing the roll is the point of this one.

Ask a helper to stand in waist-deep water next to your cockpit facing you. Interlock the little finger of your left hand with the little finger of his right hand; interlock the little finger of your right hand with the little finger of his left.

Now gently capsize toward him, keeping your fingers interlocked with his. No fair grabbing his whole hand! You are now upside down but still connected to your helper.

You will need herculean strength if you attempt to right yourself solely by pulling with your fingers in order to get your head and shoulders above water. Instead, exert pressure on your hip- and kneebraces in an effort to force the kayak to slide under you. You'll be surprised how easily the kayak does this, and how quickly you see daylight. The more hip and knee pressure, the less effort will be needed with your fingers.

Don't forget to practice the little fingers exercise capsized to the other side.

Exercise No. 4: The Paddle Brace Recovery

By now you are at ease in the controlled capsize, and you can employ good hip snap to help get yourself topside again. Therefore, with this exercise, you are advancing to the self-recovery aspect of the Eskimo roll: here you will begin to *paddle yourself upright*.

You have come far since you used a dry-land paddle brace in discovering your critical point of capsize when you were getting used to wearing a kayak. This time, though, it will be a real brace, which uses leverage on the water instead of on solid ground.

But before you start, let's take a look at your paddle again to see how it will function in this maneuver.

Get set in water no more than 3 feet (92 centimeters) deep, and have an assistant close by to effect an Eskimo rescue if your efforts get a bit scrambled before you get the knack of this new maneuver.

Lean to the right almost to the critical point of capsize. Next—still leaning—slap the face of your right-hand paddle blade *flat on the surface of the water* near your bow at 1 o'clock. Then swing your blade—still

---

Your Blade Angle in the Brace

The blades at each end of your kayak paddle are feathered, which means that they are set at a right angle to each other. Thus, when one blade is flat on the water, the other blade is stand up like a fin.

In addition the chances are 10-to-1 that the blades are scooped—that is, they have a slightly concave face, or business side, and a slightly rounded back. This spooned design makes your pull through the water more effective. However, it also means that your blade can "dive" when you swing it flat along the surface of the water in a paddle brace unless you *keep the leading edge slightly raised.*

Nonscooped blades will dive too, of course, if their leading edge is not slightly raised during a brace.

holding it flat on the water—in an arc until it's about at 3 o'clock, and you will automatically resume an upright position.

Now lean a little farther and right yourself with your paddle brace as before. Repeat, leaning more each time, until you can go well *beyond* the critical point, each time swinging the blade around to 3 o'clock in order to recover.

Eventually you'll be able to brace for several seconds while your shoulder and even part of your head are in the water, *and still recover.* At the end of your swing, you may want to draw or scull a little to assist your recovery.

The paddle brace recovery should be practiced many times on both sides. And it is a good general warm-up exercise when you first get into your kayak before attempting rapids.

Exercise No. 5: The Half Roll to the Right

This half roll contains the key maneuver for self-recovery in any Eskimo roll, and it is the final exercise before you proceed to the full roll itself.

The half roll is a controlled 180-degree capsize and recovery back up on the same side by initiating a paddle brace while you're upside down in the water, and by using "body English" mainly in the form of a strong hip snap and lay back.

You will recover without help from anybody else—but do have someone standing by in the water to assist you the first few times in case you can use a helping hand. And it would be a good idea to wear goggles or a face mask: you'll welcome a clear underwater view of the pitch of your paddle blade until you can bring off the recovery by feel alone.

Throughout the maneuver, you will be using an *extended paddle grip—* which increases the effective radius of your paddle, as you will see— and you *must maintain your blade angle by keeping its leading edge slightly raised.*

So start by holding your paddle alongside the left gunwale with your right hand somewhere comfortably near the middle of the shaft, palm down and thumb toward you. This is where the "extended" part comes in: with your hand moved back on the shaft instead of in its normal grip nearer the forward blade, you're adding about 18 inches to your paddle's range.

Lay your forward blade flat on the water near your bow, *face up* (so it will be business side *down* when you get completely capsized), and with its leading edge slightly raised. To maintain it at the correct angle and increase its leverage, reach your left hand back and, thumb down, grasp the tip of the rear blade to insure that it stands up like a fin and thus maintains your forward blade approximately flat.

A kayaker prepares for a half roll to the right. Note the correct hand and paddle positions along the left gunwale. (Ledyard Canoe Club)

With your paddle set, bend forward for a smooth capsize and turn completely over to your right.

Upside down in the water, keep your paddle close to your left gunwale and at the surface of the water in the same position it was before you capsized. You're now ready to use the pressure of a paddle brace to initiate your recovery.

Swing the forward blade in a quarter circle away from your bow, watching your leading edge through your goggles to insure that it is slightly raised and thus will skim along the surface without diving. As you bring your blade around from your bow, give a good hip snap to help get yourself upright again. Remember that the more pressure you exert against your right kneebrace, the more effective your hip snap will be, and the more readily your kayak will slide under you as you come back up again.

If you can recover successfully on your very first try at the half roll, you're some kind of athlete!

The rest of us, though, can probably use a little outside assistance. Thus:

1. Station a helper so he will be standing near the tip of your forward blade after you have capsized to the right.

Go completely over and allow your friend to guide your blade lightly in the proper arc on the surface of the water. Immediately you will feel the torsion produced by your upside-down paddle brace; at the same time, you'll sense the effectiveness of the pressure exerted by your right knee in aiding the hip snap portion of your recovery.

2. Move your helper to a position just behind your cockpit on your left. When you capsize to the right, he will reach across the bottom of

After capsizing in a half roll to the right, have a friend guide your blade in a paddle brace arc on the surface of the water. This pressure, plus the force of the hip snap, brings you upright. (Ledyard Canoe Club)

For extra help in the half roll, have your helper move behind the cockpit and gently pull on the kayak to help you roll back up. (Ledyard Canoe Club)

your hull, take hold of your left gunwale, and gently pull it back up as you work with paddle and hip snap to get yourself upright again.

As you become more proficient, he will help less and less—until, at some point unknown to you, you are accomplishing your recovery without any help from him at all.

3. In the course of your practice with a helper, you will get so accustomed to the feel of the correct angle of your forward blade that you no longer need the extra control derived from holding your rear blade by its tip. At this stage, you may wish to move your left hand up to the throat of the rear blade and control the pitch of your forward blade from there.

Exercise No. 6: The Half Roll to the Left

In many cases, people learning to roll will wish to continue working on one side until their roll is perfected. However, the "compleat kayaker" is one who eventually masters the Eskimo roll on *both* sides and thus can recover from a capsize at will, righting himself from either side as it suits his fancy at the moment.

Therefore those paddlers whose goal is to be ambidextrous in the water will want to take some time out to practice the half roll to the left. The procedure is simply a reversal of the exercise used for the half roll to the right.

With your left hand at midshaft and your right hand behind you holding the tip of your rear blade, place your forward blade on the water face up, just to the right of your bow and with its leading edge slightly raised. Capsize to the left and, when you're 180 degrees upside down, arc your forward blade back from the bow, give a strong hip snap with good pressure on your left kneebrace, lay back, and recover to an upright position. Repeat the maneuver with the aid of a helper until you have it down pat and can recover confidently on your own.

Master-sidedness may be a slight factor here. Occasionally a paddler who has cinched self-recovery on one side will take longer to perform the exercise well on the opposite side. The answer of course is to practice half rolls until there are no hang-ups with recovery on either side.

The Full Eskimo Roll

When you have nailed down the half roll and recovery, it is a simple matter to complete the full 360-degree Eskimo roll.

You merely capsize to the opposite side from the one on which you initiated the half roll, and when you're in position to start your self-

The complete sequence of steps in the Eskimo roll takes you full circle from the initial upright position (top drawing) through the capsize and recovery. (Walter Richardson)

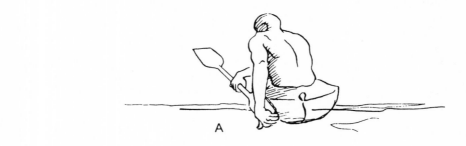

A

B

C

Continuation of sequence of the Eskimo roll.
(Walter Richardson)

recovery, you execute exactly the same paddle movement, hip snap, and lay back that brought you up from the half roll.

Thus, if you're going to recover on your right, you place your paddle on your left and capsize to your left.

If you're going to recover on your left, then position your paddle correctly on your right and capsize to your right.

On the first couple of tries, you may want a helper standing by as in the half roll practices—but the partner will be there mainly for moral support. Actually you are likely to find the full 360-degree roll easier, because you have momentum going for you as you reach the 180-degree mark in your capsize.

And remember: *how you capsize is far less important than WHAT YOU DO ONCE YOU'RE UPSIDE DOWN to get yourself topside to daylight again.*

Summing Up Key Points in the Eskimo Roll

1. Hold your paddle in an extended grip and have the forward blade positioned perfectly, then capsize.

2. Keeping the leading edge of your forward blade slightly raised— lest it dive when you swing it around in the brace movement—bring your blade flat in an arc from bow to side.

3. Exert pressure against your recovery-side kneebrace to give added strength to your hip snap.

4. Synchronize your brace, hip snap, and lay back so your boat slides under you *before* your shoulders and head emerge from the water.

The Eskimo Roll in Current

Every newcomer to the sport who has gained confidence in the roll as the result of honing his technique in pool or pond will be doubly pleased with the maneuver when it is executed with a gentle assist from flowing water.

Therefore the next step is to find a safe place in a river. "Safe" means a spot that is near the bank, is about 3 feet (92 centimeters) deep, has been thoroughly checked to be free of underwater obstructions, and has a modest current.

Which bank you choose to take off from is up to you: you are going to capsize in the current while leaning *upstream* and recover on the *downstream* side. Therefore do your very first river reading to decide how you will point your boat upstream initially to get broadside to the current.

Are you more comfortable in a recovery to the right? Then plan to have your left side upstream. If you're more proficient at recovering on the left, plan to get in position with your right side upstream.

Then put on your helmet and lifejacket and have a helper in the water standing by (these are rudimentary safety measures that show you have common water sense), paddle your kayak a few strokes to the chosen place—and try your roll.

You will be pleasantly surprised at how much easier it is to roll as the current gives you added momentum, but in the excitement of moving water, you may temporarily lose your skill in completing the roll. Don't be disheartened. This is only natural, and it happens to most of us. Simply withdraw from the moving current and practice the roll in calm water or in a pool for awhile.

When you feel completely confident about handling the roll from an upstream capsize, practice rolling from a variety of positions in the river. You might even try recovering on the upstream side: it really isn't all that difficult.

. . . Then the "Wild" Roll

Before you tackle the roll in actual rapids, simulate whitewater conditions by sprinting for at least 20 yards (about 18 meters) in relatively flat water, then capsize suddenly, without taking time to set your paddle angle or otherwise position yourself correctly before you go over. Once underwater in a full capsize, get organized for a correct recovery— and roll back up.

Practice capsizing at full speed on both sides, with correct recovery. Be sure to sprint long enough so you're slightly out of breath—as you would be if paddling hard in demanding whitewater. And as you gain confidence, capsize while holding your paddle with only one hand.

. . . At Last, in Whitewater

Later, when you have truly learned to "read the river," will come the ultimate phase of this maneuver: the Eskimo roll in whitewater.

When practicing your roll in rapids, it is more important than ever before to make sure the water is deep enough—the usual 3 feet (92 centimeters) is plenty—and that there is a quiet pool or "catch basin" just below your practice spot to give you a welcome parking place.

The difference here is that *you* choose the place and time to roll rather than having the river dictate that choice for you. Therefore you should practice rolling from different angles in whitewater, from completely sideways to heading directly up- or downstream. Always remember to assume a protective tucked-forward position as you capsize. This will provide you with maximum protection should you bump against a submerged rock. Don't be in too much of a hurry when you're upside down in whitewater—you can hold your breath long enough to do 10 consecutive Eskimo rolls. It's important to set your paddle properly in the right position before you commence the roll. Slap the paddle blade a couple of times on the surface of the water just to make sure it's at the right angle and that it's at the surface—not below.

Sometimes the water around you will appear frothy and foamy, without much substance to it. If so, just relax for a moment. You'll soon drift down the river into heavier water.

If your first attempt doesn't succeed, simply take a deep breath, go under, and carefully set up again. We have seen people make as many as 10 attempts before succeeding. That's OK; it's a lot better than swimming. Your first accidental capsize in really big water, followed by a successful roll, will be the highlight of your day. What a feeling of confidence it gives you! If, in the future, the rapids get sassy and pitch you around a bit, even tossing you over—so what? Simply roll back up and continue on your way. You may not have mastered the river, but you have mastered yourself.

The Broken Paddle Roll

Most of today's paddles are strong enough to withstand all but the worst treatment, but there's still the chance that a blade will get wedged between submerged rocks and break—possibly causing a capsize as well. A simple exercise such as the following is worth the time spent in practice: it could come in handy some day.

First get a paddle that has one blade broken and thus is useless as a lever for performing the Eskimo roll. This shouldn't be a problem, because paddles break either at the throat or somewhere on the blade itself. If you can't find a broken kayak paddle, use a canoe paddle; since it has only one blade, it will serve your purpose.

Second, pretend you don't know your paddle is broken, then capsize in the first stage of the roll and try to recover with the broken end. You'll feel immediately, as you swing the paddle around in its accustomed arc, that you are getting little or no leverage.

Third, slip back again into a fully capsized position, and simply *switch your paddle around in your hands* so you are now working with the good blade. Carefully set its angle with the leading edge slightly raised, sweep it out and around, use good hip snap, and you will roll back up with the good half of the paddle.

The Hands-Only Roll

Once you have become proficient in the Eskimo roll, you'll feel a great sense of accomplishment and achievement. You have mastered the ancient art of the Eskimos. This new skill is your best bet against getting into difficulty in the water.

Some of you, however, will want to take it one step farther. Suppose, in a capsize, you lose your grip on the paddle. It floats away out of reach. Never fear. With some practice, you can actually learn to roll your kayak back to an upright position without using the paddle at all!

Here's how it is done. First you should be totally secure with your roll with a paddle, preferably on *both* sides. You should have a good hip snap and the roll must be very reliable. Once you've achieved that through practice, you're ready to advance to the next step.

Discard your kayak paddle and replace it with a small canoe paddle; practice your roll with it. The sweeping motion is the same as you learned for the kayak-paddle-assisted roll. Once this is mastered, cut yourself two 1-inch boards about 10 inches wide and 2 feet long. (In metric measurements, you'll want two 2½-centimeter boards about 25½ centimeters wide and 61 centimeters long.) Holding one in each hand, capsize and perform the roll. You'll notice with each progressive step you are relying less and less on the "paddle" and more and more on your hip snap. Again, sweep the two boards around in that now-familiar arc to complete the roll.

At this stage, it is essential that the boat slip under you first, then your shoulders emerge, and finally your head. If your head pops up first, stop right there and go back to your paddle. Practice rolling with your head coming out of the water last.

The next step is to try it with a pair of Ping-Pong paddles. Then with only one Ping-Pong paddle, using the flat palm of your hand in place of the other paddle.

Now, cast aside the remaining crutch, the Ping-Pong paddle. Capsize, link your thumbs with your palms out flat, sweep around in the familiar arc, give it a strong hip snap, and—presto—you're seeing daylight again.

Now try it with only one hand. Tuck the other into the top of your spray cover. In each of these steps, once you have learned it on one side, you should then take time to master it on the other before moving on to the last step.

You are now ready for moving current. Head diagonally upstream and toss your paddle to a nearby companion, after making sure that the water is deep enough and that there are no underwater obstructions in the area. Allow the upstream gunwale to become caught. Over you go.

Using both hands (Ping-Pong paddles are certainly acceptable for the first few times you try it), you'll discover to your surprise how easy it really is. The secret, of course, is that when you roll over upstream and then recover on the downstream side, *you are making the current work for you*. The force of the water against your boat helps the hip snap in righting the kayak again.

When Americans first started attending the World Whitewater Championships in Europe in the 1950s and 1960s, they soon established themselves as superb rollers—perhaps because they were capsizing so much! Many of those early racers were proficient in the no-paddle roll. In 1963 one of the Americans asked multi-World Champion Manfred Schubert of East Germany if he could do a hands-only or no-paddle roll. He simply garrumphed and said, "Do I eat without a spoon?" Later that day, on a practice run, Manfred flipped and lost his paddle. He spent several cold minutes in the Leiser River in Spittal, Austria, swimming to shore with his boat. Perhaps with a spoon. . . .

Summary

Learning the Eskimo roll is essential to your becoming a competent and safe kayaker. Don't leapfrog over the exercises provided in this chapter unless you're a great athlete. For most of us, it's like learning long division in mathematics: you must first learn to add, subtract, and multiply. So it is with the Eskimo roll. Master each exercise thoroughly—on both sides of your boat—before moving on to the next skill. You'll be glad you did.

7. Driving, Stabilizing, and Turning Strokes

The Driving Strokes

Having the wet exit and the Eskimo roll under our belts, we can now concentrate on getting from here to there in a kayak. Let's start with the forward stroke, examining its components and seeing how the paddle will work in our hands.

The Forward Stroke

The forward stroke can be one of the most beautiful movements in all sport, exhilarating for the spectator and paddler alike. Knowledge and many hours of practice are required to perfect it.

A quiet day's cruise across a lake or down a stream for several miles is done in a greater degree of comfort, with less fatigue, if a good, efficient forward stroke is learned beforehand. A sea kayaker trying to reach land in a gale will be grateful for all the hours he spent perfecting his forward stroke. In whitewater, a smooth-flowing forward stroke, properly executed, does wonders toward positioning the boater safely as he negotiates the rapids. Finally, in flatwater, marathon, or whitewater races, an efficient and powerful forward stroke is absolutely vital to success.

How It Works

Basically the forward stroke is a cycling movement of arms and shoulders. It is similar in principle to pedaling a bicycle, and it must be executed with great precision and smoothness in order to be efficient. It is the economic application of effort properly done that permits the paddler to attain a greater sustained speed at less expenditure of energy.

Such a prolonged effort can be maintained only if the muscles relax in the course of the stroke. Fortunately, in kayaking the business of alternating your arms between the dip and the recovery will ensure this relaxation.

Body Position

As you settle into your kayak, maintain a naturally comfortable position with your feet firmly against the footbraces and knees against the kneebraces. Now lean forward slightly—but not too far. And don't slouch: keep your head up and look forward.

With both hands palms down, grasp the paddle in front of you so that it is parallel to the water level. Your hands should be about 2½ to 3 feet (76 to 92 centimeters) apart and approximately 6 inches (15 centimeters) up the paddle shaft from the throat. This position will make your arms create an angle of about 90 degrees at the elbows.

How the Paddle Will Turn

Virtually all kayak paddles today are feathered, and the majority of these are spooned in such a way as to require right control or left control— with right-control paddles being by far the most common.

Therefore, as you make a stroke on the right side with a right-control paddle, you will rotate the shaft a quarter turn with your right hand so the blade will enter the water in the correct position. Simultaneously your left hand relaxes a bit to allow the shaft to rotate.

To stroke on your left side, again rotate the shaft with your right hand so the left blade will enter the water properly, and then grip the shaft firmly with your left hand as you pull the left blade through the water.

The turning of the shaft with each individual stroke makes certain that the blade just removed from the water will slice neatly through the air, offering little or no wind resistance.

If you find that your paddle is left control (as mentioned earlier, this is determined by the spoon of each blade), then your left hand always turns the shaft while your right hand relaxes.

Components of the Forward Stroke

We can divide the forward stroke into three closely interrelated parts— the dip, the draw back through the water, and the withdraw/recovery.

1. *The Dip.* Lean slightly forward—but not too far. Extend your right arm forward as far as you can toward the bow and insert the right blade completely in the water. Meanwhile your left wrist should be at ear level, your left elbow pointed down and slightly away from the kayak to provide maximum leverage. The fingers of your left hand may be fairly relaxed on the shaft at this point.

2. *The Draw.* With full muscular effort, draw the blade straight back to the midpoint of the kayak *but not beyond.* Your right wrist is straight, but your right elbow flexes as the blade comes directly back alongside the kayak. To apply more power, don't hesitate to turn your body and shoulders a little to the right as you draw the blade back. Put your body into the stroke, because if you let your arms do all the work, they'll soon tire.

While your right hand was dipping and drawing back, your left hand (which controlled the other half of the paddle) pressed straight forward toward the center line of the kayak at eye level. This movement of the left arm and hand is not unlike putting the shot in track, or delivering a straight left to the jaw of your opponent in boxing.

Don't allow the dip-and-draw arm to do all the work in each cycle of strokes: if you paddle this way, you'll soon be fatigued (maybe after only a quarter mile of paddling). Instead, think of the power of the forward stroke as coming from two distinct sources: about 65 percent from your dip and draw, and about 35 percent from your forward punch with the other hand—while rhythmically moving your body and shoulders at the waist to the right and left to complement both draw and push. Both power sources working in harmony not only produce an amazingly efficient forward stroke with which you can paddle for miles, but they also create a graceful movement that is completely satisfying aesthetically.

Long-distance tourers or sea kayakers on extended trips will want to employ a modified version of this forward stroke: less forward punch with the top hand, which goes forward at neck height rather than at eye level.

3. *The Withdraw/Recovery.* Your right hand smoothly lifts the paddle from the water in a natural upward movement after the right blade passes the cockpit. Your left hand is now in a position to begin the dip of the left blade near the bow of your kayak to complete the stroke cycle.

Practicing the movement of the forward stroke doesn't have to be limited to sitting in a kayak. After you're through experimenting on the water, take your paddle home with you for the evening. Sit in an ordinary straight chair with your feet on a footstool. Then follow through the cyclical movement carefully. (Beware of chandeliers.) Have a friend observe and criticize your motions. If you have a large mirror in your house, practice in front of it. You'll be surprised at what you see.

Breathing

Even when you are in pretty good physical condition, if you're a beginning kayaker, you may suddenly find yourself out of breath after a fast spurt of forward strokes. Why? Simple: maybe you forgot to breathe!

You've been careful to keep your head up to give those air passages to your lungs a chance to work for you. Now try taking one full breath for each right-left cycle of strokes. Faster breathing will rarely permit a full exchange of used air, but a steady and rhythmic movement of the diaphragm contributes to proper circulation and helps to prevent an oxygen deficiency. A good rule to remember is: INHALE *as your right hand dips,* EXHALE *as your left hand dips.*

A

B

C

The forward stroke is basically a cycling motion of your arms and shoulders. The feathered kayak paddle is rotated during the stroke so that each blade enters the water in the correct position. The stroke includes three steps: the dip on the right side (A), the

D

E

F

draw back to the midpoint of the kayak (B), and the recovery of the blade from the water (C). The paddle is then set to begin the same sequence on the left side (D, E, F). (Robert F. George)

Wildwater kayaker Dan Johnson reaches forward with his upper hand during his powerful forward stroke. (Eric Evans)

Paddling on a full stomach impairs your breathing, not to mention ruining your digestion. Don't talk unnecessarily while paddling: it disturbs the rhythm of your breathing. Remember to keep your head up at all times, although you are leaning forward for added power.

Keeping on Track

Proper tracking—keeping a kayak running in a straight line—requires a subtlety of paddle angle and delicate paddle pressure that come only from experience. What this boils down to is making tiny corrections with each paddle stroke in order to keep the boat going straight, rather than employing one or two big forceful corrections on one side after the kayak has begun to turn off course.

Now that you have your kayak moving along in one direction by using the forward stroke, don't leave it at that. Keep paddling for a mile (1.6 kilometers) or more each day until you begin to feel your two power sources working together smoothly. Don't be discouraged—it will take time. Don't be alarmed if your craft occasionally acts like a spooked horse and veers off in some unlikely direction quite different from where you wish to go. Your kayak is merely displaying a "tracking syndrome." However, with a few miles of paddling under your keel, your kayak will recognize you as master and begin to behave.

Balance Exercises

Give yourself a change in practicing your forward strokes by leaning to the right with each dip to the right, and leaning to the left with each left dip. Lean far enough with each stroke so your gunwale is awash.

Practice leaning for a hundred yards (about 91½ meters) at a stretch without losing your rhythm. On a long paddle across a lake, this can help give you a change of pace.

When you are proficient at maintaining rhythm while leaning on your dip side, lean on the side opposite from each stroke for a hundred yards at a clip. This is a great exercise for loosening up your hips and for practicing general boat control and stability.

The Back Stroke

Normally you'll want to use forward strokes to get you where you want to go. But occasionally you'll find yourself in a situation where a good, hard back stroke can help you get in a desired position. (You'll also use this stroke in backferrying—which we'll get to when we start to practice in a current.)

Lean back a little, instead of bending forward at the waist. Without changing the basic forward stroke position of the spooned side of the blade, dip your right paddle into the water slightly behind you. The back of the blade is now your "business side" as you *push* it forward in the water, using a lot of body pressure. Meanwhile your left hand is *pulling* the left blade back in the air.

Follow the same procedure on the other side if you need to take more than one back stroke to get yourself positioned advantageously.

Even though you'll seldom need to keep backstroking, it's worthwhile to practice the cycle: then you'll have the skill to bring off a strong, precise back stroke when you want it.

The dip and push of each back stroke form a perfectly natural and easy motion and are a cinch to learn. But after you think you're pretty good at it, try leaning toward your stroking side; then try leaning away from each back stroke.

If you are honest about leaning, some interesting things can happen—including a capsize. But as a kayaker, you don't mind getting wet. And it offers a chance to practice your Eskimo roll.

A more extreme form of back stroke occurs when you twist your shoulders and head around so far that you are almost facing backward. You can twist your wrists to dig the front face of the paddle blade into the water near the stern and literally *pull* it back toward you as your body slowly uncoils. When your blade reaches the cockpit, you pivot the blade back to its proper forward position and then continue to *push* it forward toward the bow.

A

For the back stroke, dip the paddle into the water behind you (A), then push it forward through the water (B). (Robert F. George)

B

Ferrying

The ferry is a controlled sideslip across a current, the paddler using the power of the water against his partially angled kayak to carry his boat where he wants it to go—instead of pointing his bow directly toward his objective and stepping on the gas. It is most effective in whitewater, where the strong swirl of water can be the initial propellant, aiding the boater to go crabwise across the current. In a good ferry, you never have to fight your way across the river; you let the river do most of the work for you.

We have not yet graduated fully to whitewater, however, so the beginner must settle for a stream that has moving current and is clear of obstacles in which to practice ferrying. There he can learn how the forces of paddle, current, and weight distribution combine with his boat angle to bring off the exercise successfully. The fine points of the maneuver will be honed later on when he plays in real rapids.

There are two kinds of ferrying. The *backferry* (or *ferry glide*) uses back strokes to place and keep the boat in an advantageous position to sideslip as it points downstream roughly in the same direction as the current. The *upstream ferry* or *forward ferry* uses forward strokes to maintain a proper angle against the current and help propel the boat across the current.

When learning to ferry, there are two basic principles to keep in mind: *always angle your boat* slightly away from the direction of the current; *always lean downstream*, regardless of the direction you are traveling. If you lean upstream, the current will come down on your lowered gunwale and flip you over in an unplanned capsize. In addition the downstream lean offers a larger surface area for the current to work on in helping you sideslip across the river.

By putting these principles together in a coordinated action, you *and* the river join in a unique partnership to propel your kayak in the desired direction with little effort.

Pinpointing Direction

Up till now, we have used clock numbers to designate the position of your paddle in relation to the bow of your kayak. Here, though, let's use the clock to show the direction your bow is pointing, and therefore your boat's angle in ferrying.

Because there are no obstructions in the water where we are practicing, we will assume that the current flows straight down the river rather than changing direction, as it does when rounding an obstacle in whitewater. Thus "downstream" and "current" will mean the same direction for simplicity's sake, and your bow will be at 12 o'clock as you go directly downstream with the current.

In the same way, when you point upstream straight into the current, your bow will stay at 12 o'clock.

The Backferry (Ferry Glide)

In a backferry to the right while paddling downstream, apply a couple of back strokes on your left side to angle your bow toward 11 o'clock downcurrent. Then lean to the right (downstream) and apply a series of back strokes on both sides of your boat to help maintain the correct angle as you sideslip across the current. You may have to paddle a bit harder on your right side in order to maintain correct boat angle. If you are required to paddle too hard on your right side, it simply means that your ferry angle is too extreme. To correct this, you must turn your bow back toward the 11 o'clock position.

In a backferry to the left, first angle your bow toward 1 o'clock downcurrent with a couple of firm back strokes on the right side. Then lean to the left (downstream) and backpaddle briskly on both sides as you sideslip over to the left side of the river. Again, if your bow slips much past 1 o'clock on the way to 2, this will force you to paddle harder. Your ferry angle has become too extreme. Readjust your bow back to 1 o'clock.

Upstream (Forward) Ferry

In an upstream ferry, your boat must be headed roughly upstream, either because you are simply drifting downstream backward or because you have just emerged from an eddy with your boat pointed upriver.

To ferry toward your right, first angle your bow toward 1 o'clock upcurrent, then lean to the right (downstream) and use several firm forward strokes on both sides of your boat to maintain your correct angle to help propel your boat across the current. Again, as in the backferry, you may be required to paddle a bit harder on your right side in order to maintain correct boat angle.

In an upstream ferry to the left, you simply angle your bow toward 11 o'clock upcurrent, lean downstream to your left, and use several forward strokes to initiate and maintain your sideslip toward the other side of the river.

Remember, a well-executed ferry (unless it's done in water above Class III—these classifications are covered in Chapter 13) is smooth and almost effortless. You are applying the laws of physics to your kayak, and it responds as if it were self-propelled.

Stabilizing Strokes: The Paddle Braces

Having learned the half roll via the paddle brace recovery, and then the Eskimo roll, you are well acquainted with the powerful leverage your paddle blade can exert on the water. Now we're going to review the brace on its own merits and then see how it works forward, backward, and to either side.

Braces are used not for propelling, but rather to help you stabilize your boat and to make subtle directional changes. As your skill increases, you will rely more and more on your paddle blade, extended way out from the boat, to give you more and more stability.

The Forward Brace

In the forward brace on your way to the roll, you leaned to one side and slapped the face of the blade on the water near the bow. Then, as you began to tip over, you swung the blade out sideways and around from 1 o'clock to 3 o'clock. The leading edge of the blade is slightly raised at all times, preventing the blade from slicing downward through the water and thus losing its stabilizing "outrigger" effect.

In practicing the forward brace, keep leaning farther and farther each time until your head is immersed in the water and you can still recover.

The Back Brace and Stern Rudder

The back brace stabilizes a kayak. It is also used quite naturally and without any formal training by neophytes who are simply trying to steer their boats by holding their paddles on the water behind them.

The stroke consists of leaning backward and slowly pressing the rear blade—normally back side down—in a short arc on the surface of the water. By leaning to the right and sliding the blade from 5 o'clock to 3 o'clock, the back brace is completed on the right side. Sliding the left rear blade from about 7 o'clock to 9 o'clock on the left side will complete a back brace on that side.

The back brace becomes a *stern rudder* stroke if you change the paddle angle from a flat to a vertical position in the water to help steer the boat.

The back brace and the stern rudder are highly useful strokes to have in your repertoire (particularly when coming in for a landing on shore), but they do slow your forward momentum. Therefore experienced paddlers soon wean themselves from the stern rudder and back brace and use any number of forward stroke combinations to make the kayak go in the desired direction without loss of speed.

In the back brace—a stabilizing stroke—lean backward and slowly slide the rear blade in a short arc away from the boat on the surface of the water. (Robert F. George)

The Side Brace

This stroke is used almost entirely as a means of stabilizing your boat rather than as a steering mechanism. If you feel unexpectedly unstable while moving forward, extend your right blade out on the water, face down, at 3 o'clock. Place the blade as far from the kayak as possible, with the leading edge slightly raised. Lean hard to your right, with your left hand holding the rest of the paddle above your head. Surprisingly enough you'll find that you're very stable in this position—just as much as when you are sitting quietly in a kayak in still water.

From the beginning of a side brace, it is natural to move into a draw by digging the blade into the water and pulling it in toward the boat. From a side brace, you can also swing the blade forward in an arc toward the bow and then pull directly back, thus converting your brace into a standard forward stroke. You can also swing the blade back toward the rear of the kayak and transform your side brace into a stern rudder or back stroke.

Slipping into a variety of strokes from the basic side brace can be an exhilarating complement to your kayaking style.

The High Paddle Brace Position

The braces previously described are called *low braces* because the paddle shaft and both wrists are held well below eye level. A *high brace* is a more daring and powerful maneuver.

Let's start with a *high side brace* to the right. It's easier to do this while the kayak is moving, so take a dozen or so energetic forward strokes. Then, with your right hand, reach way out to the right at 3 o'clock. Hold your left hand at eye level or a little above. Simultaneously *lean* to the right.

Your first few tries may be a bit hesitant, but with practice, you can learn to lean far enough over to get your ear wet. Try the high brace position for the forward brace and for the back brace on the right side and then on the left side.

Caution

Avoid allowing your wrists to drift too far behind and above your head. This may look fancy, but in powerful water, the extreme position invites a dislocated shoulder. Therefore never let your wrists get behind your head.

The Duffek

The proficient kayaker will often find good use for the spectacular Duffek stroke, which uses forward momentum and the paddle as a pivot. This great stroke revolutionized the sport of kayaking when it was introduced to the kayaking world at the 1953 World Whitewater Slalom Championships in Merano, Italy, by the then-Czech kayaker Milovan Duffek. Prior to Duffek's application of this "hanging draw" stroke, kayakers turned their boats with reverse sweep strokes and without committing their bodies to leaning into their strokes. This conservative, slower approach to turning was turned on its ear after just a few practice runs down the slalom course by Duffek. Ever since his innovation, kayakers have not had to rely on the boat itself for stability: the paddle becomes the primary means not only of support but also for turning the kayak while in brace position. The complete story of Duffek's revolution, his subsequent escape to Switzerland at the 1953 Championships, and his brilliant kayaking career is available in *The River Masters* by Bill Endicott (see the bibliography in Part V). It is a fascinating story.

What a nifty stroke it is—particularly in whitewater! But first learn the basic idea in flatwater; otherwise you'll spend a good share of the time upside down wondering what went wrong.

To simulate moving current in flatwater, it is best to get going very fast—almost full speed in a forward direction. Then lean out as far as you can to the right. With the face of the blade at an angle of about 45 degrees to the forward direction of the boat, insert the blade at about 2 o'clock or approximately 3 feet (92 centimeters) away from the bow. Without stroking at all, hold your blade right there while your left hand is held high above your head. Presto!—the kayak will spin around to the right with the paddle acting as a pivot. Remember: never allow your

A Duffek stroke into a slalom gate. Note the forward speed of the kayaker, Bruce Swomley, as the blade is inserted into the water. (Eric Evans)

A Duffek stroke out of a slalom gate. Note that the paddle is being drawn vigorously toward the bow of the kayak. (Eric Evans)

hand/wrist to extend behind your head. In extreme cases, this could cause a shoulder separation.

The exact blade angle to use depends upon your speed, how far you lean, and how abruptly you wish to turn. The Duffek stroke can often be finished with a firm but short draw stroke to correct your balance.

If you wish to perform a Duffek turn to your left, simply hold your right hand high above but not behind your head and use your left hand to insert the left blade properly.

This is one of the most exciting moves in kayaking, but get the idea of it in flatwater, then try your luck in moving current, and then advance into eddies. As an added bonus, you will be pleased that a Duffek properly done does not cut down your speed appreciably.

Chris McCormick leaning into a Duffek stroke as he enters a gate during a slalom race in Connecticut. (Eric Evans)

Using the Extended Paddle

In automobiles we have a passing gear, which, when you press the accelerator to the floor, will give you an added surge of power; in a jet aircraft, the afterburners are fired to boost the plane over the clouds or out of the enemy's reach. In kayaking we have the extended paddle technique, which, if used judiciously, can increase your quickness and maneuverability just when you need it the most. One of the most renowned practitioners of this art is former World Champion Jürgen Bremmer from the German Democratic Republic. Bremmer most often employed the extended blade in his sweep strokes and Duffek turns.

Quite simply, the maneuver involves quickly sliding your hands along the paddle shaft until one hand is at the throat of the paddle. The other hand remains halfway along the shaft, and the far end of the paddle will be the one in the water. This increases your leverage considerably. The net effect is to provide a temporary advantage of having a much longer paddle. Once the sweep stroke or Duffek is completed, quickly slide the paddle back to its normal position in your hands.

One of the prettiest sights in kayaking is to watch a former *Weltmeister* (World Champion) such as Bremmer weave his way smoothly through a slalom course, subtly employing the extended paddle to increase his power and mastery over the rapids.

8. The K-2 and Other Decked Craft

The techniques learned in a single-seater, recreational kayak can also be applied to the two-seater kayak (K-2), which is found more often on lakes, gentle streams, and the ocean than in whitewater.

The K-2

For general recreational paddling purposes, there are several companies that manufacture the K-2 in rigid fiberglass, in polyethylene, and as a folding boat that can be dismantled in about 20 minutes and packed into two medium-large duffel bags for easy transport.

Years ago the K-2 was sometimes used for whitewater competition, but it has vanished now from the whitewater racing scene. In flatwater racing, the K-2 and the magnificent K-4 are popular classes and are splendid craft to watch when all the paddlers synchronize their strokes.

Applying Technique to the K-2

Whether the K-2 has one large cockpit accommodating two paddlers or separate cockpits fore and aft, and whether it is a collapsible folding boat or rigid, the same paddling principles apply. Using the basic maneuvers we have learned, the bow and stern paddlers simply have to put these techniques together and synchronize their movements.

For the most part, these K-2s are far more stable than the sassy little K-1s; designed for cruising, they therefore are not particularly fast or maneuverable boats. Because a K-2's main function is to go from here to there in a comfortable and pleasurable fashion—no quick turns in rough water, no standing on your ear to pivot around a rock—spray covers are not often used except while crossing windy lakes or in the ocean.

The Trim

Since two people paddle a K-2, it is important to consider the craft's trim. A stern-heavy boat wallows through the water and is sluggish to handle; a bow-heavy boat plows through the water and makes steering difficult. Therefore a K-2 when fully loaded should rest evenly on the water, neither bow nor stern heavy. If the heavier partner is in the bow, his seat should be moved back a little to compensate, just as one moves

Synchronizing their strokes, two kayakers paddle their wooden touring K-2 in the inland passage between Alaska and Seattle. These men are using spray covers, which are not always necessary in the stable touring K-2. (Chris Knight)

the heavier partner closer to the fulcrum of a seesaw to redress the balance. If the heavier partner happens to be the sternman, then either the bow seat or the stern seat (possibly both) should be moved forward a bit. Only a couple of inches can make a big difference in the trim.

In a K-2, one person should be designated as "commander" before either paddler steps into the boat. It can be either the bowman or the sternman, but it usually turns out to be the more experienced boater of the two, or the owner of the boat. Customarily the bowman steps in first while the sternman holds the boat in position for him. Then, while the bowman maintains the boat steady, the sternman slips into the rear seat and announces that the K-2 is ready to get underway. In disembarking, the bowman will step on shore first.

Bow and Stern Duties

Most of the strokes that are used in the K-1 are also applicable to the K-2. Because the K-2 is a stable craft, it more commonly calls for the traditional forward, backward, and simpler turning strokes, rather than relying so much on *hanging* (stabilizing) strokes.

As a general arrangement, the paddling duties between the bow and stern divide themselves logically between forward power and steering, respectively. This does not mean, however, that the bowman only provides power and the sternman simply sits back and steers. It is logical for the bowman to set and maintain the stroke rate, since the sternman can always see him, but he cannot always see the sternman.

The sternman, meanwhile, is the chief helmsman, and he will make frequent use of the stern rudder, the draw, and the sweep, always being careful to coordinate his strokes so he stays in rhythm with his partner in the bow. The stern paddler will provide his share of driving power with firm forward strokes in rhythm with his partner.

A K-2 is rarely put into reverse, but when the need occurs, both paddlers contribute to backing up.

A good K-2 team must practice together conscientiously in order to combine their strokes for maximum effectiveness. For example, combining a bow sweep on the right with a sharp stern rudder or stern sweep on the left side will greatly aid in spinning a K-2 toward the left.

Because K-2 paddlers often do not use spray covers, the Eskimo roll is only rarely performed in a K-2. But if they do use spray covers, they follow K-1 procedures for wet exits or rolls. Both paddlers should take care to synchronize the swing of their recovery braces (and of course do them on the same side!).

Other Decked Craft

Years ago open-decked canoes had a waterproof covering stretched across their decks to keep water out. From that primitive start, there has been an exciting revolution in the design of decked canoes, beginning with the advent of fiberglass to the boatbuilding process in the early 1960s. Today both the single-seater C-1 and the two-seater C-2 are shaped much like kayaks, although technically speaking, they are not kayaks. To the layman, the differences are subtle, and the K-1 and the C-1 are often almost indistinguishable. Back when decked canoes started to look like kayaks in whitewater competition, longtime canoe champion Bill Bickham of State College, Pennsylvania, went so far as to name his decked canoe *Notakayak* in an effort to separate himself from kayakers who "used twice the paddle but were half the man."

C-1/K-1 Comparison

A kayaker (K-1) sits in his boat and uses a double-bladed paddle, while the C-1 paddler kneels in his boat and uses a single-bladed paddle. The C-1 is wider and has a round cockpit hole, whereas the K-1's cockpit hole is shaped more like a pear or a teardrop.

The C-1 has the following advantages: it is more stable, it will turn

A touring C-1. Note the paddler's kneeling position and the single-blade paddle. (Robert F. George)

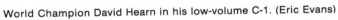
World Champion David Hearn in his low-volume C-1. (Eric Evans)

faster, and the paddler can reach out farther to put more power into each stroke. In the kneeling position, the paddler's head is at least a foot higher than that of a paddler seated in a kayak; and therefore the C-1 paddler has better forward visibility. The kneeling position also allows the paddler to rotate more of his body.

K-1s are more comfortable to sit in for any length of time, and theoretically they are faster boats. In recent years, however, C-1 scores in slalom races have often equaled, and in some cases have surpassed, the best K-1 scores.

The C-2

In the past 25 years, the two-seater decked canoe, or C-2, has also evolved into a more kayaklike shape. For many years, the bow and stern paddlers in these craft had their cockpits near their respective ends. In the mid-1970s, "center-cockpit" C-2s were developed in California and appeared on the whitewater racing circuit. In these boats, the two paddlers have their cockpits near the center of the craft to facilitate both

A C-2 ferries across a stretch of whitewater on the West River in Vermont. Note that the cockpits are located at the ends of the boat. (Robert F. George)

turning and forward power. For a thorough examination of C-2 and C-1 techniques, we recommend the American Red Cross's book *Canoeing* for touring and Bill Endicott's *The Ultimate Run* for whitewater racing (see the bibliography in Part V).

A wildwater C-2 where the cockpits are located amidships. (Eric Evans)

PART III.
ADVANCED TECHNIQUES

9. Moving Water

Water on the move is nimble as well as subtle. It is apparently made up of an infinite series of layers that seem to slip over each other with very little friction. Running water is a truly dynamic medium, especially when temporarily obstructed by irregularities in the riverbed, by rocks in the way of its flow, or by unexpected twists and turns in the river. Water that makes up the oceans of the world, when affected by wind and tide, can be among the most awesome forces of nature.

A kayaker needs to know and become familiar with all the idiosyncrasies of water on the move. Then will come the application of basic technique suited to each circumstance—and the exhilaration of paddling on moving water.

Let's define a few terms. *Whitewater* means rapids, and *flatwater* is calm water, of course. *Wildwater* refers to a specific form of racing in whitewater.

Reading the River

Water, in its headlong course toward the sea, carves for itself a highway that tries to take the path of least resistance across the surface of the land.

Basically there are three forces at work here: (1) gravity—which constantly lures water downward; (2) centrifugal force—which greatly affects a river as it swings around a bend and changes direction; and (3) power—water while moving creates one of the strongest and most irresistible forces in all of nature.

If we could cut a riverbed crossways and examine the cut end of either section, generally speaking we would notice the deepest portion of the river in the middle, with the water becoming more shallow as the sides of the riverbed slope up to meet the shore. Also, the fastest current can be found at the surface of the water in the middle part of the river. Toward the edges of the river, where the water becomes more shallow, there is greater friction for the volume of water, and the current slows down. Of course this description is true only where the riverbed runs along evenly and in a straight line.

Around the Bend

There are notable exceptions to the above rule for current, and they are dictated by the terrain through and over which the river flows. The river paddler, however, heading smoothly down a slow-moving current has little with which to concern himself. If he stays roughly in the middle of the river, he'll get the benefit of the strongest current and deepest water the stream can offer.

Sectional view of a river seen from the upstream side at the beginning of a left turn.

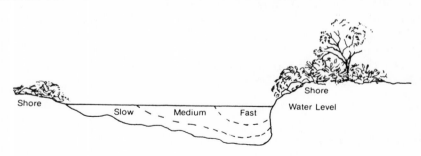

A bird's-eye view of the same turn in the river.

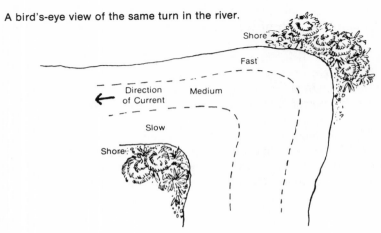

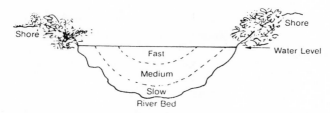

Sectional view of the river depicting differential flow of water along a straight bed.

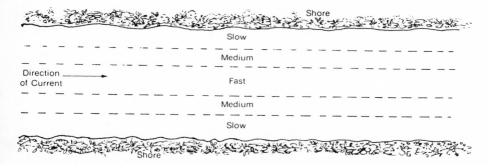

A bird's-eye view of the same river.

The simplest variation to deal with occurs when the river swings around a corner to head in a different direction. It is here that centrifugal force acts upon the water to create a lopsided river bottom, for here the deepest water will invariably be found near the *outside* edge of the river's bend. Novice river runners will be tempted to "cut the corner" and thus save several yards, but the experienced paddler will swing wide, stay with the fastest water, and beat the novice around the bend.

Classification

Most traditional whitewater rivers are babbling and shallow bottom-scratchers much of the year. Such streams depend for whitewater on the spring runoff from melting snow. They rise and fall annually, earlier in the south and later in the north; the rivers that have substantial snow bases where they rise stay higher longer. Toward the end of the white-water season, a good rainfall will restore the water level of these rivers and temporarily prolong the season.

Whitewater rivers are classified in six general categories (see Chapter 13 for details), with several factors determining classification: the complexity of the riverbed, the elevation drop per mile, the river's course, and the volume of water. The last factor—the volume of water—is the greatest variable and can alter a river's category dramatically.

Most beginning kayakers will be content with Class I and Class II water. Good whitewater touring is found in Class II and Class III. Rivers with stretches of rapids that fall into Classes IV, V, and VI—such as the great western rivers—are for experts.

Heavy Water

Paddlers often use the expression "heavy water," "big water," or "hair" when describing a stretch of rapids that looks awesome. It would be misleading to define heavy water simply as anything over a certain number of cubic feet of water per second in a river, for there are at least three other variables to consider: the size of the riverbed, the degree of vertical drop, and the experience of the boater all must be taken into account.

In terms of the riverbed and water flow, it is reasonable to classify the Olympic slalom course at Augsburg, Bavaria, as a heavy water rapids, yet there is rarely more than 900 cubic feet per second pouring through its small, narrow bed. With a wider and bigger riverbed such as that of the Housatonic in Connecticut, 900 cubic feet per second is barely enough to cover the rocks and float a boat.

For the novice, a Class III rapids may appear to be heavy water, whereas the expert might almost be bored by a "mere" Class III. As the rate of water flow increases, however, more boaters will agree that it is, indeed, heavy water. Few would deny that the Mackenzie River in Canada or the Colorado River in the Grand Canyon is heavy water.

Faster Water and Its Obstructions

As a river quickens its pace, the fun begins. So watch sharply ahead, and by observing carefully, you will find that the water before you will form an inverted V in which the wide part is upstream and the pointed end, through which the current funnels, is downstream. Generally speaking, this inverted V in the water is a guide indicating where the main current is flowing, and where you want to go. A gentle yet perceptible descent can be felt at this point.

This is what whitewater kayaking is all about: high water on a warm spring day, and a kayaker heading toward the V in a rapids. (Ledyard Canoe Club)

Riffles

When you pick up a little speed in the V as it narrows to its point, you'll notice ahead some small waves in the surface of the water. If the waves are not over a foot (31 centimeters) high, they indicate a stretch of shallow water underneath. Such small waves are called riffles, and they are caused by an unevenness—submerged rocks, ledges, or sunken logs—in the riverbed below.

Haystacks

Much larger standing waves—2 or more feet (61 or more centimeters) high—are often caused by huge submerged boulders, or they occur at the end of the chute of water from a V. These waves are called haystacks, and usually three or more come in succession. Haystacks in certain parts of the world on giant-sized rivers are so large that they appear to be hills of water in themselves.

Rock Gardens and Staircases

If the water level is low and the gradient fairly steep, the water will be churned up a bit, and lots of little rocks will barely show their heads above the surface. Boaters will often call a section such as this a rock

A series of haystacks promises a challenging ride downstream (current flows away from the viewer). Haystacks are often caused by large submerged boulders. (Ledyard Canoe Club)

garden. Navigation through a rock garden is tricky, and a paddler is lucky to get through one without at least once scratching the hull of his boat.

Another common river phenomenon is the staircase—a series of ledges or descending shelves over which the current spills. Again the cautious paddler will search out the inverted V and follow, sometimes in a zigzag course, the flow of the greatest amount of current. Parts of the beautiful Shenandoah River in Virginia are famous for their stair-caselike appearance.

Eddies

Pockets of relatively still water can sometimes be found near either bank of the river or downstream of large exposed boulders or logs out in midstream. These pockets are called eddies, and they can be either benign or malicious.

The ones with relatively little current and that contain quiet water are great places to park and take a breather, and they are fine vantage points

The current (flowing from left to right) creates a giant eddy (dark water) where it flows around a rock outcrop (at left of picture). Strong, frothing jets pour past on either side, but the kayaker can sit quietly in the protected eddy. (Ledyard Canoe Club)

from which a camera buff can photograph oncoming paddlers as they plunge toward him down the rapids.

However, not all eddies can be considered friendly or as places to linger for long. Owing to complex hydraulic phenomena working on the irregularities of a riverbed, an eddy can provide some nasty water for the unsuspecting kayaker. Often water will boil up, swirl, and twist about—even forming whirlpools—making such an eddy unpredictable as well as unpleasant as a rest stop. You feel as if some underwater monster had reached up and grabbed the hull of your boat, taking fiendish delight in yanking you from one side to another. This type of eddy is no place to relax or loiter, but well-executed braces will stabilize your boat, and several strong forward strokes will take you out into the mainstream again.

One of the most famous of malicious eddies was the one just below the formidable Avery Brundage Rock on the upper part of the 1972 Olympic whitewater slalom course in Augsburg, Bavaria. This notorious eddy was redesigned, the concrete boulder that created it pared to a smaller size for safety. Another eddy well-known to paddlers lies just below the Dumplings on the West River in Vermont. Such unstable water lures photographers, because it is here that the unsuspecting boater will provide the camera with spectacular happenings.

The Anatomy of an Eddy

In general, as the current diverges around an obstacle, it forms a very fast and powerful *chute*, or *jet*, that skirts past the head of the eddy, which lies immediately below the obstruction. The characteristic circular motion of the eddy is created in part by the passage of the jet: this milder countercurrent in the surface water of the eddy curves inward and up-

This drawing illustrates the characteristic circular motion of water in a mainstream eddy. (Walter Richardson)

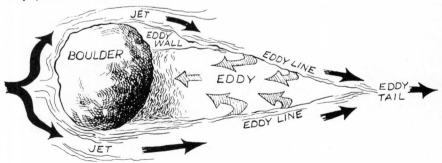

stream; then, when it meets the obstacle at the eddy's head, it peels off and heads downstream.

A sharp delineation can be seen between the chute roaring downstream and the more placid eddy water. This is called the *eddy line.*

A short *eddy wall* is sometimes formed at the top of an eddy right on the eddy line if the chute (jet) of downstream water is of unusually heavy volume and force. There can be a difference of a foot or more in this wall between the eddy water and the chute next to it.

A couple of boat lengths downstream is an area often called the *eddy tail.* Here the chute fans out and loses some of its force, which causes the eddy water itself to lose its upstream momentum, and the river water merges again.

A midstream eddy offers you a choice of moving out from either the right or the left as you proceed down the rapids, and a careful examination of the next 100 yards (91 meters) or so below the eddy from a position of safety in the eddy itself will give you a clue as to which side you may wish to leave the eddy from.

Eddies at the Side of a River

All kinds of interesting things are happening near the river bank as a river picks up speed and descends more sharply. Quite common is the *side eddy,* caused by the jut of a large boulder or point of land into the mainstream, leaving a space downstream of it where water can swirl back and return in an upstream circular motion.

A side eddy can be a welcome haven. It is an automatic "parking place" while you plan your next move downstream; it can provide ready access to shore and a chance to get out to stretch; and it's a very good place for putting in at the start of a river journey.

Bird's-eye view of an eddy on each side of a river.

A side eddy offers many opportunities to practice precision boating or just a chance to play around. And it is also a likely place to find lost paddles or other debris. The most feasible way to search for lost gear is to scout out each side eddy carefully as you proceed downriver.

Rollers and Souseholes

Among the other demanding obstructions to watch for in rapids are rollers (also called *stoppers* or *keepers*), souseholes (*suckholes* or *reversals*), or just plain *holes*.

Although there may be some technical differences in these terms, they are used somewhat interchangeably according to the section of North America you happen to be paddling in. No really precise definitions are necessary because nature can, in her own way, provide an almost infinite variety of challenges in a stretch of rapids.

Regardless of what you call them, however, they all share one basic characteristic: water at the downstream base of the obstacle recirculates back toward the obstacle in apparent total defiance of the natural downstream flow of the current. It is enough to be able to recognize that these things do exist in turbulent waters and, after recognizing them for what they are, to know what to do about them.

Rollers

The recirculating water (or turbulence) called a roller or stopper is a tricky wave that remains in the same place athwart the river; it is formed by water pouring over a large obstacle in the riverbed and plunging down into a trough below it. The term "stopper" has been applied to the roller because that is exactly what it is likely to do to your boat if you linger too long in its vicinity: if you get stuck sideways down in the trough, the roller can actually stop your forward motion downstream. If it is a giant roller with a steep wave downstream of it, it can even stop your boat if you are pointed directly downstream.

A roller or stopper is studied much more easily if you look upstream at it from the safety of the river bank rather than from the cockpit of a kayak heading downstream. It can be fairly small and localized, or it can extend most of the way across the river.

At the Quarter Mile Rapids on the White River in Vermont during unusually high water, a truly delightful roller extends diagonally all the way across the river. Another famous and challenging roller is located on the Rivière aux Sables in the northern part of Quebec in Canada, about halfway down the slalom practice area near Jonquière.

Souseholes

Souseholes, suckholes, or reversals are formed in nearly the same way as a roller or stopper, except that they are often concentrated in one central spot in the river rather than extending across the stream. They too are formed by a huge boulder or ledge, but they can also be formed by a weir or dam.

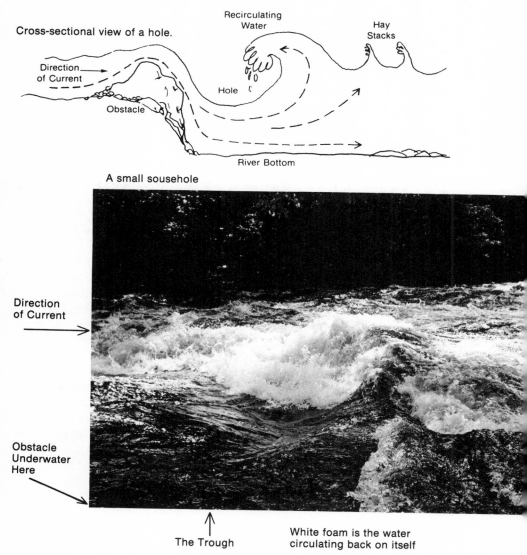

Cross-sectional view of a hole.

Recirculating Water

Hay Stacks

Direction of Current

Hole

Obstacle

River Bottom

A small sousehole

Direction of Current

Obstacle Underwater Here

The Trough

White foam is the water circulating back on itself

The water, as it plunges over the obstacle, divides itself into two main components: (1) the water that goes deep and continues on downstream, and (2) the part that is deflected back upstream toward the obstacle, creating a foaming, boiling backlash. To the unwary, it looks like the jaws of a water monster—and a sousehole deserves respect from every paddler.

A sousehole may contain a roller as part of its composition, depending upon the river's configuration at the moment, and a roller can have as part of its repertoire the makings of a sousehole.

Weirs and Dams

There are very few rivers within easy reach of civilization that are not obstructed by at least one dam or weir, and this is one of the reasons why every competent paddler scouts an unfamiliar stream before undertaking to travel it.

A weir is a small dam up to about 5 feet (about 1½ meters) in height, and sometimes it has a sluiceway at one side to conduct the water to a mill or pond. In both dams and weirs, the water spills over almost vertically and usually creates immediately downstream a roller or sousehole, which in turn tends to toss back toward the barrier any debris that has floated over it.

When you look downstream at a dam or weir, you see a *horizon line* ahead on the surface of the water. This occurs because the water usually is backed up against the barrier, and the water is likely to be calm there without much current. Then, as the water goes over the dam, it creates a straight horizontal line across the river—as if the river simply stops and drops off the earth. Larger dams, of course, have superstructures on either side of the river—and sometimes all the way over the river— making identification easier.

Every boater should always be on the lookout for these horizon lines across the river ahead, and he should pull over to shore immediately to scout out the dam *before* running it. And then, run it only with the greatest of caution, and preferably with a rescue party to assist you from shore.

The Ocean

The behavior of water in the ocean can be quite unlike that of a river. The sea can develop currents as the tide works its timeless way up and down a coastline. It is a constantly changing medium, appearing the same for only a few moments.

Ocean waves and swells are most often caused by the action of wind on the broad surface of ocean water. When waves run against the upward-sloping floor of the ocean toward dry land, the action of water against seabed creates a force that makes each incoming wave unstable. The wave is gradually forced up, is slowed down, and finally crests in white frothy foam, while the water from an earlier wave that has played itself out on shore recedes quickly back under the incoming surf.

Proper handling of a kayak in the ocean is discussed in Chapter 11.

10. Running Rapids

Until now your technique has been polished on flatwater, and you have learned what a nimble craft is the modern recreational kayak. Now, with the Eskimo roll and the basic strokes mastered and with a basic knowledge of river hydraulics, you are ready to enter the exciting world of whitewater. Few sports in the world can match the kinesthetic sensation of melding your own speed and power with that of the river.

Many laymen's perception of river running is just that: a simple, all-out bouncy ride interspersed with a few unexpected thrills as one "shoots" the rapids. The true kayaker, however, will play with the river. After studying the rapids carefully, he will then weave his way down, stopping en route to surf on a wave or knife into an eddy and then pause a moment before accelerating out of it. He may then paddle back upstream, hopping from eddy to eddy, to try a new maneuver on the same piece of whitewater. More often than not, whitewater paddling is not merely a journey on a river from point A to point B, but a water-buglike exploration of all the river's surface irregularities. Working over a stretch of whitewater in a kayak can be a very fulfilling experience. It's a real thrill to know a river well enough to use its currents, eddies, and waves to choreograph pivots, spins, glides, and even airborne pirouettes as your boat dances over the water.

Safety Measures

To save yourself embarrassment and possible loss of your boat, paddle, or even your life, adhere to the following without fail:

1. You must be a strong, competent swimmer; you should never go river running with anyone who is not a good swimmer too.

2. If you value your life as well as your boat, you'll never kayak alone in rapids. Two boats are a *minimum* for safety; three or more are better.

3. No unknown rapids should ever be run without being scouted beforehand, and maps should be studied with care. Know what you are getting into: there are bound to be stretches where it's mighty difficult, even for experts, to reach the haven of an emergency take-out spot on the river bank. A favorite river expression is "When in doubt, eddy out and scout!"

4. In addition to the PFD and helmet you should always wear, in cold weather it is smart to wear at least a part of a wet suit or dry suit, too, lest you find yourself in the grip of cold water. Water below 50 degrees Fahrenheit (10 degrees Celsius) will soon sap the energy of the strongest.

5. Have adequate flotation in both bow and stern so that your boat will ride high in the water in case of a capsize. This means flotation

bags. Half-inflated beach balls, casually stuffed inside your boat, or a thin foam supporting wall are not enough.

6. Grabloops at each end of the boat are also essential. With them your boat can be quickly controlled and pulled to shore in case of a capsize.

7. Resist the temptation to attempt any rapids beyond your ability. Be an accurate judge of your own skill, and never be teased, coaxed, or bullied into running a stretch of rapids you have serious doubts about successfully completing.

8. *Warm up.* Never attempt a rapids unless you are fully warmed up and physically loose. A warm-up can be as simple as jogging up and down the road while waiting for the car shuttle to return; or it can consist of a few exercises while sitting in your boat in a quiet eddy. Try a few bracing strokes, an Eskimo roll or two; twist and stretch your shoulders and arms. Ferry out into the stream a little way to get the feel of the moving current. Work up at least a little sweat before you take on the rapids below.

Rules of Thumb

Intelligent rapids running involves a continuous mental exercise to interpret the demands of the water as the river unfolds in front of you.

Actually "playing the river" involves two distinct things: (1) recognizing what it is you are approaching in the rapids, and (2) anticipating the appropriate move for the occasion.

Lean Downstream

When playing in the rapids, always remember to *lean downstream.* This is probably the single most important rule in all of rapids running.

It is highly unlikely that you will ever capsize if you remember always to lean downstream while maneuvering in rapids. However, the moment you get careless and allow your upstream gunwale to dip, the force of the water will grab your gunwale—and over you'll go.

Experienced boaters often refer to this phenomenon in terms of mythology. Old river runners will tell you about an underwater creature called the "Muncher" that lurks in the rapids and likes to punish boaters who disobey the basic fundamentals of river reading. The Muncher will spin your boat around if you don't pay strict attention to the currents; and if the Muncher is unusually hungry, he might even tip your boat over in the rapids. But you can always foil the critter by careful water reading, by leaning downstream, and by having a reliable Eskimo roll.

Deep Water

Generally speaking, the deepest water will lie in the middle of the now-familiar inverted V of glassy water, where the main current is flowing.

When the river is going around a bend, however, the water will be deepest on the *outside* of the turn.

Keep Going

When in doubt or startled, it is best to paddle hard *forward* rather than to try to back off with backward strokes. Never hoist your paddle above your head in despair: an "air brace" provides no stability.

Dealing with Anxiety and Fear

It is the brave person who admits fear. Only a fool tries to hide it. A certain amount of anxiety is not only natural—it can be healthy. It keeps one wide awake, sharp, and alert.

Try to bear in mind that during your very first run down a set of rapids, you probably will be frightened. After all, this is a brand new experience, in a foreign medium (water); and it is simply you, your boat, and the river. You're on your own. Your paddling companions should be sensitive to your situation and be supportive.

Anxiety is often caused by ignorance—or fear—of the unknown. Anxiety can be overcome by intelligence, skill, practice, and exposure to the river at first hand. The big, unanswerable question is—how much fear is too much? If you are paralyzed by fear, then you have obviously gone too far. Back off and try a less demanding section of the river. Work your way up more slowly. Never hesitate to pick up your boat and walk past any rapids beyond your skill level.

In many cases, though, when people are put into an anxiety-creating situation, they react well. Better yet, soon comes that tremendous feeling of accomplishment when you spin into an eddy at the foot of a rapids and look back to see what you've just passed through. Basic paddle strokes and maneuvers recently learned came into play automatically as you negotiated the rapids. You have just won a great victory—not over the river, but over yourself.

Very shortly your anxiety can be put into proper perspective. Was it simply inexperience and lack of familiarity with the situation? In a small way, you have joined the ranks of the world's great explorers and adventurers—like the first person to fly or the first person to set foot on the moon.

Experience builds confidence, but in kayaking, confidence should never turn to brashness. Always try to draw the line between being confident and being foolhardy. Don't overdo it. Reckless boaters are a danger to themselves and to their boating companions.

In summary, face up to the fact you're frightened. Analyze your fear objectively and take whatever constructive steps you can. In this way, the sport of kayaking can become a tremendously important learning process for you.

Haystacks

At some point in a rapids, you are likely to encounter a series of those large standing waves called haystacks. They are formed, as described in Chapter 9, when a fast jet of water passing over submerged rocks slows down in a rapids. Haystacks are also formed when two currents within the same river meet at an angle, as at a bend in the river where the main current hits the outside wall hard enough to be deflected back on itself.

Quite often haystacks are found toward the bottom of rapids. If they are not too large for your taste, you may wish to smash straight through them for a real roller coaster ride downriver.

If they appear more ominous than hospitable, steer slightly to one side using a draw or sweep stroke or even a stern rudder, and skirt the heavier haystacks lurking in the middle.

Haystacks don't have to be confronted from a straightforward position either. It is perfectly acceptable to approach them broadside—just so long as you always remember to lean and brace downstream.

Riding haystacks backward can also provide a thrill, but you'd better know what lies downstream of them, or you'll be in for a surprise.

Using Eddies

Your greatest ally in the rapids is an upcoming eddy. Let's say that you have spotted a side eddy to your right a hundred yards ahead downstream. From the configuration of the land or a boulder, you can anticipate the location of an eddy before it is clearly visible from your boat. Head toward it, driving hard with firm forward strokes, always bearing in mind that the jet (chute) just alongside the eddy will tend to carry you downstream farther than you expect. Therefore aim for a point higher upstream in the eddy than you really plan to go.

Keep paddling hard forward toward the eddy line and into the eddy water itself. As the eddy line extends under your boat about halfway to your cockpit, you will begin to feel the upstream eddy water grab your bow and force your boat around to the right, so that it is pointing upstream in the eddy.

Strokes for Entering an Eddy

A combination of strong forward strokes, coupled at the last minute with a strong sweep, will propel your boat into an eddy. A favorite stroke to use here is the Duffek. The most common error, though, is to begin the Duffek stroke too soon. If you perform the Duffek too far away from the eddy proper, or in the jet itself, your boat will simply wash downstream and miss the eddy entirely. Resist beginning the Duffek until you can practically lean over and place your paddle blade in the calmer water, *beyond* the eddy line. This takes skill and good timing.

At the precise moment your boat leaves the downstream jet and actually enters the eddy, you should shift your weight so as to lean *away* from the eddy. Centrifugal force plus the upstream current in the eddy will tend to pull you over to the left, so counteract this by leaning back toward the main current of the river. A little practice will give you the feel for what to do. Don't get discouraged if you tip over several times while entering an eddy, because proper anticipation and timing take a lot of experience. Once learned, this maneuver is a pleasurable one.

Leaving the Eddy

Once in the eddy, you'll have time to gather your wits, decide how to proceed out of the eddy, and get on your way down the rapids.

First, look downstream and decide where you want to go, then choose which of three possible exits from the eddy is best for you. One way is simply to drift below the eddy tail as you slowly turn to head downstream; if there are no obstructions directly downstream of the eddy tail, this is probably the easiest way to leave an eddy. Or you can choose to peel off from about halfway up the eddy; or you can continue up the eddy and peel off dramatically just inches below the rock at the head of the eddy.

The Peel-off

The peel-off is a spectacular maneuver that can be done forward or backward.

To get ready to peel off to the right, you consider directly upstream as 12 o'clock. Back down the eddy as far as you can to get a running start; then charge full steam ahead up the eddy with your *bow pointing between 1 and 2 o'clock*. The moment your bow crosses the eddy line into the jet of fast-moving current, you should continue to paddle hard and at the same time *lean hard downstream*. (It is at this point that one of the cardinal rules of whitewater kayaking will be driven home to you: *lean downstream*. Otherwise, the moment your bow hits that fast water, you'll be upside down as quick as a wink.) The closer your bow points toward 2 o'clock, the greater the chances that you'll spin quickly out of the current in an exhilarating manner and head down the river again.

For a left-side peel-off, back down for a running start, then paddle forward fast with your bow somewhere *between 10 and 11 o'clock*. Lean downstream as you hit the jet, and let the current complete your turn to the left.

Peel-offs can be done backward as well as forward. Simply turn your boat around and, by using several firm back strokes, move out of the eddy with your stern pointing between 1 and 2 o'clock if you're intending to peel off to the right (or pointing between 10 and 11 o'clock if you're peeling off to the left). Either way you'll spin around and find yourself out in the current facing upstream. And in certain situations, it could be more desirable to be facing upstream.

The Cartwheel

It is fun as well as good practice to leave and then reenter the same eddy at almost the same spot. This is called cartwheeling. For a cartwheel to the right, take off from the top of an eddy forward at about 2 o'clock (considering 12 o'clock as directly upstream), lean hard downstream, and then, with a couple of sweep strokes on the left side, guide the bow of your kayak back across the eddy line into the eddy again. The main force of the current in the jet will then catch your stern and swing it around until you find yourself safely parked in the same eddy, again facing upstream.

For a cartwheel to the left, point your bow at 10 o'clock; continue as above. Cartwheels can very quickly become a game between two kayaks to see which can make the tightest turn and lose the least amount of downstream position. It is also fun to see who can do a cartwheel with the least number of sweep strokes.

Trying cartwheels both forward and backward out of eddies from both right and left can work wonders in improving your skill in boating. What's more, it will give you a real feel for the eddy line, the power of the jet, and the eddy itself. Good cartwheelers can spin out of an eddy, sweep quickly around, and cut back into the eddy at almost the same place, all with very little loss of position.

Ferrying

Ferrying is basic to safe navigation in whitewater, and the trick is to get the massive forces of nature to do the work for you. We once saw former World Champion Jürgen Bremmer peel off out of a side eddy on the Passer River in Italy and ferry across the entire river using only one stroke. A clever ferrier can actually work his way upstream in the rapids by judicious use of ferry techniques and eddy hopping.

The Backferry (Ferry Glide)

If you want to move laterally across at least part of the river while moving downstream in strong current, you can use the backferry, sometimes also called the ferry glide.

Suppose you are heading down through rapids and see an obstruction ahead that you'd like to avoid—for example, a rock dead ahead with a clear passage to the right at 1 o'clock.

Your first and natural inclination is to point your bow to the right at 1 o'clock and paddle hard toward the clear passage.

However, the current may be stronger than you think, and your defensive efforts too late. So stop paddling forward, point your bow to 11 o'clock diagonally away from the direction you want to go, and then employ several strong back strokes while leaning downstream. The angle you have created with the boat and the water, plus the force of the current against the slowed boat, will work wonders for you.

After you have sideslipped over as far as you want, you can straighten your boat out with a forward sweep stroke so you are pointing straight downstream again. Ferry glides both to the right and to the left are standard moves all good kayakers use in picking their way down rapids.

The Upstream Ferry

Equally challenging is the upstream ferry. This is usually begun by driving hard out of an eddy upstream at an angle of not more than 1 o'clock if you are heading out to the right into the river, or 11 o'clock if you are heading out to the left into the river. Continue to paddle forward hard and remember to lean downstream when you hit the eddy line.

Getting the right angle and thrust so you'll slip across the river will take a bit of patience and practice. Here are two likely mistakes and how to avoid them:

First, if your boat keeps turning downstream like an unmanageable horse, your angle of exit from the eddy is too close to 3 o'clock if you are moving out to the right, or too close to 9 o'clock if you are moving out to the left. Make sure your bow is pointed *not more* than 1 o'clock for a ferry to the right, or 11 o'clock for a ferry to the left.

Second, if your boat ferries out nicely about halfway and then stops moving laterally across the river, the chances are your bow has crept back toward 12 o'clock. Allow it to fall off *slightly* toward 11 or 1 o'clock while paddling forward, and your ferry will begin again.

Eddy Hopping Upstream

Most people think of rapids as something for a boat to go *down* through. Yet salmon go up very swift streams in search of spawning grounds, and by borrowing a few ideas from these denizens of the river, we too can work our way upstream. If the rapids are not too severe and a variety of eddies abound, it is great fun to test your skill in eddy hopping *up* the river.

Start from one eddy and move up to its head, then charge hard out of it and ferry, maintaining strong forward strokes, over to the tail of an eddy on the other side of the river. Work your way up from the tail of this eddy to its top—where you look for the next eddy upstream.

In a way, eddy hopping can be compared to crossing from the head of one ski lift to the bottom of another farther up the mountain as you hitch to the topmost run of an Alpine ski area. In this case, the eddy acts as your ski lift—with the added bonus of having no lift lines or tickets.

Playing in Rollers

A roller can flip you over quickly if you're unprepared—as explained earlier—but a roller can also provide some wonderful opportunities for exciting whitewater boating. An entire afternoon can be spent at one single place in whitewater that has a good roller with accessible eddies on either side.

If you turn around and back slowly down into a roller, you'll soon feel the exciting sensation of having your stern rise high behind you as your bow disappears underwater at the bottom of the trough below the roller. At this moment, you may start to swerve right or left, but with a good paddle brace, you can correct your position nicely to avoid getting broadside. However, if you *do* become broadside in a roller, follow your natural tendency to do a high paddle brace—that is, bracing with an extended blade—on the downstream side, and you'll be perfectly OK.

Sometimes the roller will shoot you straight back into the air. In other cases, you will do a modest loop-the-loop or "ender," winding up up-side down. In any event, simply be patient when you find yourself capsized, and Eskimo roll back up.

Some stretches of rivers are already well known where enders can be done, such as the Endo Rapids in Westwater Canyon on the Colorado River, and the Nose Stand Rapids on the American River in California. Near the nation's capital, people can watch kayakers doing enders at Observation Deck Rapids near Great Falls on the Potomac.

A roller enjoys keeping kayaks broadside to the current so they can be bounced around a bit. If it is a worthy roller, it will challenge your ability to get out of its clutches. In small rollers, the high downstream-side paddle brace is enough to pull you out. If not, then you should combine the side paddle brace with a couple of strong forward or back strokes: these will force you to the side of the roller. At this point, as if in disgust, the roller quite likely will spit you out into an eddy or into the main portion of the river.

More daring is coasting forward downstream into a roller—but mean-while backpaddling strongly, so your boat slowly sinks into the roller itself. Then lean back until you feel your stern go deep into the trough and finally get caught by the strongest downstream current, which moves you straight downstream standing on your tail.

Modest end-over-ends can be done this way as your stern literally goes under while your bow sticks high into the air. Again, when this happens, simply wait a moment or two underwater, then complete your Eskimo roll to right yourself again.

With a handy eddy on either side of a roller, it is fun to head upstream from one eddy toward another by skimming across the top of the roller with your bow just missing the trough. Usually this creates one of the fastest upstream ferries imaginable.

Rollers with no dangerous rocks underneath can be places to strut your stuff. In the past 10 years, *whitewater rodeos,* or *hotdogging contests,* have increased in popularity. At these events, paddlers play in a roller or over a section of rapids and are judged for their creativity and tech-niques. The maneuvers that today's hot boaters such as Rob Lesser and Don Banducci can perform are mind-boggling. Many of their best air-borne stunts are done without a paddle!

On many of the really big rivers, large rolling waves will be seen. Try an upstream ferry out to the top of such a wave, then keep your bow pointed toward 1 or 11 o'clock while facing upstream. Lean slightly downstream, and the big current forcing up against your hull will slide your kayak neatly across the surface of the wave. By shifting his weight and controlling his boat, a good paddler can glide back and forth several times on the same wave.

Playing in Souseholes

Souseholes (suckholes or reversals)—even though they may be part of the roller complex in a stretch of rapids—should always be approached with great caution. The smaller, safe ones are fun to play in, but large souseholes should be avoided by everyone except the most expert boaters. For souseholes such as those found on the Colorado River in the Grand Canyon or the Bull Sluice on the Chattooga River, even top-notch paddlers wear—just in case—the big 33-pound buoyancy life-jacket rather than the lighter racing vest, which does not provide nearly as much flotation.

Of course every competent boater wears a helmet in rapids, and the importance of this protective headgear is demonstrated in souseholes. The "jaws" of a sousehole can catch you quickly, making for a very speedy capsize in all that frothy foam, which can conceal a variety of lurking obstructions.

Good boating sense dictates that you stay away from big souseholes in general, and start with the smallest ones before working your way up to larger holes as you gain knowledge of the powerful hydraulics involved.

Entering a Hole

If you wish to play in the smaller souseholes, try nosing down into the hole in a forward position, meanwhile making back strokes in order to travel slower than the rate of the current.

Another approach is to sneak from an eddy on either side into a sousehole. Move diagonally upstream out of the eddy with strong forward strokes and dive into the sousehole. More daring boaters may wish to drop down into a sousehole backward or sideways.

Once into the hole, your boat will be buffeted and bounced around a bit and will very likely turn diagonally one way or another. *At this point, always remember to lean and brace downstream.*

Small or reasonable-sized souseholes offer splendid opportunities to learn boat control. A truly expert boater can stick his bow or stern directly into the center of a sousehole and force the onrushing water to spit his boat straight back—sometimes even into the air. Or, if driven in deep enough, the bow or stern will be caught by the powerful water beneath the surface, and the kayak will be forced to go end-over-end, which can be one of the greatest thrills in kayaking.

A more constructive procedure is to use several firm forward strokes to augment a downstream brace when you are ready to exit from a sousehole. Or sometimes it is more convenient to blend that downstream brace with several firm back strokes to back your boat out of the hole.

Dealing with Larger Holes

In really heavy water (anything over 2,000 cubic feet or 56 cubic meters per second) that offers the likelihood of powerful souseholes, there are basically two schools of thought concerning procedure. The first emphasizes that a boater should—contrary to his natural instincts—paddle *hard* right through the hole itself. Here you'll have to make yourself keep paddling, but the force of your momentum augmented by the power of your strokes will see you through.

A second school of thought believes that you should relax and take it easy. Allow your boat to float along the downstream current and do not take any aggressive action at all *until* you are in the very heart of the sousehole: at that point, lean and brace on your downstream side. Practitioners of this art love to drop into souseholes or ride giant haystacks in a sideways or even backward position. It really doesn't make much difference in what direction the boat is heading as it drops into the hole, because you then can play or exit, as you wish.

Squirt Kayaking

Today squirt kayaking, or pirouetting on the ends of a kayak, is at the cutting edge of kayaking acrobatics. Led by hot recreational paddlers such as Jess Whittemore and Jeff Snyder of Friendsville, Maryland, kayaking has become a three-dimensional sport: surface currents, surface obstacles, and now underwater currents.

Squirting started as an offshoot to the radical *pivot turn* developed by the American C-1 racers in the 1970s in their low-volume decked racing canoes. In a back pivot turn, the paddler simultaneously leans backward, does a violent back sweep stroke, and dips the sharp gunwale of a racing C-1 underwater. The lower the racers drove their sterns underwater, the faster they pivoted. Voilà! The first squirt. Low-volume slalom kayaks followed suit. Soon the bow squirt appeared.

Soon thereafter paddlers found greater room for creativity in whitewater, where eddy lines and holes provided even more force to "get vertical." In the most common and basic squirt technique, a paddler enters the current from an eddy, leans upstream, and simultaneously does a downstream back stroke as far back as possible (Whittemore

Jess Whittemore surfing a hole in his squirt kayak. (C. M. Laffey)

moves his hands on the shaft of his paddle à la Jürgen Bremmer to gain even more leverage in his sweeps). The stern shoots underwater and the bow goes up in the air. Continuous back sweeps will keep the stern underwater, and the kayak will pivot on its tail in a circular motion.

Then come *bow squirts* and *pillow squirts* (using the pillow in front of a large semisubmerged rock as an eddy line; beware undercut rocks). *Splattering* is when your boat ends up on the rock during a pillow squirt. Finally there's *blasting*, in which a kayak's stern is driven under the backwash of a hole while the bow stays in the air above the oncoming water.

Squirt kayaks are usually shorter than their river running brethren, and they have flat, low profiles with little to no volume like slalom racing kayaks. Many of the paddles are also shorter with smaller, asymmetrical blades.

About Running Weirs and Dams

It is a common thing these days to see photographs of kayaks actually airborne as they sail over weirs and dams.

To the unwary thrill-seeker, this may look like the ultimate in boating. It is more likely to be an invitation to trouble.

Running a weir or a dam will inevitably cause undue stress to your boat—stress that it was never designed to take. In addition the impact of hitting the water below the dam at an awkward angle can create a physical shock to the person in the boat, possibly injuring his spine or neck. And finally, the backwash of water just downstream can pin the paddler and his boat in its grip. He then must be rescued from shore, with his boat perhaps abandoned and battered to pieces against the foot of the barrier.

Don't be fooled by the innocent appearance of a weir or dam. It may not look particularly large or ferocious, but never underestimate the power of water. The infamous Brookmont Dam across the Potomac River just above Washington, D.C., is such a place. Because it looks so benign, each year boaters have come to grief trying to run it, tragedy being the sad ending to a trip.

In general, therefore, do not run dams and weirs unless there is a sluiceway provided. Portage instead. The momentary thrill of going over the steep pitch of water is negated by the variety of dangers involved.

11. Kayaking in the Ocean

Boats

You could put to sea in almost any kind of kayak. If your purpose is simply to explore a small harbor or an inlet, a general touring kayak or whitewater play boat will suffice. But if you wish to venture out regularly into a larger estuary or poke your bow around a headland into the open sea, then a kayak designed specifically for that purpose will be more efficient, safer, more comfortable, and ultimately more fun.

In truth the general touring kayak and whitewater play boat are sluggish when paddled straight ahead for any period of time. Their bows are not meant to cope with ocean waves, and their rockered hulls are designed more for turning than for straight-ahead paddling. Sea kayaking demands less in maneuverability in design but more in efficiency and comfort in straight-ahead paddling.

In the rapidly expanding world of sea kayaking, two design extremes have emerged, each with a historical precedent and each with a dedicated group of proponents. In the past few years, these extremes have become less conspicuous.

At one end is what we might call the "Greenland approach" to design. This approach can be seen with kayaks that are low in volume, are narrow (often narrower than Olympic-style flatwater racing kayaks), and have low profiles. Patterned after the Greenland kayaks of yore, these long (approximately 19 feet, or 5¾ meters) needle-shaped boats have low flat decks and upswept ends. In short these kayaks are swift yet tippy; bracing strokes are needed when the boat is not being paddled.

At the other end of our arbitrary design spectrum is the "Bering Strait approach." These are kayaks that are shorter (approximately 14 to 18 feet, or 4¼ to about 5½ meters) and wider (up to 29 inches or 74 centimeters at the beam) with an often round, semi-vee bottom, peaked decks, and a moderate flare. In short they are slower but more stable than their Greenland counterparts.

Since Greenland was closer to Europe and, in particular, England than Alaska was, Europeans were influenced by the Greenland approach. During the past 20 years, when America turned to Europe for sea kayaking advice, the emphasis presented to us was on fast, tippy, sleek craft along with the requisite techniques to handle these craft with safety: bracing strokes, Eskimo rolls, rescue maneuvers, and hours of practice.

On North America's west coast, the Bering Straight approach was manifest: efficient yet forgiving craft that didn't require 1,001 maneuvers and practice hours in order to enjoy safely.

The boat you choose will be a reflection of your own interests and skills and the type of water you plan to paddle most frequently. In making that choice, keep the following points in mind:

1. There are several large sea kayaking symposia conducted each year throughout the U.S. and Canada. These are ideal opportunities to try many different boats and soak up advice from experts on the sport. *Sea Kayaker* magazine (see Part V at the end of this book) is the source for symposia near you.

2. Speed versus stability. All things being equal, longer generally means faster, and wider generally means slower yet more stable. If you want to get from point A to point B efficiently and quickly, then speed will be your leading criterion. If the journey is as important as the destination, then a slower, more benign boat may be what you are looking for. A skilled paddler will use his paddle to stay upright in anything, but some may want to look through a viewfinder in rough conditions, and that requires more stability.

3. Wind versus water and wave deflection. Upswept ends and/or high-decked bows will part the seas and deflect the water before it reaches the cockpit, but such features will also present more surface for the wind to strike and will create more spray.

4. Forward flare (from the bow back to the cockpit) should develop gradually. The result will be a boat that stays well on top of the water and always climbs dependably up and over waves, rather than slicing and "hobbyhorsing" through them.

Accessories

Although regular whitewater or touring-style paddles can be used at sea, lengthier paddles with longer, narrower blades are better. The propulsion is about the same but the effort seems less. The returning blade in the air offers less resistance to the wind. Asymmetrical flatwater paddles are popular, since they are light, flutter free, and comfortable. Whether the paddle is feathered or not is a matter of personal choice. It is helpful to have a sea paddle painted bright fluorescent color to make it easy for a boater to be seen. Better yet, a bright-colored deck, hat, or lifejacket will increase chances of being spotted.

With regard to clothing, one must remember that for the most part, ocean water is cold. Therefore some sort of layered protective paddling clothing is de rigueur. If your paddling plans call for lots of submersion or heavy seas with lots of spray, then go the whitewater paddler's route and opt for a dry suit with pile underneath. Wet suits would be the second choice for those days when you know you're going to get soaked.

Most sea kayaking touring involves coping with wind and, secondarily, with cold water. These more benign conditions can be handled well with paddling jackets worn over layers of pile or wool. Beware, however, that salt water has had an adverse effect on Gore-Tex and other "breathable" paddling jackets.

Helmets, which are so important in whitewater, give way to an imaginative mélange of headgear—bush hats, straw hats, and fancy sailing caps have all been seen on oceangoing kayakers. A good hat should keep your head warm and dry, protect it from the sun, and stay on in heavy wind or a capsize.

A lifejacket must be worn at sea, ALWAYS. It must have lots of buoyancy, help to retain body heat, contain pockets to carry things in, be comfortable to wear, and be easy to swim with. Compasses with luminous pointers can be fastened to the deck, ingeniously set into a visible pocket in the spray cover, or attached with a cord around the wearer's neck. When using a compass, make sure you keep it away from your walkie-talkie or other metal objects. Other important safety items for a venture at sea include flares, an automatic electronic signaling device, a flashlight or caver's headlamp, sunglasses, a whistle, and a waterproof watch.

In his Greenland kayak, Bart Hauthaway stays warm with a hat and a paddling jacket. (Bart Hauthaway)

Bulkheads and watertight hatches are better for kayaking in the ocean because in case of capsize, only the cockpit fills with water, and that can be bailed out using a deck pump. A good pump can not only bail out the cockpit, but its hose can also be placed into a companion's boat or into a flooded bulkhead or storage compartment with hatch failure to empty it. A pump provides a new and wider margin of safety for paddling at sea. One should note, however, that pumps can be slow and cold water may not allow adequate time.

Deck-mounted bungee cords can be useful for holding charts, extra gear, and spare paddles (or even paddles while you are looking at your charts!). For ocean paddling, anything on the deck stands the risk of being washed overboard if the cords are not tight. Better yet, use straps or rope. Recessed fittings—integral parts of the deck—work well, and these fittings can even be rigged with full deck lines to provide a grab point for anyone trying to hold onto the kayak while in the water. Surface fittings are also good, and either style can be used with full deck lines.

Technique

Seamanship and Common Sense

As with any type of kayaking, but particularly in whitewater or in the ocean, common sense and seamanship are the most important safety attributes a paddler can bring to his sport. Boat-handling maneuvers, Eskimo rolls, and rescue techniques are all very important, and their mastery should be sought, but nothing is as important as knowing when and where to take your kayak. For determining both, consider tidal currents and levels, weather, alternate take outs, and access.

Some Paddling Hints

Most of the basic kayak strokes are also useful in propelling and steering a kayak in the ocean. The forward, back, draw, and sweep strokes are the same. However, most of your strokes in the ocean will be forward strokes, and this will be especially true if you use a rudder. In order to keep a good forward stroke going for an extended period of time (all day), you will want to put less emphasis on the push and pull of the arms and more emphasis on the torso rotation. Finally, your upper hand will come forward at a lower level, thereby giving your deltoids a rest.

Many sea kayakers have found that an extended paddle position (hands choked up on the shaft) helps in sweep strokes by giving more leverage.

Jim Chute demonstrates an easy, relaxed forward stroke for sea kayaking. (Stan Wass)

In the standard back brace or stern rudder, the paddle blade is placed in the water at the stern with the power face angled slightly inward. The kayaker then leans on the paddle to carve a graceful arc with his boat in the same direction as the lean. Sea kayaks share many design similarities with downriver or wildwater kayaks and, thus, can also be turned by paddling forward and leaning to the opposite side of where you want your bow to head.

With long paddles, slower stroke rates are more common. Bracing strokes timed with approaching waves become very important to smooth paddling when a heavy sea is running. A paddler should always lean into a wave (as he would while surfing in the ocean or in a river), especially if the wave is breaking. The bigger the breaking wave, the harder the lean and the brace.

Launching and Landing

First get in with the kayak partially afloat, attach the spray cover, and when ready, shove off. If launching into waves, watch how far the waves roll up on the sand, then hurry your kayak down as close as possible in between waves and get in. (On the West Coast of the United States, there are commonly 8 seconds between waves, on the East Coast about 6 seconds.) When the next large wave washes up on shore, this may be enough to enable you to push off and paddle firmly out to deeper water. If not, position an upright paddle on one side of your boat. Bend forward and place your other hand down on the sand along the other side of the boat. Push down on both sides and inch your way forward toward the water. A partner on shore can also help push you out quickly into deeper water when the next waves roll up on the beach.

Launching from a rocky shore is similar to launching in a river (see Chapter 5). Be careful not to slip on the rocks; beware that a surge of incoming water doesn't lift you up and settle you down on a sharp rock. With a partner or without, you can do a "seal" launch when rocks are covered with seaweed. Simply get into your boat; use your paddle on one side and your hand on the other side to slide your boat down into the water. A partner can help by lifting your stern and giving you a shove seaward.

Landing a kayak can be a rough or smooth experience depending upon how well the kayaker can read the pattern of ingoing waves. The surf should be studied carefully. Sometimes there will be five to seven large waves rolling in, followed by a pause with a couple of smaller waves. This phenomenon results from wave interference between two sets of waves arriving simultaneously from two separate and distant storm sites. This is not necessarily a regular occurrence, so don't count on its happening every time you wish to land. In any event, study the waves until you can sense some kind of pattern; then sprint to shore just ahead of the smallest wave. As soon as you touch bottom, leap out and quickly drag your kayak up the beach out of the way of the next incoming wave.

Landing on a rocky shore is more difficult, but the principle is the same. Carefully choose a sheltered spot where you can make it in. Wait for a pause in the wave pattern and go in. Jump out of your kayak and move it quickly away from the next incoming wave. On seaweed-covered ledges, ride a surging wave into the ledge. As the water recedes, leaving the boat high and dry, jump out of the boat and move the boat and yourself to higher ground. On a rocky shore or island, there are many small coves with some protection from winds and waves for landing.

Wind

Gales

Strong winds or gales (35 miles per hour or more; 56 kilometers per hour or more) are to be avoided whenever possible. If, however, you are unfortunate and find yourself faced with a *beam wind* or *beam gale* (wind blowing at you from 3 o'clock or 9 o'clock), while making forward strokes, keep your blade low on the windward side as it returns to take another stroke on that side. For example, with a wind coming from 3 o'clock, when you finish your forward stroke on the right side, simply let the right blade skim the water on its way back forward, rather than lifting it so it is in danger of being caught by the wind. When paddling in a beam gale, always lean into the wind and time the strokes to allow paddle entry and drive as the wave crest arrives. Otherwise the boat may be tipped if the paddler's weight has shifted downwind and the windward blade is caught by a gust of wind. If a strong gust of wind does hit your raised blade, don't fight it. Relax the grip of your upper hand and allow the paddle to flip over. This will prevent a capsize.

Weathercocking

While paddling parallel to the wind and waves with any degree of forward speed, you will notice a phenomenon called weathercocking. In spite of your best efforts, your kayak may tend to turn into the wind. This can be exasperating because you are forced to paddle constantly on one side just to stay on course. This phenomenon can occur when the wind is coming at you broadside, or diagonally both fore and aft. Some designs are more sensitive than others. This effect is less of a problem when you paddle fast.

Weathercocking is caused by an imbalance of two forces acting on your boat. The wind pushing up against the exposed deck area of a kayak is called *windage*. This force must be perfectly counterbalanced by a second force—the *lateral resistance* of the area of the kayak below the waterline (see Diagram A). However, as the kayak moves forward (sideways to the wind direction), the center of lateral resistance also moves forward, thus forcing the kayak to turn into the wind (Diagram B).

Weathercocking can be counterbalanced in a number of ways. As mentioned earlier, you can simply make strong corrective forward strokes on one side. Second, a rudder can help correct the situation, but a rudder

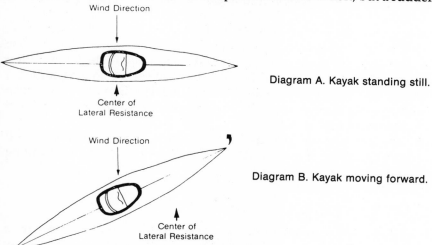

Diagram A. Kayak standing still.

Diagram B. Kayak moving forward.

creates drag and can be damaged in launching and landing. Kayaks with low deck profiles leaving very little exposed to the wind are not affected quite so much by weathercocking. The Eskimos moved forward or backward in their cockpits, because by shifting their weight fore or aft as needed, they did not have to make those exhaustive correcting strokes constantly on one side.

Some modern seagoing kayaks have a sliding seat and footbrace arrangement that can be adjusted while underway. Thus, if your kayak tends to turn into the wind, simply slide your seat forward or backward until that motion stops. What you have done is to bring back into balance windage and your boat's lateral resistance to it. (Technically it is called having a *balanced wind-water couple*.) If you significantly alter the forward speed of the kayak, you must also adjust your seat accordingly. If the force of the wind changes, you must also compensate for it by repositioning your seat. Finally, it is assumed that your spray cover and cockpit are ample enough to allow you to move your seat forward or backward.

A sliding seat may not be the complete answer, however, because such an arrangement requires a larger cockpit. The larger the cockpit, the greater the danger of having a heavy sea pound your spray cover down into your lap, filling your boat with water. In the open ocean, this is more than disconcerting—it can be dangerous. Sliding seat/bracing arrangements are less effective with a loaded kayak.

Some kayaks have an extended keel or a removable skeg that helps to keep a kayak on course. Paul Coffyn, in his circumnavigation of New Zealand, used a removable skeg to combat weathercocking.

If you lack both a rudder and a sliding seat, the "one-knee hang" is a technique that can be used. When a beam wind is blowing, simply press your knee on the leeward side hard up against the kneebrace, allowing your other (windward) knee to straighten out. This will cause the kayak to tilt toward the wind and will compensate for weathercocking. Another solution is to use an extended paddle on the windward side and transform your forward stroke on that side into more of a sweep stroke. As you can see, there are a variety of ways to attack the problem of weathercocking.

In all cases pertaining to travel in the open ocean, experiment with your gear load and the trim of your kayak near shore before heading out to deeper water.

Winds from Other Directions

In a headwind, you should develop a steady paddling rhythm, try to keep the spray out of your face, and continue to paddle briskly. It may not seem that you are making much headway, but you are. If you paddle at 3 knots and the wind costs you 2, you will go 1 knot. However, if you paddle at 4 knots into the same wind, you will actually double your speed without doubling your effort. Small plane pilots experience much the same thing with headwind and fuel economy.

If the wind is coming at you diagonally, either from bow or stern, you have a couple of choices. One alternative is to turn about 45 degrees, so that the wind is now coming from either 9 or 3 o'clock, and proceed to paddle parallel to the waves, making adjustments for weathercocking. Forty-five degrees is easier to paddle than 90 degrees (sideways to the wind). In so doing, you will not head directly toward your destination but will complete a dogleg. For instance, if you wish to cross a channel but face a beam wind at 9 o'clock, by paddling parallel to the waves, your crossing will take you downwind of your destination. As soon as you reach the leeward side of the channel, you must then turn back toward 9 o'clock and head straight up along the coast to your goal. Close to shore, those waves can still be troublesome; they crest in shallows and reflect off banks.

If, however, you find that the diagonal waves are not as troublesome as the parallel ones, continue to paddle straight toward your destination.

Waves

Waves will be your constant companion when you paddle on the ocean. Waves—their style, character, size, and ferocity—should be well known to you.

Waves consist of three basic parts: the *crest*, which is the top or highest part of the wave; the *trough*, which is the lowest part of the wave; and the *soup*, the name given to a wave after it breaks. The *length* of a wave is the distance from one crest to another, and its *height* is the distance vertically from trough to crest. The time required for two wave crests to move past a reference point is called the *wave period*. Counting the seconds between successive breaking waves on the shore also gives you the wave period.

Wind blowing against a tidal current will produce steep, choppy waves. Wind blowing across water flowing at exactly the same speed will produce no waves at all. Wind blowing in the same direction and faster than the speed of the current will produce smooth, rounded waves.

Seas and Swells

As you paddle on the sea, you will soon become aware of two broad classifications of waves: *sea* and *swell*. Seas are generated locally by wind.

They appear confused and irregular in pattern. They tend to have sharp, angular crests, and no regular wave period; the wind-whipped crests often spill forward.

Swells have often traveled thousands of miles across the broad expanse of the sea. As seas move away from their point of origin, they smooth out into long, regular crests of definite wave lengths and wave periods. These are the source of coastal surf. Calmest landing sights are those protected from these waves, not necessarily those protected from wind.

Whitecaps

When the wind blows strongly enough to whip up a deep water wave higher than one-seventh of the distance between crests, then the tops of the waves fall over, forming whitecaps. As waves move toward shore, they change some of their characteristics. As waves encounter the rising ocean bottom, their period may remain the same, but their velocity and length decrease while their wave height increases. Eventually, as with a deep water wave, they will begin to break when their ratio exceeds 1:7. When the wave gets close to shore in water only about one and a quarter times its height, the crest topples over in a breaking wave.

It is both reassuring and dangerous to know that the surf zone is actually quite shallow. Although the paddler can probably stand up after a tipover, unless he knows to lean forward against the deck as he goes over, he risks serious neck, back, or head injury if the boat rolls over him in the shallows.

Reflected Waves

Unfortunately for the kayaker, waves can be reflected into the ocean after striking piers, headlands, or even islands. Thus incoming and reflected wave patterns interfere with one another to create a very confused and choppy pattern. Sometimes the reflected wave crest is perfectly timed to meet an incoming wave, and they collide explosively. This can be dangerous, and kayaks should avoid areas where this occurs.

Plunging Waves

A plunging (or *dumping*) wave should be avoided by kayakers. Steep waves approaching a steep beach tend to plunge. This kind of wave has an overhanging curl of water that comes crashing down with tremendous impact. Launching and landing should not be attempted through plunging or dumping waves. Typically these are on steep gravel beaches, and the surf zone is very close to the beach.

Spilling Waves

Spilling waves are steep waves that approach a gently sloping beach. They are good surfing waves that break smoothly with the water tumbling down the forward slope. They lack the violence of a plunging wave and are better waves in which to surf or safely launch and land boats.

Rip Currents

While observing waves breaking and rolling up on the shore, look for strong, narrow currents of water carrying the excess water back out to sea. These are called rip currents. The water accumulates and disperses to either side, eventually to exit seaward in narrow and swift currents with waves not nearly so high. These currents can be quite strong; at high tide, they can be very pronounced. Rip channels can be found along the sides of bays and can provide a fast way of getting out into the sea.

Turning in Waves

To change direction in big waves, wait until your kayak rises to the top (crest) of a wave; then, using a sweep stroke, quickly turn your boat in the proper direction. The crest of the wave passing under the kayak

For best results in turning, turn on top of a wave. (Stan Wass)

clears the bow and stern, providing an easy pivot for turning, since both ends are in the air above water. It is much more difficult to turn a kayak when it is down in the trough of a wave. Turning will also be enhanced with some forward speed.

Tides

No one should ever launch a kayak for a trip in the ocean without being fully aware of what the tide is doing and of tidal streams and currents, if any, that will be encountered on the voyage. If you plan carefully, the tide and current can work for you and make your journey pleasant and easy. Needlessly fighting tides and currents can be taxing; eddy hopping will be required at times.

Fortunately charts and maritime booklets are available for most inhabited and mapped coastal areas of the world. To make use of the tide, it is important to keep a couple of things in mind. First, from low tide (when the tide is way out), the current gradually increases in speed until about halfway through the first tidal cycle, about 3 hours. After the midpoint of this first cycle is reached, the current slowly decreases until high tide is reached in about another 3 hours, a total of a little more than 6 hours from low to high tide. The same thing occurs in reverse from high tide back to low tide. To make it more complicated, there can be a lag between the position of a tide out at the mouth of an estuary and that farther up the estuary. There can also be a substantial lag between tidal changes and tidal current changes. Often the tide starts in well before the current starts flowing in. Crossing from the mainland to an island, one must bear in mind that the tidal stream flows faster, the narrower the gap between the two pieces of land.

Tidal streams that appear in channels and straits should not be confused with true ocean currents. For example, the famous Gulf Stream in the Atlantic Ocean is not a tidal stream, but a current. It travels toward the British Isles at a constant rate of about 3 miles per hour.

Navigating by Kayak

Poets have extolled the wonders as well as the dangers at sea. It has often been said that the sea doesn't care. The sea can be tantalizingly deceptive. For example, you can be duped into believing that the direction you aim your kayak in is the direction you actually go in. Far from it. Nature, in the form of wind, tidal streams, and ocean currents, will conspire to send you way off course. Then, if fog descends, you won't even be able to see your destination.

Werner Furrer checks his compass and his chart. (Bart Jackson)

The purpose of this section is not to provide complete information on navigation at sea. That is a science that has been studied for centuries, and many valuable books are available on the subject. Suffice to say, it is a complex subject that deserves the complete respect of anyone venturing out from the mainland in a small boat.

Navigation Aids at Sea

Fortunately most harbors and estuaries are well marked with buoys and other navigational aids. You should be familiar with all of them, so if you paddle up to one in a dense fog, you'll know exactly where you are. Since kayaks are not the only craft to ply the oceans, a kayaker should be aware of the meaning of the various ships' signals and always stay away from large vessels. In all cases, use these navigational aids to identify navigation channels and then stay out of the channels.

Fog

Generally speaking, do not venture out to sea on a foggy day, or even if fog is predicted in the weather forecast. Keep in mind that fog is caused by warm air blowing off the land over a cool sea, which chills the air down to its dew point. In parts of the world where warm air blows across a warm ocean current (the Gulf Stream, for example) and then encounters cold water, fog will form.

Should fog suddenly envelop you at sea, don't panic. Simply follow your predetermined compass course. As soon as you *feel* you are close to your destination (since you can't see it), stop paddling and start to rely on your ears. All land emits sound of some kind. It may be waves breaking against a rocky shore, dogs barking, or even the noise of birds, a chain saw, or an automobile.

Jay had an embarrassing moment in the middle of the Connecticut River on the border between Vermont and New Hampshire, just south of Ledyard Bridge, near Hanover, New Hampshire. Fog so thick descended he couldn't see either river bank. He had paddled long enough to get where he was going, but nothing showed up on the limited horizon. Apparently he had paddled in a circle. It was enormously frustrating until, far away, he heard the sound of an automobile crossing the bridge. He headed in that direction, and soon the bridge loomed up in front of him.

Transit Markers

One of the oldest navigational techniques in the world is the use of transit markers. Simply line up two identifiable objects on land that stand in the direction you wish to head. Keep one object in view directly in front of the other, and you'll be on course. Two headlands kept in line can accomplish the same purpose. Sometimes you can use two sets of transit markers at right angles to each other to pinpoint your position exactly.

Some Navigational Examples

There are two types of navigation, *dead reckoning* and *piloting*. Dead reckoning means knowing speed, direction, and time; allowing for drift, one can calculate his position. "Dead" is short for deductive, but be aware that it is often impossible to get accurate estimates of drift and velocity. Piloting is simply continuous visual orientation. This also means that if you can't see, you don't go out that day. In all navigational problems, one must consider, "What if?"

What if it is an hour and a half into a 1-hour paddle?

What if the drift is twice what was estimated?

What if we slow down because of photography, fishing, or seasickness?

Now, in Diagram A, which shows a *dead reckoning blind crossing*, what if the current is 2 knots? Or the time is 1 hour after estimated time of arrival? Or the group can't average 5 knots? Or if the current is faster than the kayaks?

A less dangerous method might be a *modified dead reckoning blind crossing* (Diagram B). The advantages are that no accuracy is required on the drift rate. The worst variable (drift rate) is not a factor. You use the eddies and weak currents lining up for the crossing, and then, in the crossing, you can cross currents that are faster than kayaks. You can also change your mind at point A if conditions worsen.

Now, once you have reached your destination (say it's a solitary lighthouse on a single point out at sea), you can make a *return trip blind crossing* (Diagram C), which is very different because you can't overshoot the shore. The advantages are that this is a simple sight-oriented crossing and it works with fast currents.

Let's assume you want to go from the start to a destination at such a distance the islands look like a continuous shoreline. Here are the pros and cons of three different strategies (see Diagram D).

Route—·—·—The advantages are that it is simple and minimizes the crossing time. The disadvantage is that you finish into the wind when the group is tired and the wind may be worse.

Route— — — — —The advantages are that you are not committed until you leave point B, it minimizes the crossing time, and you finish in protected waters. The major disadvantage is that it is hard to see the pass.

Route·····The advantages are that you are not committed until point B and that you can see the pass early (at point A). Its disadvantage is that the crossing is longer.

Most people would choose the last route because it is important to eliminate questions early and it's reassuring to see the pass.

Piloting is applicable when the visibility is good. Diagram E shows a ferry crossing in which you guess a course, then start, and make corrections en route. A more conservative approach uses the shore and the eddies to overcompensate for the drift. In piloting example 2 (Diagram F), you estimate the bearing and then start. You correct en route but stay above a straight-line course to be conservative. The advantages to this are similar to ones we have already seen: it takes minimum time in crossing, you can turn back before crossing, it does not require accurate data, and you can cross fast currents.

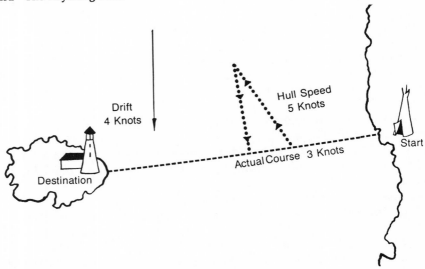

Diagram A. Dead reckoning blind crossing.

Diagram B. Modified dead reckoning blind crossing. Follow these steps: (1) Note direction of drift. (2) Follow shore upstream until drift has been allowed for (to point A). (3) Paddle on a destination heading for uncompensated time (to point B). (4) Then stop paddling and drift, or turn and paddle with the drift.

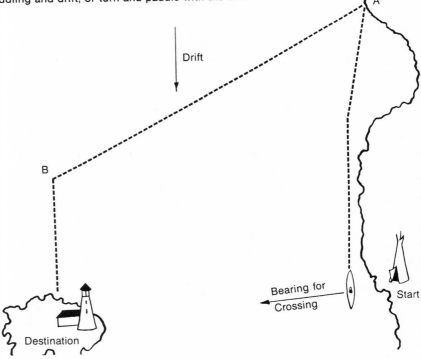

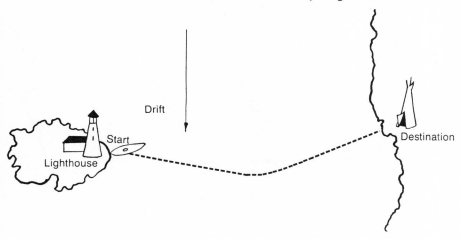

Diagram C. Return trip blind crossing. The best technique here is to make no corrections until you see shore and see that you need to veer left.

Diagram D. Three different strategies.

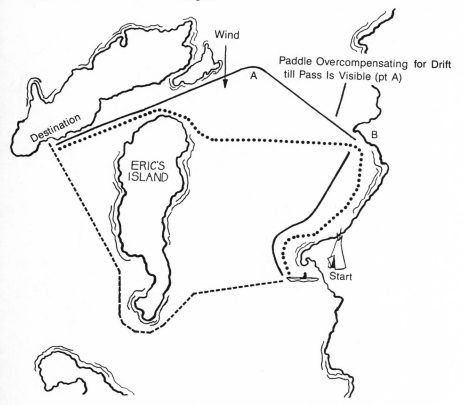

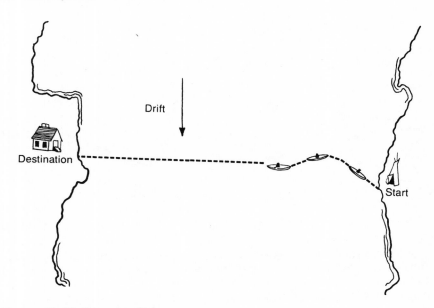

Diagram E. Piloting example 1.

Diagram F. Piloting example 2.

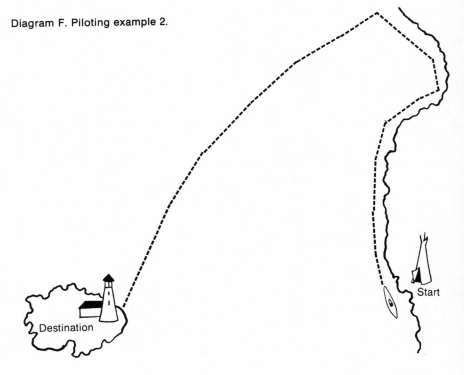

On the Sea at Night

As with fog, generally speaking, one must take care when paddling a kayak in the ocean after dark. In addition to the normal challenges of navigation, you have two additional disadvantages: you can see very little, and nobody can see you. Even if you have a headlamp or strong flashlight, most large vessels will not see you. Even if they did, they could not steer away in time to miss you. Paddling at night should be done only by the most competent kayaker who is totally familiar with the route and can identify the available shore lights—and then only under favorable weather conditions. An easily readable, illuminated compass attached to your deck is also an important accessory.

It is also essential to understand the navigational lights used by other boats. A triangle with a white light at the lower left and a red light at the lower right tells the knowledgeable paddler the ship is approaching from the right and will pass ahead of the kayak. If there are three yellow lights in a vertical stack, the paddler going close behind the boat will learn the hard way what the signal for a tow is.

Paddlers ignorant of the basic navigational lights are taking unnecessary risk in night paddling. No matter what devices the paddler uses, it is unrealistic to expect ships to see and avoid kayakers.

Sea Rescues

The river bank is never too far away when you are paddling down a rapids and something goes wrong. At sea, however, you are likely to be far from shore. Your kayak, lifejacket, and companions are your sole means of survival and rescue. Nevertheless, if you take appropriate precautions and master a variety of rescue techniques, kayaking at sea can be a safe venture.

Each of the following rescue techniques should be thoroughly practiced with your trip companions in a swimming pool or lake before you, as a group, head out for the ocean. It should also be understood that, although some of the following rescue techniques seem somewhat complicated or involved, each one should be accomplished within 60 seconds by a well-trained party.

The Eskimo Roll (See Chapter 6)

This is by far the quickest and safest means of rescue. It is your first line of defense, and the bracing strokes you acquire learning to roll will stand you in good stead in unstable conditions; you may never have to capsize. Remember to really emphasize the *lay back* when rolling a fully loaded sea kayak; hip snaps are not always sufficient.

Caution

For the sea rescue techniques described, bear in mind that, even after you have thoroughly mastered them in an unloaded boat in calm water, doing it for real in a choppy sea with a fully loaded kayak can be much more difficult. If possible all of these rescue techniques should be mastered eventually with *loaded* boats before embarking on an ocean trip.

Solo Re-entry

If you inadvertently fall out of your kayak in a capsize, it is possible to get back in and complete the Eskimo roll. Face to the rear of your over-turned boat, grab the coaming, and do a reverse somersault to get your legs back into the cockpit and fitted into the kneebraces. Then place your paddle into the correct position and roll back up.

This is not as difficult a technique or as farfetched as it appears. A sea kayak with a good bulkhead and/or flotation bags will not take in much water during a capsize, and ironically the kayak will be easier to roll with some water in it. After you roll back up, your cockpit will have lots of water in it, but at least you and the boat are right side up and you are back in the boat. You can then bail out the cockpit before re-placing the spray cover.

The Eskimo Rescue (See Chapter 6)

If you capsize and remain in your boat but cannot roll it back up, simply slap your hands hard on the exposed hull over your overturned craft. One of your companions will nudge the nose of his kayak up against your hand. Grab the bow of the kayak and pull yourself up. Be prepared to hold your breath for at least a minute. You can do it.

The Eskimo Side Rescue

The rescuer paddles quickly alongside the overturned boat and places his paddle across the capsized craft while the kayaker is still in the boat.

The rescuer grabs the kayaker's wrist and places it on the paddle shaft. The overturned kayaker can now pull himself up to an upright position while the rescuer holds the paddle firmly at a 90-degree angle across the overturned hull.

The H-I Rescue

So called because of the position of the kayaks. For this rescue, two kayaks raft up by crossing their paddles in front of them on their cockpits as they position themselves alongside each other. This forms the figure H. Next the overturned kayak, the I, is drawn up over the paddles between the rescuers' boats, emptied out, flipped over to an upright position, and then wedged between the two rescuing kayaks. The swimmer mounts and straddles the rear deck of the kayak and wriggles into the cockpit.

The Kayak-over-Kayak Rescue

Sometimes called the *T rescue* (because of the position of the kayaks). In this rescue, the rescuing kayak approaches the overturned boat at 90 degrees. With some help from the swimmer, the rescuer slides the overturned bow up over the foredeck enough to allow water to drain out of the cockpit. The rescuing kayaker flips the boat upright, slides it back into the water, and then pulls it alongside and holds it steady so the swimmer can mount and straddle the rear deck and wriggle into the cockpit.

Double T rescue employs two rescue kayaks located at the cross of the T. The capsized craft makes up the shaft of the T. It is much easier to haul the overturned boat up on to the foredeck with two rescuers working side by side. Keep in mind that a kayak with a bulkhead near the cockpit doesn't have to be brought completely over another boat; the water drains as soon as the cockpit seal is broken.

The All-In Rescue

In the worst possible case, all kayaks have capsized and all paddlers have come out of their boats. Make sure that all boats, paddles, and swimmers are connected by holding on to each other's boats and paddles. Do not allow one boat or swimmer to drift away. Then empty one kayak by drawing it perpendicularly up over a second overturned boat, making sure that this pivot boat remains upside down to keep air trapped inside the cockpit for as much buoyancy as possible. With a swimmer on either side of the pivot boat, empty the water out of the first boat, flip it over, and drop it alongside the pivot boat right side up.

Extend a paddle amidships across both boats. The second swimmer, on the outside of the overturned pivot boat, holds the paddle firmly, while the first swimmer uses the other end of the paddle as a firm brace to assist his crawling over the side and into the emptied boat.

Once the first swimmer is back in his boat, he performs a T rescue for the second swimmer and boat. Then both of them perform an H-I rescue for other overturned boats and swimmers.

Summary

The kayaker who paddles on the sea will find adventure galore. In one of the most efficient and seaworthy craft in the world, kayakers can travel where few other boaters dare to go. They can hop from one bay or island to another and avoid the roughest water by slipping in close to shore. They can ride beam to a breaking sea that is many times their own height. They can even capsize and be brought right side up again in a moment.

However, anyone who chooses to follow the path to ocean adventure must abide by the following rules:

- Use a kayak designed specifically for ocean travel; other kinds of kayaks are not suitable.
- Bring along all the appropriate equipment and know the proper ways to use it.
- Be totally skilled in all forms of rescue.
- Never venture forth with fewer than three kayaks in a group.
- Take weather, tide, wind, and currents into account before launching a kayak in the ocean.

With the above rules scrupulously adhered to, a whole new world of sport awaits the kayaker. Sea kayaking is truly the new frontier for recreational muscle-powered watercraft.

12. Surfing

Running rapids, crossing a wilderness pond at twilight, or island hopping along the ocean shore are activities for which kayaks are ideally suited. There is, however, another form of water that has attracted the attention of adventuresome people in small boats. It is the waves that ceaselessly roll off the ocean's surface and crash against the great masses of the continents. This endless activity and motion where the sea meets land has always been a source of fascination.

For years outdoor enthusiasts have used a flat board to ride these waves as they roll up on the beach. Surfboarding is well established as a respectable sport in most industrial nations fortunate enough to have one or more good seacoasts.

It was inevitable that someone, someday, would try the same thing in a kayak. At first whitewater kayaks were used, but their pointed ends occasionally dug into the sand. Soon kayaks were designed more like surfboards with a flat bottom and the seat well aft of center. Double-bladed paddles were used to get these "surfyaks" quickly back into position to take advantage of the incoming waves.

As with surfboarding, the West Coast of the United States, at least 25 years ago, became a center for kayak surfing. Today you are likely to hear the sport called "surf skiing" or "wave skiing" as well, and the British Isles, Hawaii, Australia, and South Africa have become havens for the sport in addition to both coasts of the United States.

A slalom kayak slides down the face of a wave. However, flat-bottomed surf kayaks or wave skis made expressly for surfing are easiest to control as you ride in on a large wave. (Old Town Canoe Company)

Equipment

It is possible to run almost any kayak in on the surf and enjoy an invigorating ride toward the beach. Nevertheless, thanks to modern ingenuity, the prospective kayak surfer can do better.

At first the early kayaks designed specifically for surfing were shortened and flattened slalom boats with squared-off ends. They had a tapered flat stern and a pronouncedly upswept bow. They looked something like a slipper. More recently *surf skis* and *wave skis* have emerged.

Surf skis were developed in Australia for surf rescue in the 1930s. They were long and sleek and designed to break through the surf to reach someone in trouble and then to come back directly to shore. Today these boats are generally 14 to 18 feet (4¼ to 5½ meters) in length and resemble a sea kayak in design. They are narrow and have a rudder controlled by the paddler's feet. They can be used for long-distance ocean paddling or racing in to shore on modest waves. As with wave skis, surf skis do not have a traditional "insides" like a normal kayak. Paddlers sit *on* them rather than *in* them. A divot with a molded seat and a foot well provide the boat-to-paddler contact.

A surf ski catches a wave in California. (Valhalla)

Wave skis are derived from surfboards; they are short (6 to 10 feet, or from nearly 2 to 3 meters) and blunt nosed and have a skeg (fin on the underside) for control. The seating and footbracing arrangements are similar to those found in surf skis. They are highly maneuverable on waves and, with no insides, can be righted immediately after a capsize with no worry about emptying the water. Often the paddle will be attached to the wave ski with a long elastic cord so that it doesn't get lost during a capsize.

A helmet should be worn while surfing. This is not so much to prevent the head from hitting a rock or the ocean floor as it is to protect against riderless surfboards, other surf kayakers, and stray paddles.

A lifejacket, of course, must be worn while surf kayaking. After a capsize, it can be a long swim back to shore. Or, if you are knocked away from your boat and catch a mouthful of ocean water at the same time, it is mighty nice not having to worry about struggling back to the surface and swimming energetically just to stay afloat.

Foot rests or foot wells should be designed so they cannot trap your feet, and the seat belt on a surf ski must have a reliable instant release mechanism that is not adversely affected by sand or salt water.

Wave skier Mike Petrie rides "Pinball" in Hawaii. (Shane Wave Skis)

Where to Find Surf

Playing in ocean surf means that you are entering a potentially violent environment. Surf is the whitewater of the sea. Seawater is much heavier than the fresh water found in lakes, ponds, and rivers. You will notice the difference the minute you attempt to empty ocean water out of a swamped kayak. Seawater can pack quite a wallop and should always be treated with respect.

Most beaches popular with board surfers will also be suitable for kayak surfing. Those beaches known for very gradual sloping bottoms usually make excellent spots for surfing. The best surfing conditions exist when there is little or no wind, a warm, sunny day, and large, even swells providing regular, open-ended waves in predictable patterns. Beaches where the waves wash up against a cliff or large rock formations obviously should be avoided, as should any beach that tends to produce high, dumping waves.

All wave skis don't challenge the surf. (Shane Wave Skis)

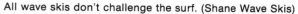

Beach Courtesy

Respect for the rights of others in the enjoyment of nature is some-thing all surf kayakers should observe. Others enjoy the surf be-sides you. Family groups with little children, swimmers, people fishing from the shore, and surfboarders all have a right to enjoy the surf.

Be sure to check with the local park service, landowner, or life-guards on duty to make sure that you may surf your kayak in an area, that it is safe, and that you will not become a danger to others. Never kayak close to swimmers, fishermen, or surfboarders. Al-ways leave plenty of room. Never kayak alone in the surf.

Riding Waves

First of all (if you are a beginner), choose a day when the waves are not too high. Anything over 2½ to 3 feet (76 to 91 centimeters) can be intimidating. Second, recall how to launch a kayak off a beach (see Chapter 11). Place your boat close to the water's edge pointing seaward. Get in, put your spray cover on, and shove your boat along the sand by leaning forward and using an upright paddle on one side and your other hand on the opposite side of your boat. Inch your boat along, and when the next wave comes rolling in, you'll be waterborne. Keep heading directly out, paddling swiftly toward the incoming waves in deep water.

Forward Running

Paddle straight out for several yards until the first breaking wave comes along. Before it reaches you, turn and point your boat directly toward shore, perpendicular to the oncoming wave. When the soup (the white, frothy part) is a few feet behind you and gaining fast, start to paddle forward briskly. The wave will soon catch up to you, and you'll feel that magic sensation of power in the wave that hurtles you toward the beach.

Place your paddle in the stern rudder position and try to maintain a straight course. When the wave plays itself out, turn around and head back for the next one. This time, however, allow yourself to be caught sideways—parallel—to the wave. NOW THE MOST IMPORTANT THING TO REMEMBER—lean *into* the oncoming wave and hang a high side brace over the soup. On small waves, you can actually place the paddle on the back side of the wave. Contrary to what you learned in whitewater kayaking about always leaning downstream and away from the current, in the surf, you lean *into* the soup. This prevents a capsize. If you lean away from a wave, the force of the water will work to overturn your boat.

After you've played around a bit getting used to the feel of the surf, sooner or later, the ocean will catch you by surprise, and you'll find yourself upside down and out of your boat. This is natural and nothing to be ashamed of. Simply grab your boat at the bow or stern and tow it back to shore, maintaining a grip with one hand on your paddle. Some surf kayaks have toggles instead of grabloops at each end, making it easier to keep control of your boat. Sometimes, in heavy surf, a boat will roll over several times, twisting a grabloop around in your hand.

Of course, with a surf ski or wave ski, you won't necessarily have to go to shore to recover after a capsize. These craft can be easily righted by just pushing up on one gunwale. To remount, lay across the seat area and bring one leg up so you are straddling the boat. Your paddle can also be used as a wing or outrigger for more balance. Surf skis will be harder to remount because they are tippier.

After you feel comfortable running straight in ahead of a wave, try going out beyond where the waves are breaking, turn around, and catch a wave by paddling forward. Allow the boat to plane along the surface of the water in front of the wave. Using the paddle in a stern rudder position, angle your kayak so that it is cutting diagonally across a wave. You may notice a tendency for your craft to turn up and out of the wave. A firm stern rudder or bracing stroke can correct this if you wish to stay on the same wave and maintain your straight course toward shore.

If a wave is large, look along the crest of it in both directions and determine on which side the wave will start to break. Turn away from the breaking side and start planing diagonally away from the soup. On a good, long wave, a competent surfer can move well over 100 yards sideways before heading appreciably toward shore.

Tricks to Try

Surf kayaks, surf skis, and wave skis are amazingly versatile craft. Here are a few stunts to add to your repertoire, some of which can be done more easily than others depending on the type of craft and design you are paddling.

The 360-Degree Turn

Fortunately a surf kayak has a flat bottom, making spinning and turning easy. As you plane down the front surface of a wave, a powerful stern rudder stroke in one direction should be enough to spin you around so that you're facing back out to sea. Complete the turn with a strong sweep stroke. Good surf kayakers can do as many as four 360s on the same wave.

Dropping and Climbing

Rather than being satisfied with running straight in to shore, try cutting back to the top of a wave, then dropping back down again. Your kayak will rise and fall on the face of the wave just ahead of the moving crest. The turns can be made by a combination of stern rudder strokes and leaning the kayak—into the wave to climb, and away from the wave to drop back down.

Cutting Back

This is a further refinement of dropping and climbing in which the boat heads down diagonally across the wave away from the soup, then turns and heads back toward the soup before turning back again to the original direction. Cutting back increases your use of the wave and lengthens your run. As before, the turns are made by strong stern rudder strokes and proper leaning of the kayak, coupled with an occasional sweep stroke if necessary.

Going Backward

Riding backward down the face of a wave can be quite a thrilling experience. Turn around so you are facing an oncoming wave. When the wave is a few yards in front of you, start paddling backward. Lean forward into the wave as soon as the angle on the face of the wave begins to steepen, and place your paddle blade near the bow to act as a rudder. This maneuver is not as easy as it sounds. The wave wants to spin your boat around into a forward position.

The Loop

Sooner or later as you surf down a steep wave, your bow will either bury itself in the sand (called *pearling* or *pole vaulting*) if the water is shallow or simply plow deep into the reverse-flowing water beneath the wave. In either case, the wave itself won't stop for you—it will hurry on by, and in doing so, it will literally push your kayak over forward in a loop. Contrary to your natural instinct to raise your head and arch your back, you should lean *forward*, duck your head, and prepare to Eskimo roll. You'll be surprised that by the time you are ready to roll, the wave has gone by, and the kayak will be rolled up in the deep water behind the wave.

Loops can be done both forward and backward. Some kayakers say that the backward loop is easier to learn because your back is presented to the water instead of your face, and your body is much nearer to the water during the loop.

The Half Loop and Flick

With the kayak in a vertical position about to be pushed over into a loop, reach down with the paddle blade into the water and make a quick sweep stroke while "flicking"—snapping your hips in the opposite direction. The kayak will spin on its axis and come down right side up facing out to sea.

The Pirouette

This is the same maneuver as the half loop and flick except that the spin is strong enough for the kayak to turn 360 degrees or more on its axis.

The Eskimo Roll Reverse Loop and Flick

Perfectly executed this can be one of the most graceful and acrobatic tricks in surfing. As the kayak falls back down the face of a wave, the stern digs in. Just before the kayak becomes vertical, the kayaker assumes an Eskimo roll position and rolls into the wave. The bow continues in its arc beyond the vertical as the Eskimo roll is completed. Surprise! The kayak emerges right side up and is now heading forward on the same wave.

Pop Ups

Sometimes called *sky rocketing* or *pop outs*, these are possible on certain kinds of waves (you'll have to try the waves to see if they are right for them); you bury the bow but do not quite do a loop. Your boat goes down deep and then acts as a Ping-Pong ball that has been immersed in a pail of water. The kayak will literally pop back up and sometimes actually clear the water.

The ultimate, of course, is an airborne 360-degree pirouette.

Summary

As you can see, surf kayaking adds a whole new, thrilling dimension to the sport of kayaking. With proper precautions taken, it is relatively safe. It can be exquisitely graceful as well as acrobatic. Since waves have so much variety to them, you can invent maneuvers that have not been tried before.

13. Touring

Exploring the waterways of the world can open an entirely new dimension for you. The spectrum is as broad as the imagination. Touring by kayak can simply mean traveling down the river that runs through your hometown or exploring the shoreline of a nearby lake. It can also mean a major trip to a famous river in another part of the country, or even an international expedition to South America or to the Himalayas, where rivers cascade from the highest peaks.

Going places, seeing unfamiliar sights, and learning new things in the great outdoors in relative safety and comfort with friendly companions can be one of life's greatest rewards. Land-based human beings are often intrigued by the smells and challenge of the sea. Urban people, surrounded by pavement, concrete, man-made noise, confusion, and visual pollution, can learn that there is natural incense in the air and a music to the wind. The world is out there for you to enjoy. A wilderness trip by kayak will renew you and refresh your senses and your appreciation of life. The kayak is an ideal vehicle to take you to some of the remote corners of the earth.

Whitewater kayaking (it's true!) at Hellgate on New York City's East River. (Eric Evans)

Taking the First Step

Whether you live in a city, in a small town, or in the country, the chances are good that you can find people who like to go kayaking. There is an extensive listing of national organizations and local clubs at the end of this book. You should check with the local YMCA, the YWCA, or the nearest college outing club. Often wilderness outfitters, such as Eddie Bauer and Eastern Mountain Sports, have personnel who are knowledgeable about kayakers in your neighborhood.

If there is a club in your area, you should consider joining it. Here you can find access to kayaks, facilities for building boats, pool sessions, and instruction. Here, too, you're likely to find companions interested in the same kinds of adventure as you.

All the ingredients for a successful outing: boats, paddles, safety equipment, and a group of enthusiastic kayakers of all ages. (Ledyard Canoe Club)

Kinds of Trips

Touring by kayak and cruising the waterways can take any of four different forms. Each has unique demands. The easiest to plan and execute, of course, is the simple day trip. Your equipment, food, travel requirements, and expenses are minimal. It can be a simple lazy afternoon float down a nearby river, a visit to a surfing beach, or a picnic on an island in the middle of a lake.

The next step up in touring is the weekend excursion. This involves an overnight or two, more meals to consider, and perhaps considerable travel. These kinds of trips are enormously popular as a welcome break from life's daily routine. It these are done in moderation, you have helped yourself to the wilderness and returned to civilization refreshed and renewed.

The third kind of trip is often hatched in the minds of kayakers on dark winter evenings when the temperature hovers well below freezing: "Let's take a couple weeks off next summer and do the Middle Fork of the Salmon River in Idaho," or "Let's do a circumnavigation of Vancouver Island." Half the fun of these major trips is in the planning. These trips are likely to be taken on vacations. They require careful logistical planning and a considerable commitment on the part of the participants.

The most exciting prospect of all, however, is the major international expedition. It can be the high point of a person's life. To say that it

Sea kayak touring off the coast of Seattle. (Bart Jackson)

requires a major dedication and commitment of time, money, and effort is an understatement, yet the rewards can be immeasurable.

Kayakers have traveled the entire navigable length of the Nile in Egypt and the Danube in Eastern Europe, as well as the Mississippi River. They have ventured into the mountain kingdoms of Nepal and Bhutan and into Australia's outback, too.

There is still much, much more to explore. All the tallest mountains of the world have now been climbed, all the deserts have been crossed, and both polar caps have been inhabited, but most of the wild rivers of the world are still waiting. Rivers tumbling down the steep slopes of the 1,000-mile-long Andes Mountain range in South America have barely been touched by kayak. For every mile of river that has seen a kayak in the huge Himalayan region of central Asia, there are hundreds and hundreds of miles still to explore. Truly the wild rivers of the world are our last major frontier on this planet.

A Word about Commercial Trips

All of the above-mentioned kinds of trips are also offered by enterprising commercial boating companies. For the most part, these companies are registered with the U.S. Forest Service or with local authorities and are perfectly reliable. They are obliged to meet certain standards of safety

Cully Erdman goes airborne on the Jata Te River in Mexico. (Eric Evans)

and wilderness usage. Your comfort and safe return are important to their success. Outdoor outfitters and travel agencies can help you get in touch with commercial trips. Perhaps the best advertisement, though, is to talk with someone who has been on the trip you are thinking of taking.

You and Your Traveling Companions

The intriguing chemistry of interpersonal relationships can either make or break a cruising trip in kayaks. When possible choose your companions carefully. Your group should be experienced enough to handle the normal hazards to be encountered on water. One paddler, weak in either boating skills or stamina, can spoil a trip for everyone. So can a hotshot boater who quickly becomes bored with slower-paced companions. There should not be too great a range in either skill level or physical conditioning of all members of the group.

You and your traveling companions should share the same basic goals. Is it agreed that this trip is to see how fast you can all paddle from point A on the river to point B? Or, are we agreed to stop and smell the flowers along the way? Tension can easily be created between those who want to push on down the river and those who wish to stay and play in a

Sascha Steinway surfs a wave on the West Branch of the Penobscot in Maine. (Eric Evans)

particularly attractive set of rapids. You should all be in agreement as to the purpose of the trip.

Unreconcilable differences in temperament among boating companions can cause unpleasantness. Naturally some differences in political outlook and temperament are welcome. A healthy blend adds spice to an outing in kayaks.

One of the most helpful things you can do is to sit down in a quiet corner somewhere and write down a personal inventory of yourself. Try to make it a really objective assessment. First consider your limitations as a boater, your skill level, and your experience. Are they compatible with those of your companions and sufficient to meet the challenges of the trip planned? Do you have any physical handicaps, such as a bad back, that might act up partway through the trip? How far can you comfortably travel by kayak in a day? Is this trip realistic for you? Would you be a drag on the others? Is this excursion well below your level of skill and interest?

Second, what do you have to offer to the group? Fishing skill, water reading expertise, campsite experience, knowledge of the area to be covered, first aid, good humor, a good singing voice, or an inexhaustible supply of jokes?

Third, you should carefully examine your personal habits. Have you ever been accused of being a "me-firster"? Are you a chowhound? Do you talk too much or too little? Are you a heavy smoker, drinker, or a penny-pincher? To what extent are you willing to share what you have with others when you don't have enough even for yourself? No person is perfect, of course, but when friends are thrown together on a kayak trip, both the best and the worst traits blossom. It is important for the success of a trip to be ever mindful of your shortcomings and not burden your companions with them. It is also helpful if you ignore the shortcomings of others.

Fourth, leadership can take many forms, and touring by kayak can provide excellent opportunities for leadership. There is no single kind of leadership that is the best. Some people prefer consensus decision making: there is no real leader, but people sit around, talk things out, and jointly agree upon what action to take. Others prefer the majority rule system, where a vote is taken on decisions of importance. Still others feel more comfortable appointing a leader whom they can trust and bestowing upon him all the decision-making responsibilities.

It would be smart before venturing out on a major kayak trip or an international expedition to do as the American Himalayan Kayak Descent did in the fall of 1981. In the words of one of the participants, "We met for a weekend at the Gauley River in West Virginia, disbursed

our equipment, and discussed the philosophy of leadership. It was decided that our leader would have final decision-making power rather
than leadership by majority rule. We also discussed chain of command,
the goals of the expedition. We listed our priorities in rank order, and
practiced rescue techniques."

As a result of such careful preparation, this expedition to a series of
unknown whitewater rivers in the remote kingdom of Bhutan was an
outstanding success in every way.

What Kind of Boat

The kind of craft you take touring or cruising may depend upon what
you happen to own, but more importantly on what kind of trip is
planned. Generally speaking, for shorter day or weekend trips, the common recreational whitewater or touring kayak is adequate. These craft
are relatively stable (kayaks really aren't tippy—some kayakers are!)
and, with their minimal draft and excellent maneuverability, are ideal
for shallow water cruising, coastal touring, and the investigation of
swamps. One can surf using a whitewater-type kayak, but it is better
and safer to use a surf kayak designed specifically for that activity. The
whitewater kayak is also suitable for open water paddling on small lakes,
since its low profile prevents its being tossed about by the wind.

For more extended flatwater cruising, your comfort is a concern.
Larger volume, touring-style kayaks, while not so maneuverable, offer
greater legroom. For the longer trips, you should consider a kayak's
cargo capacity, because you'll need to take more gear along with you.

Cruising across really large bodies of water such as the Great Lakes,
the Chesapeake Bay, or the Gulf of Mexico can be done in almost any
kind of kayak—but then, a person can enter a footrace with heavy boots
on, too, but shouldn't expect to do very well. Long, sleek, fast-moving
seagoing kayaks are available for ocean travel. Stable two-seater foldboats with built-in air sponsons are also logical choices, as are those with
sailing rigs. These craft ride the waves well, keep on course easily, and
are comfortable. In summary you should choose the type of kayak to
fit the demands of the trip, just as a skier has the choice of cross-country,
jumping, slalom, or downhill skis.

What to Wear

The two most important considerations for comfort and well-being on
a kayak trip are to be warm and dry. With a little careful preparation,

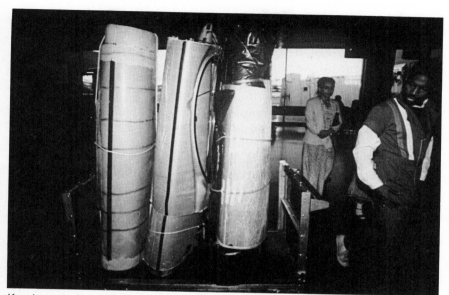

Kayaks sawed in thirds, ready for loading at JFK en route to Bhutan. (Eric Evans)

What is sawed in thirds must be rebuilt: fiberglassing in Darjeeling, India, before entering Bhutan. (Eric Evans)

you can tour all day long in a kayak in the pouring rain and still be totally comfortable. Actually, the very "defying the elements" can heighten the pleasure. If you go cruising and get wet, cold, and miserable, don't blame the weather. It is only your own shortsightedness and lack of preparation that cause the discomfort. Here's how to beat Mother Nature at her own game.

First of all, bring along a complete set of dry clothes. Leave them in the car so you can change into them at the end of the day. If you're camping out, bring them along but keep them in a waterproof bag tucked away under your deck. If you are kayaking for a couple of days or more and are not too far from civilization, make a detour to the nearest town and toss your wet clothes into the dryer at the local laundromat while you stop for gas and groceries.

Even if you usually wear a helmet while kayaking, it would be smart to bring along a wide-brimmed hat of some kind to keep the rain off while you're setting up the campsite. Always have a dry pair of sneakers and socks to sink your feet into at the end of a day. Sneakers are preferred over heavy boots, for you may wish to wear them while boating the next day. Heavy boots are not only clumsy inside a kayak but are much more difficult to swim in.

Let's face it, in kayaking your hands are going to get wet, but again, as previously explained, there are a variety of wind gloves or Pogies that are excellent in protecting your hands from the cold wind and rain. Years ago paddles came supplied with rubber drip rings between the paddle blades and where the paddler gripped his paddle. These drip rings were designed to keep water from running down the paddle shaft at the paddle was raised on the return stoke. These have pretty well gone out of fashion, but the idea is still sound.

Fortunately your spray cover and paddling jacket will do a fine job of keeping you warm and dry *while you're sitting in the kayak*. Once outside, a pair of rain pants together with your paddling jacket will come in handy and be appreciated.

There is nothing more yucky than squirming into a clammy, wet bathing suit in the morning. Take along an extra one. It doesn't take up much room, and a dry bathing suit in the morning is guaranteed to get you off to a good start.

For more rugged conditions, a wool sweater under your paddling jacket can make a noticeable difference. In the most extreme weather or cold water conditions (see Chapter 3), wet suits and dry suits are essential.

Since touring by kayak can be a wet sport, it is best to *overprepare* for cold and damp conditions rather than underprepare. It is easier to take a sweater off and stow it in your kayak, instead of shivering and wishing you had one to put on.

What to Take with You

The length and kind of trip you envision will dictate the quantity of gear you'll need to take with you. Many first-timers tend to cart along too many of the accoutrements of civilization. A good rule of thumb is "If in doubt, leave it out." This is especially true when your kayak trip goes overnight well beyond the range of your automobile. Even the larger volume touring-style kayaks have only a limited amount of room for storage. Nevertheless, here are a few tips that might prove helpful.

Everything from matches to clothing should be encased in waterproof containers. No exceptions.

Five Little Bags

One bag should hold your toiletry articles. These could include soap, toothpaste, toothbrush, Chap Stick, sunburn cream, comb, insect repellent, a metal mirror, toilet paper, and (just in case) deodorant, shaving gear, or other personal items.

A second bag should contain a first aid kit with adhesive bandages, a needle, thread, tweezers, aspirin, Ace bandage, disinfectant, small scissors, and other items you might anticipate using on the trip.

A third bag should include a repair kit with the necessary fiberglass patching materials, duct tape, and bike-tube repair material in case your flotation bags or air mattress leak. For the kayak itself, a spare take-down paddle taped to the deck is worthy of consideration—especially when going deep into a wilderness area or to sea. A sponge placed beside your seat at the bottom of your kayak will serve double duty. It can be used as a bailer to get rid of any water collected in the bottom of your boat. Then, later at the campsite, the sponge can be used to wash up or even bathe with. Don't forget to include a safety rope with the kayak.

A fourth bag—always within easy reach—should contain your camera and extra film.

Finally, have you ever looked forward longingly to lunch only to find your sandwich water-soaked? A fifth plastic, waterproof bag should contain your noon repast. Your lunch in the wilderness can be an exquisite pleasure.

A discussion of appropriate kinds of tents, sleeping bags, cooking gear, axes, and saws goes well beyond the scope of this book. There are many good outdoors manuals that treat these topics in great detail. However, the kayaker's needs are like those of the mountaineer. All items must be as light as possible, and compact. Lest you overlook something, though, make this a reminder not to forget: matches, a watch, pocketknife, can opener, and a flashlight. On a large lake or at sea—a compass, whistle, and flares.

Getting There

Classes of River Sections

Several things should be carefully considered before the actual arrival of the party at the launching site for the beginning of the trip. If you have chosen to travel a river, the section of it you intend to run will fall into one or more generally recognized classes of navigable difficulty:

Class I: moving water with maybe a few riffles and small waves. Few or no obstructions. Most flatwater rivers are in this class.

Class II: easy rapids with waves up to 3 feet (91 centimeters) high, and wide, clear channels that are obvious without scouting. Some maneuvering is required, but nothing really tricky or difficult.

Class III: rapids with high, irregular waves often capable of swamping an open canoe or a kayak without a spray cover. Narrow passages that often require complex maneuvering. Rapids of this magnitude should be scouted from the shore first to determine the best route through.

Class IV: long, difficult rapids with constricted passages that can require precise maneuvering in very turbulent waters. Scouting from shore is essential, and rescue may be difficult.

Class V: extremely difficult, long, and very violent rapids with highly congested routes that must be scouted from shore before attempting. In the event of mishap, there could be a distinct hazard to life. All boaters attempting a Class V must be well versed in all aspects of self-rescue, and a rescue party should be available at the foot of the rapids.

Class VI: difficulties of Class V carried to the extreme of navigability. To be run only by a team of experienced experts with all precautions taken.

Note: if the water temperature is below 50 degrees Fahrenheit (10 degrees Celsius) or if the river is in a remote wilderness area, then it should be considered one class more difficult than normal.

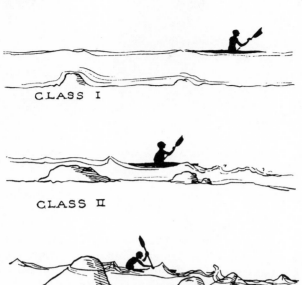

CLASS I

CLASS II

CLASS III

CLASS IV

CLASS V

Classification of rivers. Classes I-V comprise the range of navigable water. Class VI rivers—worse than Class V, if you can believe it—are avoided even by super whitewater kayakers. (Walter Richardson)

Colorado River? Guess again. The Millers River in Massachusetts in, if you can believe it, the fall. (Eric Evans)

Fortunately many of the major rivers in North America have been well described. Guidebooks are available classifying sections of rivers, from Class I to Class VI. Topographic maps of the U.S. Geological Survey are also helpful in locating dams and various access points, as well as noting elevation changes. Once you know what kind of water you can expect, you can plan your trip accordingly. This means you can change your mind on the stretch of the river chosen to be run to respond sensibly to the limitations of the group. Often a party will start their cruise just below major rapids and assure safety for all members of the party.

The river classification system is a handy yardstick, but one that should be used with caution. What might normally be Class III rapids in the spring or fall can quickly assume the proportions of a Class V after a hard rain, a heavy snow melt, or even an unexpected release of water from a dam upstream.

Put-in and Take-out

The logistics of cruising a river are interesting and fun to work out. First to be selected is the put-in point. Look for calm water where it is easy to launch kayaks. There should be ample, safe parking space for automobiles. Most important, if the put-in point is on private land, be sure to ask permission of the landowner.

The take-out point chosen should be easily recognizable from the river. Preferably it will have a gentle, sloping bank and a place where automobiles can be parked. Again, if it is on private land, you must receive the landowner's permission.

Upon arrival at the put-in point, all kayaks and gear needed on the water should be unloaded. All but two people remain at the put-in point. These two then drive two vehicles to the take-out point and leave one vehicle there. Both drivers then return to the put-in point in the remaining car to join the "expedition."

Whitewater paddling in the middle of Houston on the Astroworld whitewater ride. (Eric Evans)

Important

Make sure everybody in the party knows the whereabouts of the car keys for all vehicles stationed at either end of the river. It's embarrassing to arrive at the take-out point at the end of a very pleasant cruise only to discover that the car keys were left back at the start.

Warning

Always leave your vehicles locked, off the road, and out of the way of traffic. Leave no valuable possessions in plain sight inside the car.

Upon arrival at the take-out point, two drivers (or more) use the vehicle left there to drive back to the start, pick up the remaining cars, and return them to the take-out point. Then all boats and people can be loaded for the drive back home. Quite often the meanderings of a river make the water travel distance from start to finish much longer than it is by road. A 15-mile paddle might mean only a 6-mile drive.

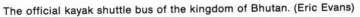

The official kayak shuttle bus of the kingdom of Bhutan. (Eric Evans)

If the party is small and only one car is used, a little more ingenuity is called for. It is possible, by prearrangement, to hire someone at a nearby cabin, farmhouse, or ranch to drive you back at the end of the day. Or perhaps your spouse has other plans for the day and can drop you off at the river, then pick you up later on. Or, you can stash a moped or bicycle at the take-out point and use that to get back to your car.

Loading Up

Whether an overnight excursion is contemplated or a more extended river trip, it will be quite a challenge to store everything properly in a kayak. However, a few simple rules can help:

Rule 1: take only what you really need.

Rule 2: pack items in formless waterproof plastic bags. (Do not stuff a frame pack into a kayak. The formless, flexible plastic bag can be fitted in much more easily and can make much better use of the limited storage space.)

Rule 3: beware of heavy articles. Take lightweight gear only. When a bag is unusually heavy, try to store it as close as possible to the center of the boat. (Perhaps tucked behind your hipbraces?) Avoid stuffing heavy objects at the extreme end of a kayak, since this will upset the trim of your boat, making steering more difficult.

Rule 4: it is OK to deflate your bow and stern flotation bags partially, since they take up so much room. Stuff them as far as possible into the extreme ends of the boat. The rest of your gear—in waterproof bags—will help displace water in case of a capsize.

Rule 5: examine your needs for the entire day. Items not needed until nightfall should be loaded first, toward the far ends of your craft. The repair kit, first aid kit, camera bag, and lunch should be packed close to the middle within easy reach. The kayaker obliged to un-pack his entire kayak at lunchtime to get at something stashed at the far end of the boat is a poor planner.

Rule 6: practice loading your kayak at home the day before you leave on the trip. This will give you ample time to redesign your gear if necessary. Such practice may sound time-consuming, but it pre-vents awkwardness on the river bank—when the others are waiting for you.

The above rules pertain to those touring by kayak, independent of any support group. For some trips, however, it simply is not practical to take it all with you. In these cases, predetermined campsites can be stocked ahead of time. But, make sure all cached gear is bear- and vandal-proof.

In cases where the river runs near a highway, a motorized escort can be arranged. This requires a person willing to carry the heavy camping gear and much of the food supply in a van or automobile. The driver sees you off in the morning, drives ahead to the evening campsite, and awaits you there. Most exotic, of course, is the periodic airdrop of supplies by a bush pilot who knows your route, timetable, and requirements.

Discipline on the Water

Under practically all conditions, the participants of a successful trip by kayak start together, stay together on the water, and arrive home safely together. Togetherness is important, not so much for sociability, but for the sake of safety, help, and rescue.

The "order of march" can be quite casual when there is no danger of rapids, fog, or other hazards, as long as *all kayaks stay within sight and shouting distance of each other at all times.* This rule holds for parties consisting of from a minimum of three to a maximum of six kayaks. Three is the smallest number for safe touring. Two kayaks is risky business—touring alone is foolhardy.

More than six kayaks can very quickly become a mob, if all try to stay close to each other in the water. When there are six or more boats in the same party, you should consider dividing into two independent groups. This does not suggest that each group can go its own way on its own timetable. Both groups should stay in reasonable proximity, but by dividing into two sections, they can prevent overcrowding on the river. Too many boats in the same place on the river can create a hazard for all concerned.

When a potential hazard appears, the most experienced boater, the one most familiar with the route, should lead. Other boats follow with plenty of space between to prevent crowding on the water. Last comes the "sweep," one of the more skillful paddlers, who trails the party, stopping to help anyone in difficulty.

Descending long rapids is often done in stages or sections. After carefully scouting from the river bank ahead of time, the party, in single file, heads through the top section and gathers at a quiet pool or eddy until all members have caught up. Should a less experienced boater inadvertently miss the stopping place, one of the more experienced kayakers should immediately peel off and head downstream in pursuit. The others should follow as soon as possible.

Everyone in the touring party should have the ability to rescue paddlers and equipment. A brief discussion of rescue procedures before running a potentially hazardous stretch can help reduce confusion in an emergency.

There will be times when some members of the party may wish to run a set of rapids while others do not. This is perfectly acceptable. No boater should ever be peer-pressured into running a stretch of water he doesn't feel comfortable trying. These people can portage their boats around the rapids; and, more important, they can post themselves at the foot of the stretch, on either side, with a throw line as a safety precaution for the others as they come through.

Rescue Drills

In addition to the Eskimo roll, there are other rescue drills valuable to practice while touring. The Eskimo roll, of course, is the best, safest, and quickest means of self-rescue. Its importance cannot be overemphasized.

The touring party should run through an Eskimo rescue drill before they go out on a trip. This procedure should be a reflex. Complete mastery of both the Eskimo roll and the Eskimo rescue is essential for all people contemplating coastal cruising or kayaking at sea or on large lakes.

In the Eskimo rescue, as described in Chapter 6, a second boater paddles quickly to the overturned boat and nudges its cockpit with his bow at a 90-degree angle. The capsized paddler can now grab the bow and, with a hip snap, pivot to an upright position again.

If it is not practical to approach the capsized kayak at a 90-degree angle, come alongside parallel. The rescuer places his paddle across both boats, holding it in place with one hand. (There should be not more than a couple of feet separating the boats.) With his other hand, he can guide the overturned kayaker's hands to the paddle shaft, so the capsized boater can haul himself upright.

What happens if the capsized person comes out of his boat? Don't despair. In a river, both boat and paddler can be towed to shore. In a large lake or at sea, it is necessary to accomplish two things. First, with the help of a third boater, water can be emptied from the capsized kayak by quickly lifting one end as high as possible in an inverted position, so the water runs out. Then, with a kayak on each side and parallel to the empty boat, with paddles crossed over in front of the cockpit and grabbed by the two rescuers, the swimmer can lift himself up on the paddles and slip back into his boat. The kayaks on either side help to

Sea kayakers practice their rescues on flatwater before heading out to the open ocean. (Eric Evans)

provide a stable platform, made secure by each paddler holding on to the other's paddle as it rests on the deck of the empty kayak in the middle. It's clumsy and it takes effort, but it works.

Incidentally, for touring far from land or in the deep wilderness, it is advisable to bring along a quick-release kayak tow assembly—just in case.

Rescue drills are fun to practice at home in a pool, or in warm, quiet water. For touring by kayak, these rescue techniques are a necessary part of every boater's skills.

Setting Up Camp

Libraries and bookstores are full of excellent guidebooks explaining in great detail the procedures for camping out in the wilderness. The following points, however, should be remembered by those kayakers who wish to camp out in comfort and safety and to respect the wilderness:

- Know where you are going to set up camp before you start out. A prearranged place is almost always better than taking potluck.
- At the end of a day's trip, make sure your kayaks are pulled completely out of the water and tied down. A heavy rain upstream during the night can raise the river and float your boats away while you snooze.
- At the seashore, always locate your campsite well above the high tide mark.

- If you can choose on which side of the river to camp, pick the one the morning sun strikes first.
- Plan your day on the water so you can erect your camp well before dark. The pleasures of a kayak trip can be greatly enhanced by making camp early.
- Avoid camping in poison ivy or in other poisonous plants.
- Avoid swampy ground near a river. Choose a higher location. It will be dryer and more bug free.
- Because of the danger of lightning, avoid camping under a tall tree.
- Be suspicious of all drinking water. Bring your own, use water purification tablets, or boil it for 20 minutes before you drink it.
- If the campsite is on private land, be sure to get the owner's permission.
- Keep all food securely battened down (or well out of reach above the ground) for the night. Your nocturnal forest friends love to scavenge through a campsite in the middle of the night.
- When striking camp, tidy up the area, carry your refuse and garbage out with you, and leave the site in *better* condition than you found it.

Kayaking for the Handicapped

By its very nature, the sport of kayaking is flexible enough to accommodate people with various handicaps. One of our earliest whitewater memories is of watching an incredibly skilled canoeist in whitewater out west. Only after the canoe finished its run below the rapids and the paddler stepped out on shore did we notice that the paddler had only one leg.

The Nantahala Outdoor Center in North Carolina has been a pioneer in devising instructional classes to aid boaters who are physically handicapped. Special fittings for arms and legs have been designed, and new techniques are being taught.

Below-the-knee amputees can make normal use of the regular knee-braces important to successful boat control. The artificial limb below the knee can work well against the footbrace. Above-the-knee amputees design their artificial limbs so that little control is lost between the upper thigh and the kneebrace on the kayak. Thanks to modern science, artificial hands and forearms are now designed so that people can hold a kayak paddle adequately.

Those with impaired sight can learn to memorize the rapids, and they should be accompanied by guides or boaters who remain close to them

A kayaking class for the handicapped at the Nantahala Outdoor Center in North Carolina. (Nantahala Outdoor Center)

to give voice signals as to which way to turn. The K-2 (two-person kayak) is marvelously suited for use by a boater and a friend with impaired eyesight.

To those who have suffered hearing loss, kayaking through the rapids may appear easy, at first glance. However, one reads water and plots a course through the waves with more than just eyes alone. The various sounds the river makes—the roar, gurgle, ripple, and swish—are all meaningful signals that, together with good eyesight, combine to help the kayaker make good judgments in the water.

Those whose hearing is impaired should act like a wise and cautious boater approaching some rapids for the first time: he walks the river bank studying the water currents and memorizing a logical course through. On the first trip down, the smart boater—whether he has a hearing handicap or not—will follow an experienced boater through.

It appears in kayaking that the biggest problem facing handicapped people is not in cockpit or paddle shaft design, but in simply becoming aware of the possibilities open to them. Handicapped persons may, naturally, be reluctant to try a new sport such as kayaking, but they can be pioneers and later help others to discover kayaking.

Listed below are a few organizations and sources that can provide more information:

National Handicapped Sports-Recreation Association
Penn Mutual Building
4105 E. Florida Ave.
Denver, CO 80221

New England Handicapped Sportsmen's Association
29 Woodcliff Rd.
Lexington, MA 02173

The Nantahala Outdoor Center
Star Rt., Box 68
Bryson City, NC 28713

National Blind Organization for Leisure Development
533 E. Main St.
Aspen, CO 81611

Norman Croucher, *Outdoor Pursuits for Disabled People*
Woodland-Faulkner Ltd., 8 Market Pasage
Cambridge CB2 3PF England

PART IV.
COMPETITION

14. Racing Kayaks

Many forms of kayak racing have evolved over the years, including racing in the ocean and surf, flatwater, marathon, and three major divisions in whitewater: slalom, wildwater, and freestyle. One of the many attractions of kayaking is the diversity of healthy competitive outlets available to paddlers to improve their skills and test themselves against the elements and their peers. In addition, within each outlet or discipline under the broad umbrella of "kayak racing," there are varying degrees of commitment required in order to participate safely and enjoyably. Whether you are a hotshot seeking to maximize your potential for the Olympics or a Sunday racer out for some exercise, each form of kayak racing offers something for you. Finally, not only will you find the pursuit of racing inherently satisfying, you will also become a better, safer paddler during your tours of rivers, lakes, and oceans.

Wave Ski Competition

Organized kayak competition in the surf is still in its formative stages in the United States but is well established in Australia, where approximately 50,000 wave skis are in use. In most cases during a wave ski competition, a point system is used, wave skiers scored by judges according to how they perform with the boat on the waves—not unlike surfboard competition.

Under the auspices of the World Wave Ski Association, the first biennial World Wave Ski Championships were held in 1984. In 1986 120 amateur competitors from Australia, Great Britain, Ireland, South Africa, New Zealand, and the United States competed in the second World Championships in Oahu, Hawaii. Australian John Christensen successfully defended his Men's Open title. The next World Championships are scheduled for Cornwall, Great Britain.

Marathon Competition

Marathon or LD (long distance) kayak racing has been popular for years in the British Isles, continental Europe, South Africa, and the United States, but only recently (1984) has this exciting arm of the sport achieved official status with the International Canoe Federation (ICF). These races are conducted mostly on flatwater, but there's no guarantee: rapids and ocean surf can also be encountered. Racers paddle flatwater K-1s or K-2s or slight modifications thereof, but you're also likely to see surf skis, wildwater boats, or just about any kind of kayak. Paddlers race against themselves and the clock, and some of the courses are many miles in length and require one or more portages. Longer races can entail even days (and nights) of nonstop paddling. Most often the official distance used in the U.S. National Championships is approximately 18 miles (nearly 29 kilometers) without a portage.

The original hotbed of marathon kayaking was the British Isles. Such well-established events as the 125-mile Devizes-to-Westminster marathon and Ireland's Liffey Descent see hundreds of contestants each year. In the United States, however, marathon racing was primarily the domain of the canoe classes until recently. Today the kayak classes are being contested with ever-growing numbers.

No official ICF World Championships have ever been held, but an international Marathon Cup event was sanctioned in 1982, and this has evolved along with a Grand Prix series of races in Europe each year. Marathon racing is the fastest-growing branch of the ICF, and a World Championship will be in the offing in the not too distant future. In the United States, there are official National Marathon Championships held every year under the direction of the United States Canoe Association and the American Canoe Association, with many different classes for canoes and kayaks spread over several days. An official U.S. Team is selected to represent the country in overseas events.

Contrary to the common, staid image of "marathon," marathon kayaking can be wild. Bedlam mass starts, where hundreds of contestants paddle furiously for position before the river narrows, are the norm. At some events, there is a Grand Prix start, where paddlers run to their boats after the starting gun; full-speed entries into tippy kayaks with other people thrashing around you are sure to draw theatrics from even the best paddlers! Then there are portages where paddlers run with their kayaks over rough terrain and reenter their boats from slippery rocks and banks. While racing, paddlers employ strategy not unlike bicycle racers by paddling just behind their competitor and riding his wake, thereby saving energy. Throw in some rapids, a few (10-foot) sideways drops over weirs, and the constant fear of dehydration (racers

Irish marathon paddlers thrash it out at the start of a long-distance race. (NORS)

Ian Pringle leads an Irish marathon race as his competitors ride wakes behind him. (Mike Feeney)

drink through tubes attached to water bottles in their kayaks so that they can continue paddling while drinking), and you have an event that's thrilling for participant and spectator alike.

Marathon racing demands the utmost in conditioning and forward stroke technique. Proper pacing, knowing when to sprint for position, wake riding strategy, and organizing the logistics of a support crew are all important aspects of marathon kayaking.

Flatwater Competition

Flatwater racing, also known as *sprint racing* or *paddle racing*, has been part of the Olympic program for many years and currently is the only form of kayak racing with the Olympic cachet. Introduced as an exhibition event on the Seine River in Paris during the 1924 Olympics, flatwater racing became an official event at the 1936 Berlin Olympics. Olympic kayak competition includes distances of 500 and 1,000 meters in six classes of kayaks:

K-1	One man in a kayak
K-2	Two men in a kayak
K-4	Four men in a kayak
K-1W	One woman in a kayak
K-2W	Two women in a kayak
K-4W	Four women in a kayak

K-2s sprint for position during a race in London. (NORS)

1984 Olympic flatwater bronze medal winner and 1987 World Champion Greg Barton. (Eric Evans)

There is also competition in single and double canoes.

International events are held under the jurisdiction of the ICF, and since 1970, this body has organized yearly World Championships with an expanded Olympic format that includes events over 10,000 meters.

Over the years, Europe has been a stronghold for flatwater racing, its greatest racers coming from the Soviet Union, the two Germanies, and Scandinavia. The greatest flatwater kayaker of all time is Sweden's Gert Fredriksson, who garnered six Olympic gold medals over four Olympics from 1948 to 1960. Over the years, American racers have done surprisingly well; in the 1984 Olympics, Michigan's Greg Barton won a bronze medal in the K-1 1,000-meter race. American flatwater racing is conducted under the auspices of the American Canoe Association, and National Championships are held each year.

Much like swimming competitions, flatwater races use separate lanes for individual boats, with up to nine starting at one time in a mass start. Large fields would necessitate heats and semifinals leading up to a finals. These events are fast and furious: 500-meter times are usually less than 2 minutes, while 1,000-meter times are usually under 4 minutes depending on the type of kayak.

Kayaks designed for flatwater racing are highly stylized. They are built for one purpose—speed through the water. As a result, these beautiful craft are sleek and sharp. They slip through the water like needles, but for the uninitiated, they are somewhat unstable and definitely not meant to turn.

Flatwater racing requires that the competitor not only be in truly superb physical condition but also have an unusually well-honed and powerful forward stroke. Serious racers maintain yearlong training logs tracking their development and progress in both categories. Their forward strokes attain machinelike precision.

Triathlons

During the late 1960s, specialty races emerged featuring various combinations of skiing, bicycling, running, and kayaking, and these have increased in diversity and popularity. Many events will begin with a mass-start 25-mile bicycle leg, follow with a 6-mile paddle in a canoe or kayak, and finish with a 10-kilometer run.

Actually, there is such a broad spectrum of possibilities for racing that almost anyone's needs and desires can be met. If yours are not, devise a competition of your own, invite a few friends, and hold your own race. Who knows? You may start a new trend.

Whitewater Rodeos

Patterned after freestyle skiing, whitewater freestyles are popular in the summer, particularly in the West, where the weather and the whitewater

Olympic kayaker Chris Spelius practices his no-paddle maneuvers. (Slim Ray)

are conducive to getting soaked while performing stunts of every kind in front of discerning judges who assign points for creativity and execution. Events of this kind are lumped under the term "whitewater rodeos" because they would include not only freestyle events but also a slalom or downriver race, movies, dances, and slide shows.

Whitewater Competition

Racing in the rapids is the most popular form of kayak competition. Two distinct disciplines have developed: slalom and wildwater. Since there are such large numbers of races of each kind held in Europe, North America, and elsewhere, each of these competitions is treated in some detail.

Slalom Racing

The first World Championships in whitewater slalom were held in Geneva in 1949, and they have been held every other year since then. In 1979 the Worlds came to North America for the first time, to Jonquière, Canada. And in 1989, the United States will host its first-ever World Championships on the Savage River in Maryland. International events are conducted under ICF jurisdiction, while American events are sanctioned by the American Canoe Association.

In 1972 the first and only Olympic whitewater slalom competition was held near Munich, Germany; it was watched by 38,000 spectators on the banks of the man-made Eis Kanal and by millions courtesy of ABC-TV. Unfortunately, whitewater slalom's inaugural success notwithstanding, the International Olympic Committee decided not to continue whitewater slalom on the Olympic program, because it felt that the sport was too costly and that not enough countries worldwide participated in this form of kayaking. Recent World Championships have belied these assertions, and plans have just been completed for bringing whitewater slalom back into the Olympics in 1992.

During the past 10 years, the United States has been blessed with a dedicated coach, Bill Endicott of Bethesda, Maryland, who has helped to develop numerous World Whitewater Champions in various classes. He has published three excellent books on the sport and worked tirelessly on behalf of many paddlers. As a result of his efforts, U.S. kayakers will represent themselves very well at our first World Championships in 1989.

Former World Champion Cathy Hearn cuts sharply around a slalom pole. (Eric Evans)

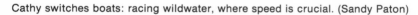

Cathy switches boats: racing wildwater, where speed is crucial. (Sandy Paton)

U.S. Whitewater Team coach Bill Endicott explaining techniques to his charges on the Feeder Canal outside Washington, D.C. (Abigail Endicott)

The Anatomy of Slalom

Whitewater slalom consists of paddling, in the fastest possible time, a stretch of challenging rapids whose demands have been increased ten-fold by the introduction of additional, and artificial, obstacles. These obstacles are the gates—wooden poles dangling from a crossbar suspended over a stretch of highly turbulent water not more than 600 meters (over 655 yards) long.

There is no such thing as a standard championship slalom course like the 100 meter hurdles in track-and-field events. Rather each slalom is laid out to create a unique series of challenges posed by the natural obstacles in the rapids in concert with the placing of the gates. Almost any number of gates will do, ranging from 12 or 15 in smaller local races to the 25 gates at most international competitions. The racer must go through each gate in the proper order (each is numbered), and in the proper direction. The gates must be run either downstream (two green-and-white poles) or upstream (two red-and-white poles). In a full slalom course, most of the 25 gates will be downstream gates. There must be a minimum of 6 upstream gates.

Paddlers race separately against the clock, each trying for the least amount of time—and the fewest number of penalities for touching a gate or failing to follow the course correctly. The racer is given two runs on the course; the better run counts. The score is the total number of seconds taken to complete the course, plus the number of penalty points accrued, added in seconds.

"Fishpole" gates mark the course in this beginners' slalom race. (Ledyard Canoe Club)

An artificial slalom course in the middle of South Bend, Indiana. (Sandy Paton)

Penalty Points

If you touch a pole while negotiating a gate, 5 points (seconds) are added to your total time. If you get swept downstream, miss a gate entirely, and never get back to do it: 50 points added. If you manage to get close enough to touch a gate, but your body doesn't pass between the poles in the proper direction: 50 points added.

If you capsize as you go through a gate: 50 points added. If you get confused and pass through a gate in the wrong direction: 50 points.

There are other fine distinctions in the judging of gates, but these will do as starters. The thing to remember is to make your boat go through the gates properly *without touching*.

The Downstream or Forward Gate

This is the most common gate in whitewater slalom. In most situations, the downstream gate should be taken at full speed, without interrupting your stroke, and at an angle that will line up your boat for getting quickly to the *next* gate.

COMMON MISTAKES

Hitting a pole with the paddle as you stroke through the gate.

Not being lined up properly before you go through the gate.

Allowing your stern to touch a pole as you leave the gate.

Looking back as you go through the gate to see if you have cleared it. (It is too late for you to do anything at that point, and it will break your concentration on the next gate.)

Offset Downstream or Forward Gates

Two or more downstream (forward) gates in sequence set across the current from each other constitute offset gates. They can be quite difficult to reach, to say nothing of being negotiated swiftly and efficiently.

Offset gates can be done in three or four strokes. As you approach the first gate, aim for the outside (left) pole. A boat length in front of the pole, your first stroke should be a strong sweep on the left followed instantly by a Duffek stroke on the right. The Duffek should be planted just before your body passes between the poles. Those two strokes pivot your boat. Now finish the Duffek with a sharp draw and a strong forward pull to slip through the gate unscathed.

If it appears that in pivoting, your stern may touch the outside (left) pole, employ a forward sweep on the left with your boat flat on the water and you leaning back slightly in the cockpit. This will help get your stern to slip under the pole.

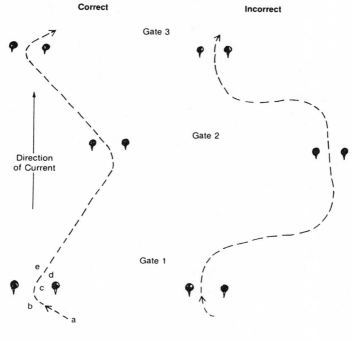

Correct   **Incorrect**

Gate 3

Gate 2

Direction
of Current

Gate 1

a. Aim toward the outside (left) pole
b. Sweep stroke on the left side
c. Duffek stroke as you enter the gate
d. Draw-pull stroke as you leave the gate
e. Sweep stroke on left side, boat flat, and leaning back.

Offset gates.

Remember, the quickest way to run offset gates is by turning *in* the gates.

COMMON MISTAKES

Turning well before or after you have negotiated the gate. (This wastes time.)
Allowing your stern to touch the outside pole.
Touching the inside pole as you plant the Duffek stroke.

The Upstream Gate

This gate, often placed in eddies behind rocks, can cost the racer a lot of time if his route is not carefully planned. The idea is to slip through the gate with the fewest strokes in the least possible time. This calls for unusually accurate depth perception as your boat closes in on the gate.

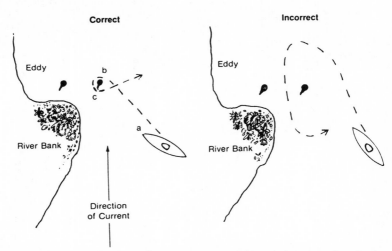

Correct   Incorrect

Eddy   Eddy

River Bank   River Bank

Direction
of Current

a. Aim boat toward a point upstream of the gate depending upon how strong the current
   is just outside the near pole.

b. Duffek stroke on left around the pole

c. Sweep stroke on the right to clear gate and get on to the next gate

Upstream gate.

As you bear down hard on the approach, aim your boat upstream of the gate, because the downstream current will carry you farther down beyond the gate than you need to go. If the pole near you is high off the water, you should sneak as much of your bow as possible under the pole (without touching it) as you Duffek into the gate. When conditions are right, an upstream gate can be negotiated in fewer than 4 seconds using only two strokes: the Duffek for the pivot, followed by a sweep stroke to clear the gate.

Upstream gates are often located near the shore where the water is shallow (on the shore side) and a rock or two stands out prominently on the river bank. If this is the case, don't hesitate to practice pushing off from the rock with your paddle—*if* this will speed up your gate negotiation. Be careful, of course, not to get the paddle caught on the rock or allow it to slip.

COMMON MISTAKES

Swinging too far below the gate into the eddy. (The current will tend to move you farther downstream than you expect.)

Misjudging the eddy current and thus making an outside (or inside)

Chris McCormick cuts crisply around the pole during an upstream gate. (Eric Evans)

Bruce Swomley exits an upstream gate with a sweep stroke. (Eric Evans)

touch on a pole as you swing into and through the gate. (Study the current and the eddy carefully beforehand.)

Swinging out too far upstream after clearing the gate.

The Reverse Gate

There may be infrequent moments when you want to go through a gate in reverse or sideways in order to line yourself up better for an ensuing gate. In approaching a reverse gate, continue paddling forward toward it as long as possible. Paddling forward is always faster than paddling backward, so you obviously want to spend as little time as possible in backward paddling. Make your turn in front of the gate, taking advantage of the current by swinging your stern around into the faster-moving

Reverse gate.

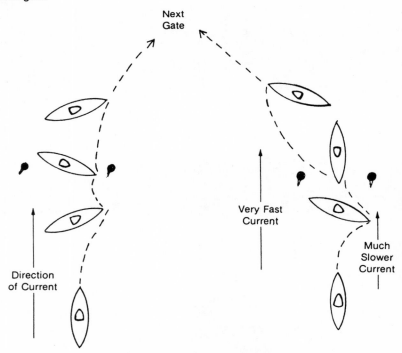

Above are depicted two ways to do a reverse gate depending upon current flow and the location of the next gate down the course.

water. Make the water work for you rather than trying to turn against the current.

If the poles are high off the water, both your bow and stern will sneak under without danger of touching. If one pole is low to the water, you will have to turn your boat more before entering the gate to avoid touching the pole. Studying how other boaters negotiate a reverse gate and how the current affects their boats can be very helpful to you in deciding how to use the water in front of the gate to your benefit, as well as which poles, if any, can be sneaked under. As you pass through a reverse gate, keep your paddle in a vertical position and well down into the water. This will maintain positional control of your boat.

Proper exit from a reverse gate is as important as proper approach. Be sure to angle your boat so you are in position to go for the next gate in the sequence in the fastest possible time.

COMMON MISTAKES

Not looking at the gate soon enough as you approach it.

Not keeping your eye on the pole constantly as you turn in front of the gate.

Turning before the gate either too early or too late.

Floating through, rather than powering your way through, the gate.

Dropping below the gate too far (even an inch) after your body has cleared the line between the two poles.

"Pivotitis"—looking first over one shoulder, then over the other shoulder as you approach the gate. (If you are closing in properly on the nearer pole, you automatically know exactly how far away you are from the other one.)

Not twisting your body around enough so that *both* eyes can concentrate on the pole.

Putting the Slalom Together

MEMORIZING THE COURSE

From a close study of the course, preferably from both river banks, you must get the entire route firmly planted in your mind. Ideally it is best to arrive at the race site a day or two in advance to get settled, but short of that, you should plan to get out early on the morning of the race to acquaint yourself with the water conditions and all details of the course.

By this intensive study, you should develop a clear-cut program of attack and get it firmly in mind. Take along a notebook and a pencil.

Read from the Bottom of the Page Upward

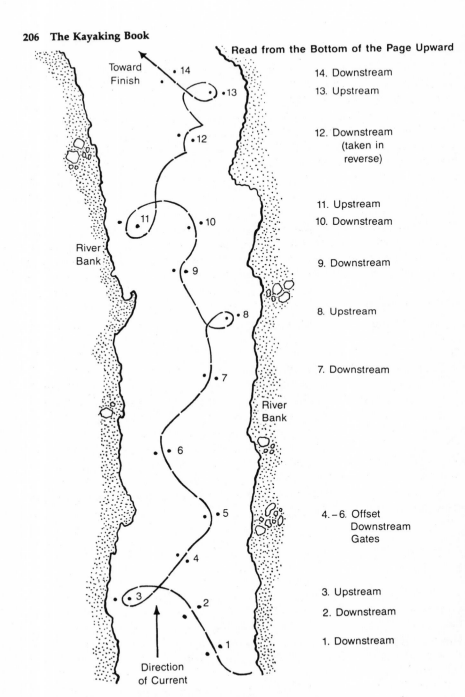

14. Downstream

13. Upstream

12. Downstream
    (taken in
    reverse)

11. Upstream

10. Downstream

9. Downstream

8. Upstream

7. Downstream

4.–6. Offset
    Downstream
    Gates

3. Upstream

2. Downstream

1. Downstream

Bird's eye view of a slalom course (looking downstream).

Watch carefully to see how the good boaters do it if free practice is allowed on the course ahead of time. Those who have difficulty remembering a whole course might try clumping the gates in their minds. Think of several gates as a unit, and go over in your mind how you plan to tackle them.

THE DECISIONS INVOLVED

At each gate, you must make three decisions:

1. At what angle should I approach so I get the fastest line on to the next gate?

2. Exactly where will I place my paddle the very moment I am clear of the gate?

3. If something goes wrong, can I duck into the nearest piece of friendly water and make a second attempt at the gate? (It is better to use an extra 15 seconds than to settle for a permanent 50-point penalty for missing the gate altogether.)

THE WARM-UP

Most people simply don't warm up enough before the race. A good warm-up prepares the body for the large load it will soon be asked to bear, and—even more important—it helps to reduce nervous tension. If the race is held in the morning, you should get up at least several hours before your run to make sure that you are operating on all cylinders by race time.

Always remember that a full stomach prevents good breathing, so don't eat anything for at least a couple of hours before the race.

You should paddle hard for 10 minutes somewhere upstream of the start, out of the way. If this is impossible, jog and sprint along a nearby path or road, and do some limbering-up and stretching exercises. Your pulse rate should be up around 100, and you should have developed a pretty good sweat just before the countdown.

THE START

Shake your arms, shoulders, and wrists to loosen them. Relax your trunk muscles and take a few deep breaths to fill your lungs with oxygen. Make a final check of your spray cover. Listen carefully to the cadence of the countdown for other racers, so you can anticipate the split second when "Go" is called for your boat. (If the timing is by an electronic eye, you won't have to worry about that.)

At the start, a standing boat must be brought into motion, and to overcome inertia and accelerate to top racing speed requires considerable strength. Also at the start, keep your boat pointed a few degrees inside of the direction line you wish to follow, so your first maximum-power forward stroke can be employed without the immediate necessity of making a correcting stroke.

When the start is electronic, *if it is permissible*, back off a bit to try to get one or two strokes in so your boat will be well underway before the electric eye is triggered.

IT's A RACE

You can waste much of the advantage gained from good gate technique if you loaf between gates. Keep in mind that an American National Slalom title was lost not too many years ago by 0.6 second! In World Championship competition, many a gold, silver, and bronze medal has been lost by less than half a second. Most gates are about 20 yards (18¼ meters) apart, so you have a chance to gain a little between gates if you hustle.

After the last gate is behind you, really pour it on and *sprint* not just to the finish line, but to a point at least one full boat length beyond. This will guarantee that your boat crosses the real finish line in the fastest possible way.

BETWEEN RUNS

After your run, get into dry clothes as soon as possible. Get comfortable, but don't eat anything right away. Anything you ate, even pure sugar, wouldn't give you any energy until long after the end of the race, anyway.

You will probably wish to walk slowly up the course carefully studying how the other racers are negotiating the gates. Don't waste your time watching inexperienced boaters or engaging in idle distracting conversation. Keep your mind clear for the second and final run. When the time comes for your run, be sure to warm up as thoroughly as you did for your first run.

And good luck!

Wildwater Racing

Wildwater racing has become popular for one major reason: it is a simple, pure race. Your rewards are directly proportional to your skill, your experience, and the quality of effort you put into the event. After many years of trying, the United States won its first World Wildwater K-1

A Code for Whitewater Racers
(Slalom and Wildwater)

Whitewater racing is marvelously rewarding, thanks in part to its prevailing spirit of good fellowship and fair play. To make sure that this spirit is not eroded as the competitions grow, we propose the following code for racers.

Be realistic about your degree of competence. There are increasing numbers of boaters anxious to race who have not yet perfected the Eskimo roll, the most reliable way to get out of trouble. The answer to this problem rests largely in the hands of the race officials, who will determine that only competent kayakers may enter events that tax their skills. The kayaker has an obligation not to oversell his or her abilities.

Never enter a race without studying the course beforehand. Skill seldom compensates for bad judgment arising from ignorance of where obstacles lie. So get out to the river where the race will be run and study its haystacks, rollers, eddies, and chutes. Walk along its banks, spotting obstructions that lurk underwater.

Race with all the equipment necessary for safety. You owe it to yourself and everybody else to ensure that a mishap does not become a full-fledged emergency because you, and your boat, are not properly outfitted. This means lifejacket, helmet, and wet suit (if it is indicated) for you; grabloops and flotation bags for your boat. To protect yourself against chill, use Pogies or gloves and have warm clothing handy at the end of your run.

Bring your own equipment for every race. Borrowing equipment is poor form indeed, aside from being a nuisance. Bring an extra paddle, if possible. Have your name on each piece of your gear.

Follow the rules of any competition you enter. Race organizers have good reasons for the regulations they make. Therefore don't ask for special dispensation or consideration. Send your entry form in on time—completely filled out and with the correct entry fee attached. On race day, be patient with race organizers and be alert for chances to be helpful. Protest only for the most valid reasons.

Be gracious, win or lose. The true sportsman will congratulate the winner and will never be a sore loser. (And a thank-you note to the committee after the race will certainly be appreciated!)

Championship medal when Jon Fishburn of Montana won the bronze at the 1985 Worlds.

What at first appears to be mainly physical labor is, in reality, very highly concentrated mental discipline. Each stroke is meaningful. You must constantly follow the shortest and fastest route down the river. The kayaks used are beautiful, highly specialized racing machines built primarily for speed. Training is less complicated than for slalom, and there is very little need for extra equipment such as gates, wires, and a communications network. As a bonus, the scenery of the course can be spectacular.

Basically a wildwater race consists of a start somewhere upriver with a finish line anywhere from 2 to 15 miles (3¼ to 24 kilometers) or more downriver. No penalty points are involved, and the winner is the racer with the shortest elapsed time between start and finish. While slalom rarely exceeds 4 minutes, a wildwater race will take anywhere from 9 to 30 minutes or more, depending upon the length of the course. The trick is to find the swiftest route through the rapids.

The Fastest Route

Familiarity with the course not only is helpful technically but gives the racer a great psychological boost. Every rock in the river, every new view around the bend should be a familiar, beckoning sight. Running the course many times at the same water level at which the race will be conducted, and experimenting with different routes, will add the knowledge necessary for winning.

Avoid eddies that will catch your bow and spin you around, and be wary of rollers and stoppers that slow your forward movement. Avoid "bottom drag"—an insidious braking action that measurably slows your boat when the water is too shallow.

Once the fastest route has been determined, go over each part of it in your mind just as carefully as you would the gates of a slalom. Develop a mental picture of it section by section.

The Start

In most wildwater races, paddlers are started singly, with 1-minute or 30-second intervals between boaters. If this is the case, simply leap off that starting line as fast as possible and do everything in your power to close the gap between you and the boater who took off ahead of you.

In a multiple start (two or three boats at a time) when the field is particularly large, it is important to sprint out in front immediately and stay there. Let the rest of the pack jockey for position behind you.

Overtaking

If you catch up to a boater, it is legal to ride his wake—assuming that he takes what you *know* to be the fastest route!

If you overtake another boater and are ready to pass him, he must give way to allow you room to pass. Simply yell "Track!" as in skiing, and he is obliged to move over.

Splits

Splits can be a handy way of keeping track of your speed in comparison with other boaters in a wildwater race. You need a confederate with a stopwatch, a bicycle or car, and a good working knowledge of the backroads and paths near the river.

Good Samaritans

Since much wildwater racing involves stretches of rapids in a canyon or valley away from civilization, any racer who sees another boater in trouble and in need of help must stop, discontinue racing immediately, and go to the kayaker's aid. Failure to do so can mean disqualification forever. You'll be glad you helped. You can always race another day.

For example, your friend knows that the person you would like to beat is 2 minutes ahead of you in the starting order. The split-taker will be stationed at some mutually agreed-upon place down from the start (bridges are always handy). He'll start his stopwatch as your adversary goes by. If you haven't gained on your opponent, then you should also pass by when the split-taker's stopwatch reaches the 2-minute mark. If you appear in 1 minute and 40 seconds, this means that you have gained 20 seconds on your opponent. The message will be shouted to you loud and clear by your friend on the bridge, and welcome news it is. And if you have fallen behind, the information thus relayed to you should give you renewed determination to step up the pace.

The Finish

As soon as the finish line comes into sight is the time for an all-out sprint. No need to conserve energy or to pace yourself any longer. Just keep constantly in mind that some races are won or lost by a fraction of a second. At the World Championships in 1987, the difference between a bronze and a silver medal in wildwater K-1W was only .21 second over a 17-minute course.

As in slalom, always paddle *through* the finish line, not simply *to* it. Then paddle around a bit to "warm down" until your pulse rate is reduced. Don't eat anything for at least half an hour after the race.

15. Organizing Whitewater Races

The popularity of whitewater competition is such that race organization requires efficiency and long-range planning. Running a race can be a source of enormous pride and satisfaction at seeing an event unfold smoothly, or it can turn into an endurance contest. By following a reasonably strict timetable spread over several months, it is possible not only to organize a race successfully but to enjoy it as well. The better the preliminary work behind the scenes before race day, the better the race turns out.

Most, if not all, of the principles in this chapter may be applied to other kayak races including flatwater and marathon events.

Six Months before the Race

Where/When/Who

Choose the site, the time of the race, and the kind of race you want—slalom, wildwater, or possibly both. Obtain permission of the landowners on each side of the river where you propose to hold the events. Next decide what kind of race it should be: experts only, beginners, or an allcomers race open to anyone. Determine what classes to offer. The ICF recognizes K-1, K-1W, C-1, C-2, and C-2M; you may want to add divisions for junior, senior, beginner, intermediate, and expert boaters. You might wish to consider having a "cruiser" or "plastic fantastic" class for paddlers with general whitewater play boats. Many river runners like to compete infrequently in slalom but won't if they are forced to obtain a fancy low-volume racing kayak in order to do so. Decide the number of entries you can safely handle in terms of available manpower, camping, parking, and toilet facilities.

Publicity

After the basics have been decided, make sure the race gets listed with the American Canoe Association, the National Organization for River Sports, and all the major paddling magazines (see Part V) including the *Whitewater Racing Program*, so people will learn about the event. Since most publications go to press months in advance of their cover date, be sure to check on the deadlines for getting your information to the editors.

At the same time, ask the American Canoe Association for sanction. Write for permission to hold the race, listing the date, location, kind of race, any limitations, and the name and address of the person who has been designated to provide information. The American Canoe Association can also offer race insurance for those races they sanction.

Finding a Sponsor

Races cost money to run. Quite often the local kayak or canoe club or a combination of clubs will bear the costs of organizing a race. Some businesses may be willing to underwrite at least part of the expenses of a race in return for a bit of advertising. As a race organizer, you can offer the business pre-race publicity, racing bibs and race programs bearing the sponsor's name, and results printed on the sponsor's stationery.

Finding sponsors also helps to bring the local community into the spirit of the event. It is nice to have the local townspeople take an active interest in a recreational event taking place in their community.

Three Months before the Race

Paperwork

Entry forms for a well-run race should be mailed out a month to 6 weeks before the race date. Be sure to allow for the time it will take to prepare and print the forms and mail them out. Entry forms should include the following: time, place, date, starting time; description of the course, race categories, water conditions; liability release; entry fee and deadlines; and an address to which entries should be sent.

It is helpful, but not necessary, to mention whether there will be a shuttle service or food for sale and to give the addresses of conveniently located motels and campgrounds in the race area.

Manpower

Assign one person as the race registrar to keep track of all the entrants and whether or not they've paid the entry fee, so at any time, he can report how many racers have entered and who is racing in what class. The registrar's duties last until race day is over and are linked closely with those of several other committees.

You should line up 50 percent more manpower than you think you'll need (most of your help will be volunteers, and therefore many well-meant promises might not be kept at the last minute). For a slalom race, the following positions need to be filled: registrar, timers, scorers, recorders, gate judges, safety crew, gate-adjustment crews, protest committee, results coordinator, press officer, communications crew, and starters.

For wildwater all these positions need to be filled except the gate judges and gate-adjustment crews needed for slalom races.

Numbering/Amenities/Water Level

The race registrar can also distribute and collect numbered racing bibs on race day. Bibs are available from ski areas and outing clubs, canoe companies, and some sports clothing outfitters. Paper bibs, which are beginning to replace the traditional cloth ones, will hold up well enough in whitewater to last a weekend, and they make a nice souvenir of the race to take home. Over the years, we have had good luck ordering our paper race bibs from Reliable Racing Supply in Glens Falls, New York.

Occasionally one will see a large white decal pasted on the deck of the boat with the racer's number written on the decal. This system works fine unless two racers want to use the same boat—in which case the first decal must be removed and a new decal applied in its place.

Check with groups that might want to set up food concessions. Inform local police about the race and alert them to any possible traffic problems.

If there is a dam upstream of the race site, investigate the possibility of having a water release timed for your race.

One of the nicer touches we have seen at races is the enormous bulletin board that Ken Fisher of Brattleboro, Vermont, hangs each year at the finish line for the West River races. On the board are pictures, biographies of the leading racers, race information, and historical data. The board is covered with a plastic sheet to withstand rainy days. It is not only a delightful courtesy to folks unfamiliar with the sport, it saves the race organizer hours of explaining what's going on that day.

Equipment

Collect all the needed equipment several months in advance of a race, including gates, wire, rope, string, communications materials, clipboards, scoreboards, typewriter, safety gear, and first aid equipment.

A Slalom Primer

The Course

A good slalom course should take advantage of the natural obstacles in the rapids yet should be laid out so that an expert racer can make a smooth and penalty-free run. Whenever possible there should be as many upstream gates (or "break-outs," as the British say) to the right as to the left.

A full-blown slalom course of 25 gates will meet international specifications, but for most competitions, 18 to 20 gates will do nicely.

The Slalom Gate

A slalom gate consists of a wooden crosspiece with a pole dangling from each end. A small board hangs from the middle of the crosspiece to display the gate number. The gate hangs from a wire that has been stretched across the river high enough to let each dangling pole just clear the surface of the water.

The simplest form of gate has the poles permanently attached to the crosspiece, with the entire gate capable of being raised or lowered by adjusting the suspension wire over the stream. This rudimentary gate is not really satisfactory, however, because one pole should hang higher than the other if the rapids below are uneven. It is important in a race that *each pole*, regardless of its length, hang just clear of the water.

Gate Components

Crosspiece boards should be 6 or 7 feet (about 182 to 213 centimeters) long to allow for adequate spacing of the poles. According to ICF regulations, the width of the gate must be at least 1.2 meters (about 4 feet) and no more than 3.5 meters (just over 11 feet). At most slalom races, the gates are between 4 and 5 feet wide. Decide on the width of your gate and space two metal screw eyes that distance apart, equidistant from the ends of the crosspiece. Also at the ends of the crosspiece, attach shower-curtain rings or metal loops through which a wire can be threaded when stringing gates across a river.

Two poles are needed for each gate. Poles for downstream gates should be painted using alternating bands of green and white, while upstream gates will consist of two poles painted with bands of red alternating with white.

A *gate-number board* about 15 inches (38 centimeters) square hangs from the crosspiece between the poles to identify each gate. Paint both sides of the board yellow, with the gate number in black; add a diagonal red

While a gate crew holds the lines that regulate the height of each pole, a crew on the other side of the river will pull this gate into position over the water. (Ledyard Canoe Club)

stripe on the backside of the board in the international sign for "no entry," so the racer knows which direction to approach it from.

Stringing a Gate

For the uninitiated, gate stringing seems quite a puzzle, but basically the setup is similar to that of a clothesline on pulleys, stretching between a porch and a garage. Just as you haul clothes toward you by pulling on the line, gate stringers move a gate from one side of the river to the other on a lead line.

The gate itself hangs from a wire; the gate's position is controlled by separate lines attached to the ends of the crosspiece. Another set of lines holds the poles to the crosspiece; these lines should be run from both poles to the same shore, so that individual poles can be adjusted easily from only one side of the river.

On Race Day

Safety

No matter what sort of waiver a racer may sign to release the organizing committee from liability for damage suffered during a race, the organizers are morally responsible to some degree for every boater's safety. There are increasing numbers of boaters eager to race before they've learned how to handle themselves in an emergency, much less come to the aid of anyone else.

Preventive Measures

The most important preventive measure is simple: *make sure each boater's ability is equal to the difficulty of the water.* A beginners' race should always be held in easy water. If you are holding a race in difficult water, pre-screen the entrants and allow only qualified boaters in the race.

Another precautionary measure is holding a boat inspection before the race, not so much to see that the boats are of legal length, width, and weight as to make sure they have ample flotation and a grabloop in both bow and stern for controlling the boat and towing it to shore after a capsize and wet exit.

We vividly recall the Mascoma River (New Hampshire) slalom several years ago, which took place under flood conditions. As the chief official, Jay allowed only the best-qualified 13 out of 50 entrants to race in that dangerous water. Some people were angry that day, but he preferred that they be disappointed rather than injured.

Rescue

The best rescue of course is self-rescue, and for that, nothing quite compares with a reliable Eskimo roll.

The trouble comes with racers who have not perfected the roll. For them a variety of arrangements for rescue from shore have been developed over the years.

A rescuer on shore throws an inner tube and line to a capsized boater. The kayaker has remembered to hang on to the boat and paddle. (Ledyard Canoe Club)

A very effective measure is to ask at least *two boaters* to wait in their boats at the finish line while a third completes the course. This makes it easy to pick up paddles that come floating through, and to nudge a capsized boat toward shore.

Skin divers can be a great help—if they are familiar with the dynamics of rapidly moving water.

Throw-line rescue bags have now been perfected so that they can be very effective when thrown properly. (See Chapter 4.)

In preparing for a whitewater race, it is important to arrange for a standby emergency vehicle staffed by qualified emergency medical technicians to be *at the race course*. Large races draw spectators and other recreational boaters, some of whom might also need first aid assistance.

Communications

Effective communications are the key to a successful slalom. You need some means of knowing what's going on at the starting point, at a command post partway down the course, at the primary gate-checking stations, and at the finish line. At major ICF races, there is a gate checker with a portable telephone reporting to the command post the penalties at every gate as they happen. However, at less luxurious competitions, one telephone often will have to cover at least five gates, with the other gate judges signaling the penalties to the telephone operator.

Walkie-talkies also make an efficient communications system. Of course you'll make sure that the sets are powerful enough to cover the length of the course.

Scoring

Scores must be posted promptly. The Dartmouth instant-scoring system, devised by Sandy Campbell, a member of the 1972 Olympic team, is a good one for either telephones or walkie-talkies.

From the race starter, the recorder at the command post gets the name, class, and run number of the racer about to depart. The recorder writes this information on an individual score sheet on a clipboard to which a stopwatch is attached. Over the walkie-talkie, the recorder hears the starter give the racer the countdown and starts his stopwatch as the racer begins. As the racer takes each gate, the gate judge reports any penalties over a walkie-talkie. The recorder follows the racer through the course, noting penalties as they are incurred, and clicks the stopwatch when the finish-line judge's report is heard that the boat has

A scoreboard should be accessible and easy to read, and scores should be posted soon after a racer finishes the course. (Ledyard Canoe Club)

crossed the line. The recorder then hands over the stopwatch and score sheet to a scorer, who puts the results on the board for all to see.

In large, well-established races and U.S. Team trials, more sophisticated means are used, not only to provide quick race results, but also to insure greater accuracy.

Timing a Wildwater Race

In wildwater kayak racing, the most important single item, aside from safety, is *timing*. Make sure the timers are at the finish line when the first racer arrives. Synchronize the watches before the race begins so that the finish-line timers don't have to appear at the start at all.

Timers at the finish line need to have cool heads and keen eyes, because sometimes boats will cross the finish in a wild sprint and closely bunched, and it may be hard to see the race numbers.

A full finish-line crew should include one person who does nothing but read off the exact time, down to the nearest fraction of a second, as a given boat crosses the line. To verify the timekeeping, at least one assistant should be there with a backup stopwatch. In addition there should be two recorders ready to write down the racers' numbers (and/ or names) and times as they cross the finish line. The cards can then be arranged according to time and class so the results can be posted immediately after the race. If the timing is electronic, there still should be a backup hand watch.

After the Race

Judge and Jury

In the event of a close call in slalom, a gate judge must have written down what happened, in case the race jury asks him to testify to decide a protest. All protests should be submitted by a team captain in writing immediately after the posting of scores. The jury's decision is final.

The boater is probably the poorest judge of all as to whether he touched a pole or not: he simply is not able to see the entire length of his boat on both sides simultaneously.

Awards

Decide well ahead of time what kind of awards you will give, and be sure they are on hand the day of the race. There is nothing like trophies to stimulate interest and enthusiasm among inexperienced racers. Utilitarian-minded race organizers sometimes offer paddles for awards, or mugs. I've seen pewter candlesticks given, and a nice leather briefcase was the prize for placing tenth in the K-1 class at Merano, Italy.

No matter what the awards are—mugs, cups, ribbons, or whatever— the important thing is for the awards ceremony to take place immediately following the race.

Dealing with the Press

When dealing with the press, remember that the Fourth Estate has the last word as well as the first word, and, at its discretion, no word at all. However, many sportswriters welcome the chance to report such a refreshingly different event as a kayak race.

Good press relations are important, and detailing a couple of people to act as a publicity committee can help. The committee should send out a *factual* news release to local and regional papers before the event. Committee members should be on hand at the race to escort reporters, if necessary, and to supply them with facts about the events and information about the competitors, plus any real human interest angles. A copy of the race results should be placed in each reporter's hands pronto.

In addition send all race results to the American Canoe Association and to kayaking magazines.

16. Getting in Shape— Physically and Mentally

Racing and serious river running or exploration demand total body performance and mental concentration. They call for stamina as well as strength, varying from a maximum output of effort of a couple of minutes in a slalom race or 500-meter flatwater race to 30 minutes in a wildwater race to even days in a long marathon contest. If your body is conditioned to putting out concentrated, sustained effort for the required period of time, you will be able to focus on the immediate obstacles of the race, how to deal with them, and technique.

How Fit Are You?

If you wish to take up racing seriously, you should take an objective look at yourself. What kind of shape are you in *now*? First get medical clearance. Then find out how far you can jog or run in 12 minutes. According to Dr. Kenneth Cooper's book *Aerobics*, an average active person can do up to 1.75 miles (2.8 kilometers) in 12 minutes, while a

Olympic kayaker Leslie Klein undergoes physiological testing in a slalom kayak at SUNY Buffalo. Dave Pendergast and his assistant stand on the movable platform, which will rotate around the circular water tank at whatever speed the paddler can maintain. (SUNY Buffalo)

gold-medal-category athlete can cover 2.25 miles (3.6 kilometers) or more.

After you have established your current physical fitness category, you can lay out a program for working up to your potential. You should have your doctor's permission to train. You should warm up thoroughly before each workout. Figure on a period of at least 6 months before expecting any substantial improvement, and try to work out at least 5 days each week. Above all else, remember that conditioning should be *specific* to the type of activity you are pursuing; the best training for paddling is to paddle. Other forms of training should take on a secondary role. Only if you can't paddle should you look to alternative forms of training.

Building Stamina

Any or all of the following exercises will increase your stamina. If you can't do them for the prescribed length of time, simply do them for as long as you can and gradually work up. If these exercises are too easy for you, you're only cheating yourself unless you set your sights higher.

Interval Training

When water is available, get into your boat and try 50 rapid maximum-effort forward strokes followed by a 10-second rest. Repeat this exercise six times or more. On land run six 200-yard (182-meter) sprints, keeping track of your time. Try to lower your time with each sprint.

Tempo Training

Paddle at full racing speed for 20 percent of the length of time it takes to cover a race. If you are training for slalom, try paddling all out for 1 minute; for wildwater, paddle all out for 2½ to 3 minutes, once for each quarter of the race. Repeat about five times. If you don't have access to water, run six consecutive ½-mile (0.8-kilometer) stretches in not more than 3 minutes each, taking a 1-minute rest between each ½ mile.

Distance Training

Ideally this involves prolonged paddling for 30 minutes to an hour at racing speed against a stopwatch. Try to increase the distance you cover from week to week. If you can't get to water, jog or run for at least an hour nonstop.

Building Strength

Strength is the power your body has available to accomplish a particular task. Stamina and strength go hand in hand as essential ingredients for good physical fitness. Do these exercises at least every other day. The important thing is to establish a definite routine and keep at it until it becomes a regular part of your life.

Chin-ups

How many you can do will depend on your body weight and frame, but if you are not physically out of proportion, you should aim for two groups of 25 each in a period of a couple of minutes. Chin-ups develop the biceps and the muscles of the forearm and upper back.

Push-ups

Push-ups work wonders to develop the triceps as well as the upper chest. Aim for three groups of 40 push-ups in a couple of minutes.

Sit-ups

Do three groups of 20 sit-ups (knees bent) in a couple of minutes. Hold your hands behind your head and your body rigid at a 45-degree angle for 20 seconds afterward, until those abdominal muscles really begin to shout for relief.

Circuit Exercises

A six-station circuit exercise that requires only a barbell and weights, a 1-inch-diameter (2½-centimeter-diameter) wooden dowel, and about 5 feet (1½ meters) of rope is recommended. Complete the "circuit" three times in a row, allowing about 5 minutes for rest between each station.

1. With a 10-pound (3¾-kilogram) weight held behind your head, do 20 *sit-ups*.

2. Lying on your back with weights equal to two-thirds of your body weight attached to the barbell, *bench-press* the barbell 10 times.

3. Standing, with a quarter of your body weight attached to the barbell and with your arms at your sides, palms out, raise the barbell to your chin, then lower it back to waist level; do this *curl* 10 times.

4. Standing, with a quarter of your body weight on the barbell and with your hands at your sides, palms in, raise the barbell to your chin with elbows high, then lower it; do this *upright row* 10 times.

5. Sit with your forearms resting on top of your thighs, wrists extending just beyond kneecaps and palms facing out; *wrist-curl* the barbell up as high as you can until your forearms leave your thighs, 50 times.

6. Stand with your arms fully extended in front of you, grabbing the dowel with both hands. Roll the dowel up, turning it so that a rope attached to the dowel will gradually lift a 10-pound (3¾-kilogram) weight tied to the other end of the rope; do this *roll* 10 times.

Pulley weights used by a paddler sitting on a bench are very specific for paddling. (Eric Evans)

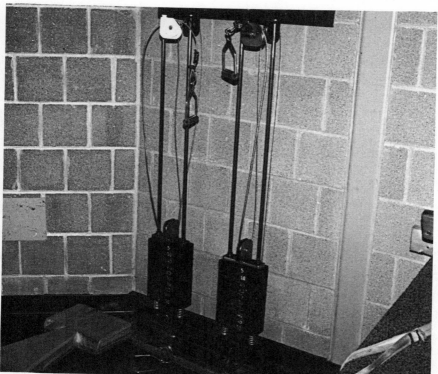

Another specific dry-land training method is to use wall pulley weights. By sitting on a bench and either facing the weights or facing away from them, you can simulate the pull and then the push of the kayak stroke.

Race Training

Although there are many different kinds of kayak races, luckily training will cover all of them. There is much overlap in technique from one kind of racing to another. The following exercises will help you train for almost any kind of race.

Pool Training

There are municipal or private indoor pools in most communities. The local kayak club can usually organize pool sessions by arrangement with public or private owners.

Pool training offers several advantages. The space limits make coaching easier, and there is guaranteed lighting for the use of visual aids. The trick is to devise basic training techniques that call for very little water space but at the same time simulate outdoor conditions.

Pool training. (Evans Associates)

The Eskimo Roll

Above all, that pool water is warm! Those trying to conquer the Eskimo roll on their weak sides will find this a great help. You can make a game of it. Anyone can learn to roll using a paddle—eventually—but how about with a pair of Ping-Pong paddles, or better yet, using hands only?

Stunt men will be interested in seeing how many rolls they can do in 60 seconds. A competent roller in reasonably good physical condition should be able to complete up to 20 rolls in a minute. (The first time you try it, though, you'll believe that it is the longest minute of your life.)

The English Gate

The English Gate—developed in England, where it's called the "Wiggle Test"—is a complicated, back-and-forth, in-and-out maneuver to add flavor to flatwater, in which a paddler goes all around and through a single gate without touching a pole. It is particularly effective training for slalom and helps develop the quick, precise movements you need for wildwater racing. It can be practiced in a pool indoors, or outdoors in a river.

The English Gate.

Phase I

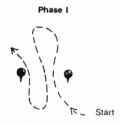

Forward through three times

Phase III

Reverse down outside, then reverse through twice

Phase II

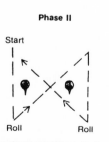

Reverse down outside, roll, forward through on both sides

Phase IV

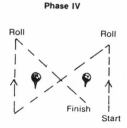

Forward down outside, roll, reverse through, on both sides

In the days before low-volume slalom kayaks, the English Gate was a valuable exercise. Today it is not used by top racers in their low-volume boats, but it is still a valuable exercise for beginners in larger boats that won't sneak under the poles immediately after the body passes through the line between the poles.

First, pass through the gate in a forward direction three times. Next, back your kayak down the outside of a pole, roll, then go forward through the gate and repeat the process on the other side. In the third phase, move again down the outside of a pole, pivot, and then go backward through the gate. Once through, pivot again and go backward through the gate. For the final phase, move forward past the outside of a pole, roll, then go backward through the gate and repeat the process on the other side.

The English Gate should be done flat out at full speed. The occasional weekend racer really ought to complete an English Gate in 80 or 90 seconds.

The Rack

A rack consists of two wooden two-by-fours connected by wooden crosspieces like a ladder, with a molded kayak seat set in the middle. Attach the rack firmly to the side of the pool so that it projects directly out into the water, and support it from below so that it won't move. Place a full-length mirror in front of the kayak seat so that a boater can see his own strokes.

Using a stopwatch, take a stroke a second and paddle in the rack for 5 minutes without once breaking rhythm. This exercise begins to simulate the physical strain that a boater experiences during a 20- or 25-gate slalom. You can vary the 5-minute time limit for interval and tempo training.

Don't try the rack with a full-bladed paddle: it has too much water resistance. Take an old paddle and shave the blades to about 3 inches (7½ centimeters) wide.

Pool Games

The Chase

A three-man chase lasting for 5 minutes straight adds zest to any practice. At top speed, the paddler in Boat No. 1 leads the other boats on an unpredictable route for 5 minutes, through and around 4 or 5 gates that have been strung across the pool; he can also include an occasional Eskimo roll. The object of the chase is for the lead boat to gain enough on his followers to approach and touch Boat No. 3 from the rear. All gates must be negotiated without touching the poles.

Sprints

A fast start is important in track racing and equally so in kayak racing. Line three or four boats up at one end of the pool and start them off at a given signal to sprint almost the entire length of the pool. The sprinting should be backward as well as forward, and even sideways using sculling and draw strokes.

Sequences

One of the most popular ways to train for slalom is to design a course through several gates. The leader makes a demonstration run while the other boaters watch and try to memorize the course. Then, by starting a couple of boats only 10 seconds or so apart, it is possible to maintain two racers on the course at a time—always under the relentless hand of the stopwatch.

Backward paddling, especially through a gate, is an art often neglected in this era of no "official" reverse gates. Entire sequences can be designed in which all the gates are negotiated in reverse. To add a little spice, throw in an Eskimo roll or two as well.

Exergenie Contests

An *exergenie* provides extra drag against which the boater must paddle. It is a small metal tube through which you thread a rope, twisting the rope inside: the amount of twist determines the degree of resistance. Exergenies are for sale in sport shops.

Thread a nylon rope as long as the pool through the exergenie and fasten one end of the rope to the stern grabloop of a kayak. At a signal, the boater springs forward, drawing the entire length of rope through the exergenie to the far end of the pool. When a boater has pulled the rope the length of the pool under a stopwatch several times, he is usually quite ready to suggest switching places with the timers. This exercise is best done with a fairly narrow-bladed paddle.

Kayak Polo

Kayak polo, a favorite sport in England, can be played in an indoor pool (two boats per side) or outside in flatwater (three or four boats per side) in either K-1s or C-1s. A good fast game builds stamina, increases paddling skills and maneuverability, and is a worthwhile change from formal training.

Players use their paddles as mallets and try to hit a volleyball or water-polo ball into the opponent's goal (a loose net inside a rectangular frame about 3 feet, or 91 centimeters, above the water). Every boat should have a rubber tip on its bow, and players should wear helmets. Players cannot use hands or elbows to touch the ball, an opponent, or a boat. Some polo games are played with bat boats—kayaks with rounded ends to prevent injury.

Outdoor Training

If you are fortunate enough to live near water with a moving current or rapids, you can have a lot of fun working out various practice routines to develop basic moves and skills during the warm-weather months. Most of the exercises and games recommended for pool training are just as effective outdoors, especially sequences, sprints, the chase, and, of course, kayak polo. Unless vandalism is a problem, or the sensitivities of fishermen are involved, you may be able to set up permanent gates on a river.

Many members of the U.S. Slalom Team practice twice a day on the Feeder Canal just upstream from Washington, D.C., on the Potomac River. Even during the low-water months, there are enough waves and eddies over 500 yards to set over 50 (!) gates for any number of racers to practice on at any one time.

You don't need to have real rapids and lots of whitewater in your backyard in order to train outdoors. Check the topographic maps; visit the nearest dam. There is more whitewater around than you may think. You don't need much. The Czechoslovakian National Whitewater Team, for example, conducts much of its practice in moving current under a bridge in the heart of the city of Prague.

Mental Preparation

Lots of attention has been paid to getting in shape physically for a kayak race, and attention has also been paid to proper technique, but we are still at the threshold of knowledge about mental preparation. Physical gains are easily measurable and obviously noticeable. However, scientific data on sports psyche are still quite limited. How does one measure concentration, nervousness, anxiety, or fear of failure?

Fear of Failure

Until significant breakthroughs are made in this fascinating field of inquiry, we are limited to personal observation, coupled with the practice of strict mental discipline. Those who have entered competition are well aware that many races have been lost not because of poor physical conditioning (a National Championship was won not too many years ago by a person who had been bedridden with a 102-degree fever) or poor technique, but as a result of fear of failure. More often racers complain about the judges, the condition of the race course, the water level, the weather, the food they ate or didn't eat, the wind, the lack of sleep the night before, or the long drive to the race site. All of these items are common excuses for a deeper, underlying symptom—fear of failure.

Fear of failure, especially in our success-oriented society, is a common malady that afflicts us all in one degree or another. The thing to do is simply to recognize it for what it is, then treat its symptoms. Fear of failure manifests itself as tension. The entire body becomes tight. Movements and maneuvers that were easy in practice now feel awkward under race conditions. Fear of failure makes you think about where you're going to place in the race rather than how to get the job done. It is far better to take the approach that you are going to go out there on the river and do the very best you can. If someone is lucky enough to do better, then that person deserves to win.

A second method of dealing with tension caused by fear of failure is to get plenty of racing experience. The more you sit in that starting gate, the more you will feel accustomed to it. Experience is a wonderful banisher of worries.

Concentration

Another major mental facet of kayak racing is concentration, control of the flow of thoughts that pass through your head while on the race course. Avoid thoughts that destroy your concentration on the task at hand, such as

> "I've simply got to win this one."
> "Why do I feel so tired so early in the race?"
> "Who is that person standing on the shore?"
> "Someone shouted at me and I should answer back."
> "What if I goof gate 13?"
> "My foot is going to sleep."

Thoughts that improve concentration center on the immediate task at hand: get off to a fast start, remember to exit left immediately after gate 1, shave the upcoming rock close to the right, sneak the green pole on gate 2, head directly for gate 3, plant the Duffek immediately in front of gate 4, on to other gates and the finish.

Rarely does everything go according to plan in a race. Surely something unexpected will pop up to throw your concentration off. If such an eventuality occurs:

- Don't fuss over the problem. Utter no cry of despair or curse; don't slam your paddle down in frustration. All this does is to draw attention to the mistake and allow the valuable seconds to tick away.
- If an error has been made, there is nothing you can do about it now. Put it out of your mind instantly and start concentrating on the next item coming up on the course. Don't dwell—even for a fraction of a second—on the mistake. You have no way of knowing how well or how poorly others may be doing.

At a National Slalom Championship held in the Northwest, one racer got a 50-point penalty near the start of the course by hitting gate 2. Instead of losing heart—because there was no way he could win the national title with a 50-point penalty—he *increased* his concentration for the rest of the course and turned in such a remarkable score that he won the silver medal.

Concentration is an acquired habit. Practice it, master it, and you might reap enormous rewards later in life, where it really counts.

Just remember, nervousness, anxiety, and tension are all natural feelings that spring from fear of failure. Recognize them for what they are. Get as much experience as you can, and keep winning (or at least trying to win) in its proper perspective. A loss is not the end of the world, and a victory is only for today.

PART V.
USEFUL INFORMATION

Glossary

ACA. The American Canoe Association.

Aft. Toward the stern or rear of a kayak.

AMC. Appalachian Mountain Club.

Amidships. Midway between the bow and stern.

ARCC. American Rivers Conservation Council.

Astern. Behind the kayak.

Asymmetry. Hull shape having its widest point behind dead center front to back.

AWA. The American Whitewater Affiliation.

Backferry. See ferry.

Baidarka. Russian term for the covered skin boats of the North Pacific.

Ballast. Weight concentrated at the bottom of a kayak that increases its stability by lowering the center of gravity of the boat.

Bat boat. A shortened version of "bath boat," a snub-nosed kayak popular in the British Isles for training in indoor pools.

Beam. The transverse measurement at the kayak's widest part.

Bilge. In a cross section of a kayak hull, the point of greatest curvature between the bottom and the side.

Blasting. A squirt boat maneuver whereby a kayaker drives his stern down under the backwash of a hole and lets his bow shoot into the air above the oncoming wash.

Blind drop. Rapids, the end of which cannot be seen from the top.

Boil. A (water) current welling up into a convex mound. Often found in big eddies.

Broaching. Running a kayak up sideways against an obstacle in the river, or veering broadside to the wind or waves in a lake or in the ocean.

Bulkhead. Sealed compartment fore or aft in a kayak used for storage or flotation.

Buoyancy. The characteristic that provides good flotation for a lifejacket or for a kayak.

Cartwheel. A training exercise in which a kayak peels out of an eddy, spins around, and reenters immediately. It can be done both forward and backward.

Center of gravity. The single point of resolution of all weight in a kayak.

CFS. Cubic feet per second, the volume of flow in a river.

Channel. A navigable route through rapids or a designated stretch of water in a harbor or estuary.

Chine. The line of intersection between the side and bottom of a flat-bottom or V-bottom kayak.

Chute. A gap or drop in rapids, steeper than the surrounding water.

Coaming. The raised lip around the cockpit of a kayak.

Cockpit. The open hole in the deck of a kayak to accommodate the boater.

Crest. The highest point of a wave.

Deck. The covering for the hull of a kayak to prevent water from entering.

Draft. The vertical distance from the bottom of a kayak to its waterline.

Draw stroke. A basic kayak stroke in which the paddler plants his paddle out and away from the kayak and pulls the boat toward the paddle.

Duct tape. Common plumber's gray or silver tape used in the repair of boats. Sometimes called gray tape.

Duffek stroke. A high bracing stroke, named after the Czechoslovakian kayaker Milovan Duffek.

Ebb. The falling away of a tide.

Eddy. An area of relatively motionless water in a river, often found directly downstream of an exposed obstacle or downstream from an outcropping from a river bank.

Eddy line. The line of demarcation between the main current and an eddy. It is sometimes marked by turbulence and small whirlpools. In heavy water, this is sometimes called an eddy fence or an eddy wall.

Eddy turn. A maneuver used by a kayaker to enter an eddy.

Ender. A situation in which a kayak stands momentarily on end in a vertically upright position while surfing or playing in a roller or sousehole. Enders are also called pop ups, endos, end-overs, nose-stands, or tail-stands.

Endo. See ender.

End-over. See ender.

English Gate. A timed training exercise around a single gate. It also involves four Eskimo rolls. It helps to develop quick, precise movements and boat control. In England it is called the Wiggle Test.

Eskimo roll. A self-rescue maneuver in which the kayaker rights his capsized kayak, bringing it and himself back into an upright position.

Extended paddle roll. An Eskimo roll in which the paddle is slid forward in the kayaker's hands to obtain greater leverage.

Faltboot. See foldboat.

Feather. To recover the paddle upon completion of a stroke by leading with one edge to reduce wind or water resistance.

Feathered blades. The blades on a kayak paddle that are set approximately at right angles to one another.

Ferry. A movement laterally across a river or an ocean swell. The kayak is paddled diagonally against the current. When facing upstream, it is called an upstream ferry. When facing downstream and paddling in reverse, it is called a backferry or setting. Sometimes the maneuver is called ferry gliding.

Flatwater. Lake, river, or ocean water where no rapids or strong current exists.

Foldboat. A collapsible kayak consisting of a frame covered by a waterproof material. The kayak can be dismantled and packed into two bags. Sometimes called a Faltboot (German).

Footbraces. Part of a kayak's internal bracing system, designed to support a kayaker's feet.

Freeboard. The vertical distance from the waterline to the lowest part of the kayak's gunwale. The freeboard plus the draft should equal the kayak's depth.

Freestyle. A type of whitewater competition where judges give points based on the creativity and expertise of the kayaker in a rapids. Also called hotdogging contests or whitewater rodeos.

FRP. Fiberglass-reinforced plastic. Woven fiberglass cloth held rigid in a matrix of resin.

Gate. Two wooden poles, separated by a crosspiece, suspended over rapids. The poles are color-coded and the crosspiece is numbered to inform the slalom racer in what manner he should pass his kayak between the poles.

Grabloop. A coil of rope at each end of a kayak. Used for lifting, carrying, and tying down a kayak.

Gradient. The average rate of descent of a section of a river, usually specified in feet per mile.

Gunwale. The uppermost portion of the hull of a kayak, all the way around.

Hanging strokes. Basic maneuvers employing a paddle in which the kayaker leans out away from the boat and relies on the paddle blade in the water for stability.

Hatch. Access port on front or rear deck of a touring kayak.

Haystacks. A succession of standing waves often found toward the end of rapids.

Heavy water. Big rapids: a very large volume of water passing down a river, characterized by fast current and large standing waves.

High brace. A hanging stroke in which a kayaker leans out away from the boat with the upper paddle blade high and away from him while the lower blade digs into the water.

Hipbraces. Interior supports for the hips in the cockpit so the body will fit snugly.

Hip snap. A movement of hips, lower torso, and knees to adjust the position of a kayak. An important part of the Eskimo roll.

Hole. A depression in river water where a portion of the current is recirculating or falling back on itself. Also called: sousehole, roller, stopper, keeper, and reversal.

Hypothermia. Loss of enough body heat so that the body's core temperature begins to drop. Can lead to death if not treated promptly.

ICF. The International Canoe Federation.

Kayak. It is believed this word evolved from the Eskimo expression for a hunter's boat. It describes a small streamlined craft paddled by one or more people using double-bladed paddles.

Keel. A projecting strip along the bottom of a kayak located on the outside of the hull to improve tracking and prevent sideslipping.

Keeper. See hole.

Kevlar. An aramid fiber often used in combination with fiberglass in building kayaks.

Kneebraces. Interior support for the knees just forward of the cockpit.

Lateral resistance. The resistance of the part of a kayak below the waterline to being pushed sideways by the wind.

Lay-up. An expression used to describe the soaking in resin of two or more layers of fiberglass cloth in a mold. When done by hand, it is called a hand lay-up.

Ledge. The edge of a rock stratum in the riverbed that acts as a natural low dam or as a series of such dams.

Lee, Leeward. The sheltered or downwind side.

Left bank. The left side of a river looking downstream.

Lining. Allowing a kayak to drift down the edge of rapids while the kayaker walks along the shore holding the kayak under control with a rope. Or, pulling a kayak up rapids from shore with a rope.

Low brace. A bracing stroke in which the paddler pushes down on the water usually with the back side of a paddle blade, holding his arms and wrists in a low position.

Mold. A specially prepared shaped form from which a kayak can be constructed.

Nonpower face. The face of a paddle blade that is not being used to push water.

Nose-stand. See ender.

Paddling Jacket. A waterproof parka or anorak type of outer clothing designed to protect the kayaker from splashing waves.

Painter. A line attached to the bow or stern of a kayak.

Pawlata roll. An Eskimo roll performed with the paddle extended beyond the normal grip to increase leverage. Named after the Austrian Hans Pawlata, the first modern European to master the Eskimo roll.

Pearling. A burying of the bow in the sand or the reverse-flowing water beneath an oncoming wave.

Pillar. A structure on the interior of a kayak that reinforces the top deck. Often made of foam.

Pillow squirt. Squirt boating using the pillow in front of a large rock in rapids.

Pirouette. A maneuver in which a kayak, while doing an ender, turns before assuming a horizontal position again.

Pitch. A steep section of a rapids. Sometimes also referred to as a drop.

Pogie. Waterproof and windproof mitts that attach directly around the paddle shaft to protect the kayaker's hands. Also called wind gloves and smittens.

Polyethylene. Thermoplastic material used in construction of kayaks.

Pool. A section of the river where the current is slower and the riverbed deeper than normal.

Pop up. See ender.

Port. The left side of a kayak, facing forward.

Portage. The act of transporting a kayak between two stretches of water, or carrying it overland around a rapids.

Power face. The concave side of a paddle blade. Sometimes called the business side of the paddle.

Put-in point. The location on a river at the start of a kayak trip.

Reversal. See hole.

Reverse sweep. The same as a normal sweep except that it starts at the rear of the kayak and arcs widely out toward the front.

Riffle. A stretch of shallow water producing small waves and a little turbulence.

Right and left control. Right control indicates that the kayak's right hand remains fixed during the normal forward stroke. In left control, the kayaker's left grip remains fixed.

Right bank. Looking downstream, the right side of a river.

River left. A directional term indicating the left side of the river, looking downstream.

River right. A directional term indicating the right side of a river, looking downstream.

Rocker. The amount of upward curvature in the hull of a kayak from the center toward the bow and stern.

Rock garden. A stretch of rapids in a river heavily obstructed by rocks and boulders.

Roller. See hole.

Rudder. Directional control device on some touring and racing kayaks. Can be fixed or adjustable via foot controls.

Screw roll. An Eskimo roll performed with the paddle shaft gripped in the normal paddling position.

Sculling. A series of figure eight strokes on one side of a kayak that provides stability for the kayaker while at the same time tending to pull the kayak toward that side.

Setting. See ferry.

Shaft. The handle of a kayak paddle between the blades. Sometimes called the loom.

Sheer. The upward curve of the sides of a kayak's hull from amidships to the ends.

Shuttle. A transportation arrangement in which vehicles are parked at both the start and finish of a kayak run on a river.

Skeg. The fin on the underside or hull of a kayak, used for control.

Slalom. A race through the rapids usually not over 600 meters in length, the object of which is to pass through a numbered series of gates in order from start to finish in the shortest time.

Soup. The name given to that part of a wave that breaks and forms white foam (whitecaps) in front of it.

Sousehole. See hole.

Splash cover. See spray cover.

Splattering. A squirt boat maneuver whereby in a pillow squirt, the boat lands on the rock.

Spray cover. A neoprene or cloth material that fits over the cockpit rim and snugly around the kayaker, making the cockpit waterproof. Sometimes called a spray deck, a spray skirt, or a splash cover.

Spray deck. See spray cover.

Spray skirt. See spray cover.

Squirt boating. Pirouetting on the ends of a kayak while on flatwater, an eddy line, or in rapids.

Standing wave. A permanent wave in a river that is formed when water flows over a submerged obstacle.

Starboard. The right side of a kayak when facing forward.

Stopper. See hole.

Strainer. A river obstacle, such as partially submerged trees or bushes. If current flows through a strainer, it is possible for an unwary boater to become trapped.

Surfing. A kayaker balances his boat on a standing wave in a river. Also riding ocean waves on to a beach at the seashore.

Surf skis. Long, narrow kayaks used in the ocean.

Swamp. To fill the inside of a kayak with water.

Sweep boat. The last kayak down a stretch of river. It is the sweep's responsibility to make sure no kayakers are left behind.

Sweep stroke. A widely arcing stroke that creates a turning motion to the opposite side. There are both forward and back sweep strokes.

Tail-stand. See ender.

Take-out point. The location on the river where the kayaker finishes his run and leaves the water.

Throat. The section of the paddle shaft just above the blade.

Throw-line rescue bag. Rescue device incorporating a long rope coiled inside a nylon bag.

Thwart. A transverse brace, from gunwale to gunwale.

Tip. The extreme end of a paddle blade.

Tongue. The final stretch of smooth water at the top of a rapids at the point of a V.

Tracking. The ability of a boat to hold a straight course due to its hull design.

Trim. The angle to the plane of the water surface at which the kayak rides. A kayak can ride down at the stern or down at the bow or be trimmed evenly.

Trough. A hollow depression between two waves.

Upstream ferry. See ferry.

USCA. United States Canoe Association.

V. The angle formed by flatwater as the river approaches the top of rapids. The pointed part of the V extends down into the rapids a short way.

Volume. A measure of the total enclosed space within the shell of a kayak. Volume can also refer to the amount of water in a river.

Wake. The wave(s) a kayak makes as it travels through water.

Wave ski. A short, maneuverable kayak used for surfing.

Weathercocking. The turning in a beam gale or diagonal wind of a kayak into the wind unless proper correction is made.

Weir. A low level dam on a river.

Wet exit. The maneuver by which a kayaker extricates himself from a kayak while underwater, instead of performing an Eskimo roll.

Wet suit. A close-fitting garmet of neoprene rubber that helps hold body heat.

Whitewater. Rapids filled with a lot of aerated water.

Wildwater. A stretch of untamed rapids. Also a type of kayak race.

Windage. The wind acting on the exposed area of a kayak above the waterline.

Wind gloves. See Pogies.

Windward. The direction from which the wind is blowing.

Wind-water couple. A balance in the kayak between windage and lateral resistance so that the kayak will not turn into the wind.

Wrap around. A situation where a kayak has broached against an obstacle and is bent around it by the force of the current.

A Selected Bibliography

Below is a representative, alphabetic sampling of books and manuals for readers who wish to delve further into the sport of kayaking. All of these books may be ordered directly from the American Canoe Association, P.O. Box 1190, Newington, VA 22122 (telephone 703-550-7523) or the National Organization for River Sports, P.O. Box 6847, Colorado Springs, CO 80904 (telephone 303-473-2466).

Special Editions

The A.C.A. River Safety Report 1982–1985. By Charles Walbridge. 1986. 58 pages. $2.95. An update on *The Best of the River Safety Task Force Newsletter 1976–1982*, it contains reports of a number of fatal accidents, near-misses, and the latest ideas for safer equipment and better educational programs.

The Bark Canoes and Skin Boats of North America. By Edwin Adney and Howard Chapelle. 1964. 242 pages. $19.95. A beautifully illustrated and diagramed history of the development of hand-paddled watercraft.

The Best of the River Safety Task Force Newsletter 1976–1982. By Charles Walbridge. 1983. 99 pages. $2.95. Includes reports of 16 fatal accidents, 10 near-misses, and 6 safety programs.

The River Masters. By William Endicott. 1979. 186 pages. $9.00. A complete history of the World Championships of Whitewater Canoeing and Kayaking.

Rushton and His Times in American Canoeing. By Atwood Manley. 1968. 203 pages. $11.95. A saga of nineteenth-century American canoeing and the roots of today's multifaceted sport.

Books About Skills

Boat Builder's Manual. By Charles Walbridge. 1982. 165 pages. $10.95. A revised edition of the complete handbook for building fiberglass canoes and kayaks.

Canoeing: An Olympic Sport. By Andy Toro. 1987. 400 pages. $20.00. A thorough treatment of Olympic-style canoe and kayak racing by a former Olympic medal winner and current ICF official.

Danger Zone. By William Endicott. 1985. 365 pages. $23.00. The only full-length book on downriver (or wildwater) canoe and kayak racing in any language.

Derek Hutchinson's Guide to Sea Kayaking. By Derek Hutchinson. 1985. 122 pages. $12.95. An invaluable guide to coastal touring or touring on large bodies of water.

Kayak Cookery. By Linda Daniel. 1987. 200 pages. $9.95. A guide to kayak camping and cooking with menus and packing hints.

River Camping. By Verne Huser. 1981. 154 pages. $12.95. An introductory overview of river camping written by one of the West's most knowledgeable river experts.

River Rescue. By Les Bechdel and Slim Ray. 1985. 220 pages. $9.95. Describes the latest advances in river rescue strategy and equipment with an emphasis on preparation and prevention.

Sea Kayaking. By John Dowd. 1981. 240 pages. $8.95. A complete book for touring on open water; intended for the aspiring sea kayaker with prior background in kayaking.

The Ultimate Run. By William Endicott. 1983. 524 pages. $19.95. A must for every slalom racer, this book is an exhaustive look at whitewater racing at the international level.

Kayak Films and Videos

There has been a proliferation of films and videos pertaining to kayaking in recent years. For a current list of films and videos covering all aspects of the sport—including instruction, touring, whitewater expeditions, safety, racing, sea kayaking, and wave skiing—we recommend that you contact the following groups, who rent or sell these movies:

American Canoe Association
P.O. Box 1190
Newington, VA 22122
703-550-7523

Canadian Recreational Canoeing Association
P.O. Box 500
Hyde Park, Ont., Canada NOM 1Z0
519-473-2109

Gravity Sports Films, Inc.
P.O. Box 520553
Salt Lake City, UT 84152
801-485-3702

National Organization for River Sports
P.O. Box 6847
Colorado Springs, CO 80904
303-473-2466

Another source of information is a book available through the A.C.A.: *Filmography: A List of Canoe, Kayak, Raft, and River Conservation Films.* By Bruce Stratford. 1983. 64 pages. $5.00. The book contains an anthology of over 250 films and where to obtain them.

Manufacturers and Distributors

North America

Alaskan Kayaks
SR-1, Box 2425
Chugiak, AK 99567

Ally Pak Boats
R.D. #2, Box 165
Enfield, NH 03748

Alp
244 N. Hwy. 101
Encinitas, CA 92024

America's Cup
P.O. Box 2009
La Puente, CA 91746

Apple Line
146 Church St.
Amsterdam, NY 12010

Aquaterra
P.O. Box 1357
Easley, SC 29641

Aqua-Ventures
75 Parkton Rd.
Jamaica Plain, MA 02130

Avoncraft Canada
P.O. Box 249
Halifax, N.S., Canada B0J 2L0

Baldwin Boat Co.
R.F.D. #2, Box 268
Orrington, ME 04474

Barryville Kayak
Rt. 97
Barryville, NY 12719

Bart Hauthaway
640 Boston Post Rd.
Weston, MA 02193

Barton Paddles
6201 23½ Mile Rd.
Homer, MI 49245

Bermudes
51 Milina Dr.
E. Hampton, NY 11937

Blue Water Kayaks
Rt. 2, Box 3422
Lopez Island, WA 98261

Body Glove
530 Sixth St.
Hermosa Beach, CA 90254

California Canoe and Kayak
229 Tewksbury
Pt. Richmond, CA 94801

California Rivers
P.O. Box 1140
Windsor, CA 95492

Cal Tek Engineering
36 Riverside Dr.
Kingston, MA 02364

Campmor
817 Rt. 17 N.
Paramus, NJ 07652

Carlisle Paddles
Box 488
Grayling, MI 49738

Cedarcraft Canoe
R.R. #2, Box 1118
Clearwater, B.C., Canada V0E 1N0

Chicagoland Canoe Base
4019 N. Narragansett
Chicago, IL 60634

Class VI Whitewater
3474 S. 2300 E.
Salt Lake City, UT 84109

Colorado Kayak Supply
P.O. Box 3059
Buena Vista, CO 81211

Concorde Surf Skis
417 N. Avalon Blvd.
Wilmington, CA 90744

Current Designs
1437 Store St.
Victoria, B.C., Canada V8W 3J6

Curtis Enterprises
Hemlock, NY 14466

Dagger Paddles
P.O. Box 132
Long Creek, SC 29658

Dauber Canoe and Kayak
P.O. Box 59
Washington Crossing, PA 18977

Delta Lifejackets
110 Condor St.
East Boston, MA 02128

Dirigo Boatworks
Box 478
Blue Hill, ME 04614

Dri-Flex
34202 Johnson Landing Rd.
Scappoose, OR 97056

Dunn's Custom Built Kayaks
8991 Gowanda State Rd.
Eden, NY 14057

Easy Rider Canoe and Kayak
P.O. Box 88108, Tukwila Branch
Seattle, WA 98188

Eco-Marine Ocean Kayak Ctr.
1668 Duranleau St.
Vancouver, B.C., Canada V6H 3S4

Eddyline Kayak Works
Painefield S. Complex
Bldg. 302
Everett, WA 98204

Feathercraft
1334 Cartwright St.
Vancouver, B.C., Canada V6H 3R8

Folbot, Inc.
P.O. Box 70877
Charlestown, SC 29405

Gillies Canoes
General Delivery
Margaretville, N.S., Canada B0S 1N0

Great Canadian Canoe
65–45 Water St.
Worcester, MA 01604

Grey Owl Paddle Co.
62 Cowansview Rd.
Cambridge, Ont., Canada N1R 7N3

Harishok
R.D. 2, Box 922
Canaan, NH 03741

Hawaiian Island Wave Ski Co.
P.O. Box 579
Kalaheo, Kaua, HI 96741

Helly Hansen Drysuit
P.O. Box 1030
Redmond, WA 98052

Hoefgen Canoes
H.C.R. 1, Box 137
Menominee, MI 49858

Hydra Kayaks
3645 N.W. 67th St.
Miami, FL 33147

Hydra Tuf-Lite
5061 S. National Dr.
Knoxville, TN 37914

Iliad Paddles
208 Cherry St.
Sunbright, TN 37872

Inland Water Travel
P.O. Box 13375
Wichita, KS 67217

Innovative Sports
P.O. Box 21
Hudsonville, MI 49326

Jersey Paddler
Rt. 88W
Brick, NJ 08724

Kayak Specialties
P.O. Box 152
Buchanan, MI 49107

Klepper America
35 Union Square W.
New York, NY 10003

Kokatat
5350 Ericson Way
Arcata, CA 95521

L.L. Bean
Freeport, ME 04033

Laser West
1769 Pacentia Ave.
Costa Mesa, CA 92627

Logan Boat Co.
7318 North Honore
Chicago, IL 60626

Malibu Ocean Kayak
20585 Seaboard
Malibu, CA 90265

Mariner Kayaks
1005 E. Spruce
Seattle, WA 98122

Merlin Kayaks
R.R. #2
Yarker, Ont., Canada MAG 1W6

Mitchell Paddles
Canaan, NH 03741

Mohawk Paddles
P.O. Box 668
Longwood, FL 32750

Morley Cedar Canoes
P.O. Box 147
Swan Lake, MT 59911

Mustang Lifejackets
P.O. Box 5844
Bellingham, WA 98227

Natural Designs
4849 W. Marginal Way S.W.
Seattle, WA 98106

Necky Kayaks
#22 31550 S. Fraser Way
Clearbrook, B.C., Canada V2T 4O6

New Wave Kayak Products
2535 Round Top Rd.
Middletown, PA 17057

Nimbus Kayak Specialists
2330 Tyner St., Unit 6
Port Coquitlan, B.C., Canada V3C 2Z1

Nippenose
330 Government Place
Williamsport, PA 17761

Noah Company
71 Maple Springs Rd.
Bryson City, NC 28713

Nona Boats
322 E. Dryer Rd.
Santa Ana, CA 92707

Norse Paddles
R.D. 1
Spring Mills, PA 16875

Northstar Kayak
40 Ayer Rd.
Locust Valley
Long Island, NY 11560

Northwest Design Works
3512 N.E. 92nd
Seattle, WA 98115

Northwest Kayaks
14307 N.E. 193rd Place
Woodinville, WA 98072

Northwest River Supplies
P.O. Box 9186
Moscow, ID 83843

Ocean Kayaks Ltd.
47-664 Kam Hwy.
Kaneohe, HI 96744

Ocean River Sports
560 Johnson St.
Victoria, B.C., Canada V8W 3O6

Old Town Canoe Co.
58 Middle St.
Old Town, ME 04468

Omega Lifejackets
266 Border St.
East Boston, MA 02128

Outdoor Endeavors
840 Water St.
Fitchburg, MA 01420

Outdoor Sports Center
80 Danbury Rd.
Wilton, CT 06012

Pacific Canoe Base
2155 Dowler Place
Victoria, B.C., Canada V8T 4H2

Pacific Water Sports
16205 Pacific Hwy. S.
Seattle, WA 98188

Paddle Ski
50 Commercial St.
Plainview, NY 11803

Parkway
241 Raritan St.
S. Amboy, NJ 08879

Patagonia
P.O. Box 150
Ventura, CA 93002

Perception
P.O. Box 686
Liberty, SC 29657

Phoenix Products
P.O. Box 109
Berea, KY 40403

Poseidon Kayak Imports
Box 120
Walpole, ME 04573

Prijon/Wildwasser Imports
P.O. Box 4617
Boulder, CO 80306

Quitus Enterprises
444 Lake Mary Rd.
Flagstaff, AZ 86001

Rainbow Boatworks
Box 159
Newport, VT 05855

Rivers and Mountains
2000 Broadway
Redwood City, CA 94063

Rockwood Outfitters
699 Speedvale Ave. W.
Guelph, Ont., Canada N1K IE6

Rutabaga
820 S. Park
Madison, WI 53715

Sea Trek Ocean Kayak Center
Schoonmaker Pt., Spring St.
Sausalito, CA 94965

Seaworthy Design Ltd.
1840 N.E. Ravenna
Seattle, WA 98105

Seda Products
P.O. Box 997
Chula Vista, CA 92012

Sevylor Inflatables
6371 Randolph St.
Los Angeles, CA 90040

Sidewinder Paddles
1692 Second St.
Richboro, PA 18954

John R. Sweet
118 S. Buckhout St.
State College, PA 16801

Thule Roof Racks
One Westchester Plaza
Elmsford, NY 10523

TK Kayaks
234 San Miguel Ave.
Salinas, CA 93901

Ultrasports
3051 Edison Way
Redwood City, CA 94063

Valhalla Surf Ski Products
2148 Fairfield St.
San Diego, CA 92108

Valley Mill Boats
15101 Seneca Rd.
Germantown, MD 20874

Venture Sport
1195 N.E. 121st St., Suite 302
N. Miami, FL 33161

Voyageurs Ltd.
P.O. Box 409
Gardner, KS 66030

Wabash Valley Canoes
616 Lafayette Ave.
Crawfordsville, IN 47933

Wenonah Canoes
P.O. Box 247
Winona, MN 55987

West Side Boat Shop
7661 Tonawanda Creek Rd.
Lockport, NY 14207

White's Kayaks
P.O. Box 845
Niagara Falls, NY 14302

Wildwater Designs
230 Penllyn Pike
Penllyn, PA 19422

Yakima Roof Racks
820 N St.
Arcata, CA 95521

Great Britain

A.C. Canoe Products Ltd.
P.O. Box 62
Chester, England

Avoncraft
Burrowfield Industrial Estate
Welwyn Garden City, Herts AL74SR
    England

Baron Canoes Ltd.
Hatch Moor
Ind. Estate Great Torrington
North Devon, England

BMS Plastics (Midlands) Ltd.
Tollerton Aerodrome
Tollerton, Nottingham, England

Canoesport U.K.
97 High St., Hampton Wick
Kingston-upon-Thames
Surrey, England

Capel Canoes Ltd.
Five Oak Green
Nr. Tonbridge, Kent, England

CYMRU Canoes
St. Hilary's Rd.
Llanrhos Llandudno
Cwynedd LL30 1 PU Wales

Dolphin Wetsuits
2/4 Ashwell St., St. Albans
Herts, England

Gaybo
Bell Lane Bellbrook Industrial Estate
Uckfield, East Sussex TN22 1QL
 England

Granata Boots (CN) Ramsey
Huntingdon, England

Harishok Ltd.
Unit 3 Clarendon Trading Estate
Hyde, Cheshire, England

Howarth Sports
18 Brookdale, Belmont
Bolton, England

Insports
31–39 High Bridge
Newcastle on Tyne NE1 1ES England

Lendal Products Ltd.
18/20 Boyd St.
Prestwick KA9 1LG Ayrshire
England

Ottersports Ltd.
Ash St.
Northampton, England

P & H Fibreglass Ltd.
Old Stanley Colliery Station Rd.
West Hallam Ilkestom, Derby DE7 6JA
 England

Palm Canoes and Kayaks
Unit 15 Marsh Lane, Easton-in-Gordano
Nr. Bristol BS20 ONW England

Seasports
119 Seamer Rd.
Scarborough
YO12 4EY England

Shepperton Design Studios
76 The Green
Twickenham, England

Trylon
Wollaston Northants
NN9 7QS England

Valley Canoe Products Ltd.
Private Road Colwick Estate
Nottingham, England

Wye Kayaks
31 East St.
Hereford, England

Kayak Schools and Clinics

(See also Organizations and Clubs.)

The following organizations offer instruction in kayaking. They may range from one day or weekend clinics to courses lasting several weeks in length. The United States appears first; Canada is at the end.

P = Private Location   C = City Recreation   I = Institutional

ALABAMA

Cahaba Canoe & Kayaks Too (P)
2468 Cuchura Rd.
Birmingham, AL 35244
205-967-9241

Canoe Trails (P)
Broad & Dauphin St.
Mobile, AL 36608
205-344-6433

ALASKA

Alaska Sea Kayaking
P.O. Box 1386
Palmer, AK 99645
907-745-3487

Alaska Treks 'n' Voyages
P.O. Box 625
Seward, AK 99664
907-288-3610

Canoe Alaska (P)
1738 Hilton
Fairbanks, AK 99701
907-456-2999

Valdez Medical Clinic (P)
Box 789
Valdez, AK 99686
907-835-4811

ARIZONA

Grand Canyon Youth Expeditions (P)
R.R. #4, Box 744
Flagstaff, AZ 86001
602-774-8176

ARKANSAS

Buffalo Outdoor Center
P.O. Box 1
Ponco, AR 72670
501-861-5514

Moore Outdoors (P)
1001 N. Arkansas
Russellville, AR 72653
501-968-6324

Ozark Canoe School (P)
Rt. #2, Box 387
Springdale, AR 72764
501-756-9514

Ozark Outdoor Supply (P)
5514 Kavanaugh
Little Rock, AR 72207
501-664-4832

Take a Hike (P)
2611 Kavanaugh
Little Rock, AR 72205
501-664-2423

CALIFORNIA

Adventure Sports (P)
303 Potreo #15
Santa Cruz, CA 95060
408-423-3648

American River Recreation
11257 S. Bridge St.
Rancho Cordova, CA 95670
916-635-4479

American Touring Association (P)
1307 Harrison St.
Oakland, CA 94612
415-465-9355

Beaver Creek Lodge (P)
P.O. Box 121
Klamath River, CA 96050
916-465-2246

Big Foot Recreation (P)
30841 Walker Rd.
Horse Creek, CA 96045
916-496-3313

California Canoe and Kayak
249 Tewksbury Ave.
Pt. Richmond, CA 94801
415-234-0929

California Rivers (P)
P.O. Box 468
Geyserville, CA 95441
707-857-3872

EPIC Adventures (P)
550 S. 1st St.
San Jose, CA 95113
408-294-5676

Long Beach Water Sports (P)
738 E. 4th St.
Long Beach, CA 90802
213-432-0187

National Outdoor College (I)
11383 Pyrites Way
Rancho Cordova, CA 95670
916-638-7900

Open Passage (P)
Box 753
S. Laguna, CA 92677
714-645-7217

Otter Bar Lodge (P)
Forks of the Salmon, CA 96031
707-444-3044

Robbins Mountain Shop (P)
7257 N. Abbey Rd.
Pinedale, CA 93650
209-431-7152

Sea Trek (P)
Foot of Spring St.
Sausalito, CA 94965
415-332-4457

Sierra Kayak School (P)
P.O. Box 682
Lotus, CA 95651
916-626-3461

Ultrasports Kayak School (P)
P.O. Box 581
Lotus, CA 95651

Western Mountaineering (P)
550 S. 1st St.
San Jose, CA 95113
408-298-6300

World of Whitewater (P)
P.O. Box 708
Big Bar, CA 96010
916-623-6588

COLORADO

Aspen Kayak School (P)
P.O. Box 1520
Aspen, CO 81612
303-925-6248

Bill Dvorak's Kayak and Rafting
Expeditions, Inc. (P)
17921 Hwy. 285
Nathrop, CO 81236
303-539-6581

Boulder Kayak School (P)
2510 N. 47th St.
Boulder, CO 80301
303-444-8420

Outdoor Leadership Training (P)
P.O. Box 20281
Denver, CO 80220
303-333-7831

Rocky Mtn. Outdoor Center
10281 Hwy. 50
Howard, CO 81233
303-942-3214

Roger Paris Kayak School (P)
0171 Ute Trail
Carbondale, CO 81623
303-963-2433

CONNECTICUT

Clarke Outdoors
Rt. 7, Box 302 West
Cornwall, CT 06796
203-672-6365

Main Stream Outfitters (P)
590 Old Albany Rd.
Canton, CT 06019
203-693-6353

DELAWARE

Wilmington Canoe Trips, Inc. (P)
Wilmington Trail Club
P.O. Box 1184
Wilmington, DE 19899
302-751-5370

FLORIDA

Sea Touring Kayak Center
Key Largo, FL 32564
305-451-1108

IDAHO

Boise City Recreation (C)
Fort Boise Community Center
Boise, ID 83702
208-384-4256

Leonard Expeditions (P)
P.O. Box 98
Stanley, ID 83278
208-774-3656

INDIANA

Fluid Fun Canoes (P)
200 E. Jackson Blvd.
Elkhart, IN 46514
219-848-4279

St. Joe Valley Canoe & Kayak Club (P)
200 E. Jackson Blvd.
Elkhart, IN 46514
219-295-6915

Water Meister Sports (P)
P.O. Box 5026
Ft. Wayne, IN 46895
219-432-0011

IOWA

Mid America River Voyageurs (P)
Box 125
Spencer, IA 51301
712-262-5630

KANSAS

Trail Phernalia (P)
6404 E. Central
Wichita, KS 67218
316-684-8129

LOUISIANA

Canoe & Trail Shop (P)
624 Moss St.
New Orleans, LA 70119
504-488-8528

Delta Wilderness Outfitters (P)
1817 Veterans Blvd.
Metairie, LA 70005
504-835-1932

Outdoors Adventures (P)
410 N. 6th St.
West Monroe, LA 71201
318-387-0128

MAINE

Eastern River Expeditions (P)
P.O. Box 1173
Greenville, ME 04441
207-695-2411

Sea Touring Kayak Center (P)
123 Elm St.
Camden, ME 04843
207-236-9569

Unicorn Expeditions (P)
P.O. Box T
Brunswick, ME 04011
207-725-2255

MARYLAND

The Potomac Kayak School (P)
P.O. Box 30061
Bethesda, MD 20014
301-530-8733

MASSACHUSETTS

Aqua-Ventures
75 Parkton Rd.
Jamaica Plain, MA 02130
617-524-6239

Berkshire Outfitters
Rt. 8
Adams, MA 01220
413-743-5900

Hampshire College Kayak Program (I)
Robert Crown Center
Amherst, MA 01002
413-549-4600

Outdoor Center of New England (P)
8 Pleasant St.
Millers Falls, MA 01349
413-659-3926

MINNESOTA

The Cascaders Kayak & Canoe Club (P)
710 W. 98th St.
Bloomington, MN 53420
612-884-4315

MISSOURI

Mountain People, Inc. (P)
836 N. Glenstone
Springfield, MO 65802
417-869-0775

San Souci River Sports (P)
Rt. #5, Box 121
Joplin, MO 64801
417-623-0253

Wilderness Access (P)
4110 Baltimore
Kansas City, MO 64111
816-531-6185

MONTANA

Outdoor Resources Center (I)
University of Montana
Missoula, MT 59801
406-243-5072

The Trailhead (P)
501 S. Higgins
Missoula, MT 59801
406-543-6996

NEW HAMPSHIRE

Ledyard Canoe Club (I)
Dartmouth College
Hanover, NH 03755
603-646-2753

Saco Bound (P)
Box 113
Center Conway, NH 03813
603-447-2177

NEW JERSEY

Boats & Paddles (P)
11 Hillview Dr.
Madison, NJ 07940
201-377-5569

NEW YORK

Wild Waters (P)
P.O. Box 157
Warrensburg, NY 12885
518-494-3393

NORTH CAROLINA

Nantahala Outdoor Center (P)
Star Rt., Box 68
Bryson City, NC 28713
704-488-2175

New River Outfitters (P)
P.O. Box 433
Jefferson, NC 28640
919-246-7711

University of North Carolina at Charlotte (I)
Cone University Center, UNCC Station
Charlotte, NC 28223
704-597-2521

OHIO

Base Camp, Inc. (P)
1600 W. Mill Ave.
Peninsula, OH 44264
216-657-2110

Blackhand Gorge Canoe Livery (P)
1101 Staddens Bridge Rd.
Newark, OH 43055
614-763-4000

River Horizons, Inc. (P)
Box 395
Neapolis, OH 43547
419-875-5292

OREGON

Aquarian Enterprises (P)
1088 S.E. Oak St.
Milwaukie, OR 97222
503-233-9009

Rivers West (P)
2909 Hilyard
Eugene, OR 97405
503-686-0798

Sundance Expeditions (P)
14894 Galice Rd.
Merlin, OR 97532
503-479-8508

PENNSYLVANIA

Bottoms Up Canoe Club (I)
R.D. #2, Box 266
Pittsfield, PA 16340
814-563-7138

Coats Canoes (P)
1 Walnut Valley Rd.
Chadds Ford, PA 19317
215-388-7613

Love's Canoe Rentals (P)
Hilltop Dr., Box 17
Ridgeway, PA 15853
717-776-6285

Pocono Whitewater Center (P)
Box 44, Rt. 903
Jim Thorpe, PA 18229
717-325-3656

Riversport School of Paddling (P)
213 Yough St.
Ohiopyle, PA 15424
814-395-5744

Whitewater Challengers (P)
P.O. Box 8
White Haven, PA 18661
717-443-9532

Wildwater Outfitters (P)
46 S. Pershing Ave.
York, PA 17401
717-846-3132

RHODE ISLAND

Everett River and Mountain (P)
P.O. Box 723
Wakefield, RI 02879
401-783-4547

SOUTH CAROLINA

Alpine Outfitters (P)
P.O. Box 18143
Hillcrest Shopping Center
Spartanburg, SC 29318
803-583-8688

Wildwater Ltd. (P)
General Delivery
Long Creek, SC 29658
803-647-5336

TENNESSEE

C&C Canoe Crunchers (P)
Box 42, Rt. #1
Winchester, TN 37398
615-967-3008

Cumberland Transit (P)
2807 West End Ave.
Nashville, TN 36734
615-327-4093

Nolichucky Expeditions (P)
P.O. Box 484
Erwin, TN 37650
615-743-3221

TEXAS

Far Flung Adventures (P)
P.O. Box 31
Terlinga, TX 79852
915-371-2489

Goynes Canoe Livery (P)
Rt. #1, Box 55R
Martindale, TX 78655
512-357-6125

Whitewater Experience (P & I)
3835 Farnham
Houston, TX 77098
713-721-7299

UTAH

Bear River Kayak School
943 McClelland St.
Salt Lake City, UT 84105
801-533-9090

Moki Mac River Expeditions (P)
6829 Bella Vista Dr.
Salt Lake City, UT 84121
801-564-3361

Slickrock Kayaks
P.O. Box 1400
Moab, UT 84532
208-462-3639

Timberline Sporting Goods (P)
3155 Highland Dr.
Salt Lake City, UT 84106
801-466-2101

Whitewater Sports (P & I)
3495 W. 8245 S.
West Jordan, UT 84084
801-255-2295

VIRGINIA

Appomattox River Company (P)
P.O. Box 68, 610 N. Main St.
Farmville, VA 23901
804-392-6645

James River Experience (P)
11010 Midlothian Tpk.
Richmond, VA 23235
804-794-3493

New River Canoe Livery (P)
P.O. Box 188
Ripplemead, VA 24150
804-626-7189

Wilderness Challenge School (P)
P.O. Box 809
Norfolk, VA 23501
804-547-0117

Wind & Water Sports (P)
7720 Lisle Ave.
Falls Church, VA 22043
703-821-1053

WASHINGTON

NWOC (P)
2100 Westlake Ave. N.
Seattle, WA 98109
206-281-9694

Whitewater Sports, Inc. (P)
817 N. 1 St.
Tacoma, WA
206-627-8068

WEST VIRGINIA

Appalachian Wildwater (P)
P.O. Box 126
Albright, WV 26519
800-624-8060

Class VI River Runners (P)
P.O. Box 264
Fayetteville, WV 25862

Class VI River Runners (P)
P.O. Box 78
Lansing, WV 25862
304-574-0704

Cooper Canoes (P)
401 Dunbar Ave.
Dunbar, WV 25064
304-965-3552

North American River Runners (P)
P.O. Box 81
Hico, WV 25854
304-658-5276

Trans Montane Outfitters (P)
P.O. Box 325
Davis, WV 26260
304-259-5117

WISCONSIN

American Outdoor Learning Center (P)
Star Rt., Box 133
Athelstane, WI 54104
715-757-3811

Hike Out Ltd. (P)
#3 Menard Plaza
Wausau, WI 54401
715-842-0805

Steeds Wolf River Lodge (P)
White Lake, WI 54491
715-882-2182

Wheel & Sprocket (P)
10575 N. Forrest Home Ave.
Hales Corner, WI 53130
414-425-7930

Whitewater Specialty (P)
White Lake, WI 54491
715-882-5400

WYOMING

Snake River Kayak School (P)
P.O. Box 3482
Jackson, WY 83001
307-733-3127

Teton Mountaineering (P)
P.O. Box 153
Jackson, WY 83001
307-733-3595

CANADA

Canadian Outward Bound School (P)
P.O. Box 370
Keremos, B.C., Canada
604-499-5582

Geoff Evans' Kayak Centre (P)
Box 97
Cultus Lake, B.C., Canada V0X 1H0
604-858-6775

Madawaska Kanu Camp (P)
2 Tuna Court Don Mills
Toronto, Ont., Canada M3A 3L1
416-447-8845

Temagami Wilderness Centre (P)
RR #1(s)
Temagami, Ont., Canada P0H 2H0
705-569-3733

Publications

North America

The American Canoeist
P.O. Box 1190
Newington, VA 22122
(Newsletter of the American Canoe Association)

American Whitewater
6 Farnum St.
Cazenovia, NY 13035
(Journal of the American Whitewater Association)

Anorak
Box 444
Tuckahoe, NY 10707
(Newsletter of the Association of North Atlantic Kayakers)

Canoe
P.O. Box 3146
Kirkland, WA 98083
(Four-color magazine covering canoeing and kayaking)

Canoe News
R.R. 1, Box 262
Royal Center, IN 46978
(Newsletter of the United States Canoe Association; marathon racing coverage)

Currents
314 N. 20th St.
Colorado Springs, CO 80904
(Newsletter of the National Organization for River Sports; coverage of river rights and conservation)

Kanawa
Box 500
Hyde Park, Ont., Canada N0M 1Z0
(Journal of the Canadian Recreational Canoeing Association)

Messing About in Boats
29 Burley St.
Wenham, MA 01984
(Newsletter covering small boats)

Ocean Sports International
6-A Hangar Way
Watsonville, CA 95076
(Coverage of wave skiing, surf skiing, and sea kayaking)

Paddler
157 Silber Burch Ave.
Toronto, Ont., Canada M4E 3L3
(Newsletter with focus on Ontario canoeing and kayaking)

Paddles Up
333 River Rd.
Vanier City, Ont., Canada K1L 8H9
(Newsletter for the Canadian Canoe Association with emphasis on Olympic-style racing)

River Runner
P.O. Box 697
Fallbrook, CA 92028
(Four-color magazine covering river running)

Sea Kayaker
1670 Duranleau St.
Vancouver, B.C., Canada V6H 3S4
(Four-color magazine covering sea kayaking)

Small Boat Journal
P.O. Box 1066
Bennington, VT 05201
(Emphasis on small boats with occasional kayaking article)

Europe

Aguas Vivas
Federacion Espanola de Piraguismo
Cea Bermudez, 14
Madrid-3, Spain
(Spanish Canoe Federation magazine)

Canoa
Via Tadino 29
2014 Milan, Italy
(Italian four-color canoeing magazine)

Canoeing International
F.I.C.K. Viale Tiziano 78
00196 Rome, Italy
(Official International Canoe Federation magazine)

Canoeing Magazine
Ocean Publications
34 Buckingham Palace Rd.
London SW1, England

Canoeist
43 Primrose Close
Purley on Thames
Reading, Berks. RG8 8DG
England

CanoeKayak
403 rue de Poissy
78670 Villennes-sur-Seine
France
(French four-color magazine)

Kanu-Sport
Deutscher Kanu-Verband
Berta-Allee 8
41 Duisburg 1
West Germany
(Official magazine for the West German Canoe Federation)

Australia

Wave Ski
P.O. Box 191
Hornsby, N.S.W. 2077
Australia
(Australian surf and wave ski coverage)

National Organizations

American Canoe Association
P.O. Box 1190
Newington, VA 22122
703-550-7523

American Red Cross
17th and D Sts.
Washington, DC 20006
202-737-8300

American Rivers Conservation Council
322 4th St. N.E.
Washington, DC 20002

American Whitewater Affiliation
6 Farnum St.
Cazenovia, NY 13035
315-475-7499

Association of North Atlantic Kayakers
Box 444
Tuckahoe, NY 10707

Canadian Canoe Association
333 River Rd.
Vanier City, Ont., Canada K1L 8H9
613-784-5623

Canadian Recreational Canoeing Association
Box 500
Hyde Park, Ont., Canada N0M 1Z0
519-473-2109

Canadian Whitewater Association
12843 Crescent Rd.
Surrey, B.C., Canada V4A 2V6
604-531-8205

Eastern Professional River Outfitters
530 S. Gay St., Suite 322
Knoxville, TN 37902

Friends of the River Association
Bldg. C, Fort Mason Center
San Francisco, CA 94123

Inflatable Boat Association of America
National Marine Manufacturers Association
353 Lexington Ave.
New York, NY 10016

National Association of
Canoe Liveries and Outfitters
P.O. Box 88866
Atlanta, GA 30356
404-393-8171

National Organization for River Sports
314 N. 20th St.
Colorado Springs, CO 80904
303-473-2466

Trade Association of Sea Kayakers
P.O. Box 84144
Seattle, WA 98124

United States Canoe Association
R.R. 1, Box 262
Royal Center, IN 46978

United States Inflatable Boat
Manufacturers Association
1800 K St., Suite 1000
Washington, DC 20006

Western River Guides
7600 E. Arapahoe, Suite 114
Inglewood, CO 80112

State Organizations and Clubs

(See also Kayak Schools and Clinics)

United States

ALABAMA

Birmingham Canoe Club
P.O. Box 951
Birmingham, AL 35201

Gunwale Grabbers
1003 Inverness Lane
Birmingham, AL 35243

North Alabama River Runners
8120 Hickory Hill Lane
Huntsville, AL 35802

ALASKA

Alaska Kayak Club
5413 Emmanuel Ave.
Anchorage, AK 99504

Alaska Rivers Company
P.O. Box 827
Cooper Landing, AK 99572

Alaska Whitewater Association
Bill Kenyon
Glenn Allen, AK 99588

Juneau Kayak Club
P.O. Box 1898
Juneau, AK 99802

Knik Kanoers and Kayakers
P.O. Box 101935
Anchorage, AK 99510

Valdez Alpine Club
P.O. Box 1889
Valdez, AK 99686

ARIZONA

Arizona River Runners
25 S. Lazona Dr. #26
Mesa, AZ 85204

Dry Wash Canoe and Kayak Club
Chemistry Department
Arizona State University
Tempe, AZ 85281

Northern Arizona Paddlers Club
Rt. 4, Box 948
Flagstaff, AZ 86001

ARKANSAS

Arkansas Canoe Club
Box 1843
Little Rock, AR 72203

The Bow and Stern
1408 Rockwood Trail
Fayetteville, AR 72701

Ozark Kayak Association
Rt. 1, Box 193
Ravenden Springs, AR 72460

CALIFORNIA

Alpine West
1021 R St.
Sacramento, CA 95805

American Guides Association
P.O. Box B
Woodland, CA 95695

Antioch Whitewater Club
40 North Lake Dr.
Antioch, CA 94509

Bay Area River Touring
257 Pacheco St.
San Francisco, CA 94116

Bay Area Sea Kayakers
229 Courtright Rd.
San Rafael, CA 94901

Bear Boaters
6925 Wilton Dr.
Oakland, CA 94611

Cakara
675 Overhill Dr.
Redding, CA 96001

California Kayak Friends
Suite A-199, 1425L Culver Dr.
Irvine, CA 92714

Chasm Outing Club
Box 5622
Orange, CA 92667

Echo Wilderness
2424 Russell St.
Berkeley, CA 94705

Feather River Kayak Club
1773 Broadway St.
Marysville, CA 95901

Haystackers
212 W. Bygrove St.
Covina, CA 91722

Humboldt River Touring
650 10th St.
Arcata, CA 95521

Idlewild Yacht Club
800 Market St.
San Francisco, CA 94102

Lera Canoe Club
200 Almond Ave.
Los Altos, CA 94022

Loma Prieta Paddlers
19141 Barnhart Ave.
Cupertino, CA 95014

Lorien Canoe Club
4211 Holly Lane
Bonsall, CA 92003

Marin Canoe Club
1024-C Los Gamos
San Rafael, CA 94903

Monarch Bay Canoe Club
24371 Barbados Dr.
Dana Pt., CA 92629

National Outdoor College
P.O. Box 962
Fair Oaks, CA 95628

Offshore Canoe Club
3857 Birch St. #333
Newport Beach, CA 92660

Outdoor Adventures
688 Sutter St.
San Francisco, CA 94102

Outdoors Unlimited
Millberry Union Recreation Dept.
500 Parnassus
San Francisco, CA 94143

Powell Boating Club
Univ. California Berkeley
5499 Claremont Ave.
Oakland, CA 94618

RAFT Kayak School
Box 682
Lotus, CA 95657

Redwood Paddlers
P.O. Box 1164
Winsor, CA 95492

River City Paddlers
P.O. Box 161792
Sacramento, CA 95816

San Diego Sea Kayakers
2803 Morningside Terrace
Escondido, CA 92025

Shasta Paddlers
Box 3756
Redding, CA 96049

Sierra Club R.T.S.
629 22nd St.
Richmond, CA 94801

Sierra Club T.S.
1760 Walnut St.
Berkeley, CA 94709

Southern California Canoe Association
3966 S. Menlo Ave.
Los Angeles, CA 90037

The Confluence
P.O. Box 224
Vallecito, CA 95251

The Wheels of Industry
P.O. Box 4899
Arcata, CA 95221

Tomales Bay Kayak Club
Box 468
Pt. Reyes Station, CA 94956

Trisphere
16291 Magellan Lane
Huntington Beach, CA 92647

Truckee River Kayaks
Box 1592
Tahoe City, CA 95730

Valley Canoe Club
341 Manzanita Dr.
Los Osos, CA 93402

Ventura Olympic Canoe Club
3427 Gloria Dr.
Newbury Park, CA 91320

Voyageur Canoe & Kayak Club
12814 Arminta St.
N. Hollywood, CA 91605

West Coast Wave Ski Club
1652 Birchfield St.
Tustin, CA 92680

Western Mountaineering
550 S. First St.
San Jose, CA 95108

Whitewater Voyages
River Exploration Ltd.
1225 Liberty St.
El Cerrito, CA 94530

YMCA of San Joaquin County
640 N. Center St.
Stockton, CA 95202

COLORADO

Colorado Kayak Club
University of Colorado
Boulder, CO 80309

Colorado Rivers
P.O. Box 1386
Durango, CO 81301

Colorado Whitewater Association
7600 E. Arapahoe Rd.
Englewood, CO 80112

CSU Whitewater Club
P.O. Box 531
Fort Collins, CO 80522

Fibark
Box 151
Buena Vista, CO 81211

Otero Junior College Recreation Club
La Junta, CO 81050

Pikes Peak Whitewater Club
6436 Dewsbury Dr.
Colorado Springs, CO 80907

Rocky Mountain Canoe Club
2900 Gaylord
Denver, CO 80205

Telluride Navy
P.O. Box 888
Telluride, CO 81435

Yarmon Kayak Club
9362 W. Kentucky Place
Lakewood, CO 80226

CONNECTICUT

AMC Connecticut Chapter
50 Meadow Brook Rd.
Hamden, CT 06517

AMC Connecticut Whitewater
116 Westmont
W. Hartford, CT 06177

Amston Lake Canoe Club
Deepwood Dr.
Amston, CT 06231

Columbia Canoe Club
Lake Rd.
Columbia, CT 06237

Connecticut Canoe Racing
785 Bow Lane
Middletown, CT 06457

Connecticut River Oar and Paddle
18 Riverside Ave.
Old Saybrook, CT 06475

Fairfield Whitewater Association
100 Vermont Ave.
Fairfield, CT 06430

Farmington River Club
P.O. Box 475
Canton, CT 06019

Good Earth Inc.
539 Broad St.
Meriden, CT 06450

Great World
Riverdale Farms
Avon, CT 06001

Greenwich High School Kayak Club
10 Hillside Rd.
Greenwich, CT 06905

Hong Gong Snakes Kayak Club
22 Bushing Hill Rd.
Simsbury, CT 06070

Housatonic Canoe and Kayak
Box 105
Lakeville, CT 06039

OGRCC Family Paddlers
20 Arcadia Rd.
Old Greenwich, CT 06870

University of Connecticut Outing Club
Box 110
Holcom Hall
University of Connecticut
Storrs, CT 06268

Waterford Canoe Club
Box 111
Waterford, CT 06385

Water Works
Jewett Hill Rd.
Sharon, CT 06069

Westminster School Outing Club
Simsbury, CT 06070

DELAWARE

Buck Ridge Ski Club
R.D. #1, Box 426 E
Arthur Drive, Wellington Hills
Hockessin, DE 19707

Wilmington Trail Club
Box 1184
Wilmington, DE 19899

DISTRICT OF COLUMBIA

Potomac Boat Club
3530 Water Street N.W.
Washington, DC 20007

Washington Canoe Club
3700 K Street N.W.
Washington, DC 20007

FLORIDA

ARC
624 Court St.
Clearwater, FL 33516

Bounty Canoe Club
345 2nd Ave. N.E.
St. Petersburg, FL 33701

Buffalo Creek Canoe Club
910 E. McBerry St.
Tampa, FL 33603

Citrus Paddling Club
Rt. 1, Box 415
Floral City, FL 32636

Everglades Canoe Club
909 S.W. 27th Way
Boynton Beach, FL 33435

Florida Competition Paddling
503 67th St. N.W.
Bradenton, FL 33529

Florida Sport Paddling Club
P.O. Box 656
Ozona, FL 33560

Mugwump Canoe Club
9025 Sunset Dr.
Miami, FL 33173

Pack and Paddle Club
5080 Ponderosa Lane
W. Palm Beach, FL 33406

Polivalues
101 Maplewood Ave.
Clearwater, FL 33515

Seminole Canoe Club
3348 State Rd. 13
Switzerland, FL 32043

GEORGIA

Atlanta Whitewater Club
P.O. Box 33
Clarkston, GA 30021

Camp Merrie-wood
3245 Nancy Creek Rd. N.W.
Atlanta, GA 30327

Canoochee Canoe Racing
P.O. Box 8
Claxton, GA 30417

Central Georgia River Runners
P.O. Box 5509
Macon, GA 31207

Columbus College Canoe Club
Columbus, GA 31907

Coweta County Canoe Club
P.O. Box 1218
Newman, GA 30264

Dean's Club
6277 Roswell Rd. N.E.
Atlanta, GA 30328

Explorer Post 49
1506 Brawley Circle
Atlanta, GA 30313

Georgia Canoeing Association
Box 7023
Atlanta, GA 30309

Ogeechee Canoe Club
119 Oxford Rd.
Savannah, GA 31419

Rome YMCA WW Club
P.O. Box 727
Rome, GA 30161

HAWAII

Haleakala Canoe Club
98-410 Koauka LP, #21-C
Aiea, HI 96701

Hanalei Canoe Club
P.O. Box 814
Hanalei, HI 96714

Hawaiian Canoe Racing Association
169 S. Kukui St.
Honolulu, HI 96813

Healani Canoe Club
3455 Campbell Ave.
Honolulu, HI 96815

Honolulu Canoe Club
99-1648 Analio Place
Aiea, HI 96701

Hui Nalu Canoe Club
P.O. Box 26342
Honolulu, HI 96825

International Hawaiian
1724 Kalauokalani Way
Honolulu, HI 96814

Kailua Canoe Club
P.O. Box 177
Kailua, HI 96734

Kaiola Canoe Club
P.O. Box 3502
Lihue, HI 96766

Kai Oni Canoe Club
355 Auwinala Rd.
Kailua, HI 96734

Kai Opua Canoe Club
P.O. Box 99
Kailua Kona, HI 96745

Kanaka Ikaika Inc. Kay Club
P.O. Box 438
Kaneohe, HI 96744

Kau-I-Ke-Aouli Canoe Club
P.O. Box 4415
Kailua Kona, HI 96745

Kawaihae Canoe Club
P.O. Box 856
Kamuela, HI 96743

Kayak Club
P.O. Box 747
Kamuela, HI 96743

Keoua-Honaunau Canoe Club
P.O. Box 592
Honaunau, HI 96726

Kihei Canoe Club
25 Kaluanui Rd.
Makawao, HI 96768

Lanikai Canoe Club
P.O. Box 501
Kailua, HI 96734

Leeward Kai Canoe Club
89-889 Nanakuli Ave.
Waianae, HI 96792

Loa'a Outrigger Canoe Club
47-357-B Ahuimanu Rd.
Kaneohe, HI 96744

Maui Co. Hawaiian Canoe Association
59 Koki Place
Kihei, HI 96753

Moku O Hawaii Canoe Racing Association
400 Hualani St., #355
Hilo, HI 96720

Na Kai Ewalu
P.O. Box 483
Kahului, HI 96732

Oahu Hawaiian Canoe Race Association
933 Lunahelu St.
Kailua, HI 96734

Queen Liliuokalani Canoe Club
P.O. Box 1532
Kailua Kona, HI 96740

Waikalua Canoe Club Inc.
45-557-J Keaahala Rd.
Kaneohe, HI 96744

Wailani Canoe Club
395 Todd Ave.
Hilo, HI 96720

IDAHO

American Indian Center Canoe Club
115 N. Walnut
Boise, ID 83702

Sawtooth Wildwater Club
1255 Elm St.
Mountain Home, ID 83647

Idaho Alpine Club
P.O. Box 2885
Idaho Falls, ID 83401

Idaho Whitewater Association
1812 N. 21st
Boise, ID 83702

ISU Outdoor Program
Box 8118
Pocatello, ID 83209

ILLINOIS

American Youth Hostels
3712 N. Clark St.
Chicago, IL 60613

Belleville Whitewater Club
No. 3 Oakwood
Belleville, IL 62223

Caterpillar Canoe Club
344 W. Arnold Rd.
Sandwich, IL 60548

Central Illinois Whitewater Club
2502 Willow St.
Pekin, IL 61554

Chicago Whitewater Association
1343 N. Portage
Palatine, IL 60067

Decatur Paddlers
32 Whippoorwill Dr.
Decatur, IL 62526

Elgin Voyagueur Brigade
Rt. 1, Box 285
Elgin, IL 60120

Fox Brigade
14 Steves Farm Dr.
Elgin, IL 60177

GLOP Kayak Club
1510 Lombard Ave.
Berwin, IL 60402

Grosse Pointe Voyageur Brigade
2024 McCormick Blvd.
Evanston, IL 60201

Illini Downstreamers
4821 Wallbank
Downers Grove, IL 60515

Illinois Paddling Council
9 Pfiffer Lane
Lemont, IL 60439

ISU Whitewater Club
220 N. Main St.
Normal, IL 61761

La Brigade d'Illinois
R.R. 1, Box 548
Cary, IL 60013

La Brigade des le Loutres
815 Oakton St.
Des Plaines, IL 60018

Lincoln Park Boat Club
2737 N. Hampden Court
Chicago, IL 60614

Little Grassy Lake Camp
372 Prairie Ave.
Brookfield, IL 60513

Mackinaw Canoe Club
#711, 1st National Bank Bldg.
Peoria, IL 61602

Mt. Zion Canoe Club
30 Benton Rd.
Mt. Zion, IL 62549

Pontiac Paddlers
Motorola Dr.
Pontiac, IL 61764

Prairie Club Canoeists
703 W. Millers Rd.
Des Plaines, IL 60016

Prairie State Canoeists
3825 N. Kildare Ave.
Chicago, IL 60641

St. Charles Canoe Club
901 S. Jackson St.
Batavia, IL 60510

Sauk Valley Canoe and Kayak
507 W. 4th St.
Sterling, IL 61081

Sierra Club Canoeists
625 W. Barry
Chicago, IL 60657

South Illinois Canoe & Kayak
Rt. 2
Makanda, IL 62958

Tippee Canoers
R.R. 2, Box 55
Sullivan, IL 61951

University of Chicago Whitewater Club
933 E. 56th St.
Chicago, IL 60637

INDIANA

ARC Canoe Club
P.O. Box 3862
Evansville, IN 47737

Bloomington Canoe Club
501 E. Univ.
Bloomington, IN 47401

East Race Waterway
P.O. Box 4692
South Bend, IN 46634

Elkhart YMCA Canoe Club
200 E. Jackson Blvd.
Elkhart, IN 46516

Evansville Canoe Association
R.R. 4, Box 331C
Evansville, IN 47712

Hoosier Canoe Club
5695 N. College Ave.
Indianapolis, IN 46220

Kekionga Voyageurs
Box 110, FWNB Trust/ALBTN
Fort Wayne, IN 46801

LaFayette Canoe Club
2536 LaFayette Dr.
LaFayette, IN 47906

Maumee Whitewater Club
9962 Diebolo Rd.
Fort Wayne, IN 46825

Michiana Watershed Inc.
P.O. Box 1284
South Bend, IN 46624

Northwest Paddle Pushers
Court St.
Crown Point, IN 46307

Prairie Club Canoeists
364 Rose Ellen Dr.
Crown Point, IN 46307

Purdue Canoe Club
Purdue University
W. LaFayette, IN 47906

St. Joe Valley Canoe
200 E. Jackson St.
Elkhart, IN 46516

Sugar Creek Paddlers
R.R. 3
Crawfordsville, IN 47933

Tukunu Club
952 Riverside Dr.
South Bend, IN 46616

Whitewater Valley Canoe
1032 Cliff St.
Brookville, IN 47012

Wildcat Canoe Club
2212 Glenora Court
Kokomo, IN 46901

IOWA

Iowa Canoe Association
211 N. Olive
Maquoketa, IA 52060

Mid America River Voyageurs
Box 125
Spencer, IA 51301

KANSAS

Johnson County Canoe Club
7832 Rosewood Lane
Prairie Village, KS 66208

Kansas Canoe Association
Box 2885
Wichita, KS 67201

KENTUCKY

Blue Grass Pack & Paddle Club
216 Inverness Dr.
Lexington, KY 40503

Bluegrass Wildwater Association
Box 4231
Lexington, KY 40504

Four Rivers Canoe Club
523 Alben Barkley Dr.
Paducah, KY 42001

Kentucky Canoe Association
2006 Marilee Dr.
Louisville, KY 40272

Louisville Paddle Club
1951 Lewiston Dr.
Louisville, KY 40216

SAGE Outdoor School
209 E. High St.
Lexington, KY 40507

South Kentucky Paddlers
P.O. Box 265
Bowling Green, KY 42101

Viking Canoe Club
4410 Amelia Court
Louisville, KY 40222

LOUISIANA

Bayou Haystackers
624 Moss St.
New Orleans, LA 70119

Broken Paddle Whitewater
208 Bradford Dr.
Carencro, LA 70520

MAINE

Appalachian Mountain Club
R.R. 2, Box 2
Bridgton, ME 04009

Bangor Parks & Recreation
224 Fourteenth St.
Bangor, ME 04401

Bates Outing Club
Bates College
Lewiston, ME 04240

Hebron Academy Outing Club
Hebron Academy
Hebron, ME 04238

Mattawamkeag Wilderness Park
P.O. Box 104
Mattawamkeag, ME 04459

Penobscott Paddle & Chowder Society
77 James St.
Bangor, ME 04401

Rumford Rotary Club
625 Washington St.
Rumford, ME 04276

Saco Bound Canoe & Kayak Club
Fryeburg, ME 04037

UMM Outing Club
University of Maine at Machias
Machias, ME 04654

York Hospital Canoe Club
R.R. 1, Box 117B, Harbor Rd.
Kittery Point, ME 03905

MARYLAND

Appalachian River Runners Federation
Box 107
McHenry, MD 21541

Baltimore Kayak Club
3934 Old Columbia Pike
Ellicott City, MD 21043

Explorer Post 440
13113 Vandalia Dr.
Rockville, MD 20851

Greater Baltimore Canoe Club
P.O. Box 591
Ellicott City, MD 21043

Mason-Dixon Canoe Cruisers
222 Pheasant Trail
Hagerstown, MD 21740

Monocacy Canoe Club
Box 1083
Frederick, MD 21701

Montgomery Sycamore Island
23 Grafton St.
Chevy Chase, MD 20815

Potomac River Paddlers
18505 Kingshill Rd.
Germantown, MD 20874

St. Mary's Canoe & Kayak
St. Mary's College of Maryland
St. Mary's City, MD 20686

Terrapin Trail Club
Student Union Building
University of Maryland
College Park, MD 20742

MASSACHUSETTS

Appalachian Mountain Club,
Berkshire Chapter
Knollwood Dr.
E. Longmeadow, MA 01028

Appalachian Mountain Club,
Boston Chapter
5 Joy St.
Boston, MA 02108

Brockton High Boating Club
Azure Bldg.
Brockton High School
Belmont St.
Brockton, MA 02178

Canoe Association, Northeast
8 Cherry St.
Belmont, MA 02178

Cochituate Canoe Club
99 Dudley Rd.
Cochituate, MA 01760

Experiment with Travel
281 Franklin St., Box 2452
Springfield, MA 01101

Foxboro Community Canoe Club
Dept. 852, Bldg. 51
Foxboro, MA 02035

Greenfield Community College
College Dr.
Greenfield, MA 01002

Hampshire College Kayak Program
Hampshire College
Amherst, MA 01002

Kayak & Canoe Club of Boston
Bolton Rd.
Harvard, MA 01451

Lake Chaogg Canoe Club
P.O. Box 512
Webster, MA 01570

Massachusetts Canoe Association
P.O. Box 96
Whitinsville, MA 01588

Merrimack Valley Association
18 Alderbrook Rd.
Andover, MA 01810

MIT Whitewater Club
R 6432 MIT
Cambridge, MA 02139

Northeast Sports & Recreation Association
2 Fairmont Terrace
Wakefield, MA 01880

Northeast Voyageurs
West St.
Kingston, MA 02360

Outdoor Centre of New England
8 Pleasant St.
Millers Falls, MA 01349

Pioneer Valley Paddlers
7 Evangeline Dr.
Wilbraham, MA 01095

Puritan Canoe Club
1819 William J. Day Blvd.
S. Boston, MA 02127

Rat Pack Paddlers Inc.
P.O. Box 372
Athol, MA 01331

River Runners Canoe Club
44 Pine Hill St.
E. Taunton, MA 02718

University of Massachusetts Outing Club
R.S.O. Box 309
University of Massachusetts
Amherst, MA 01033

Upper Housatonic Canoe Recreation Club
8 Bank Row
Pittsfield, MA 01201

Wampanoag Paddlers
13 Borden St.
N. Scituate, MA 02060

Westfield River Whitewater Canoe Club
Ingell Rd.
Chester, MA 01011

MICHIGAN

Clinton River Canoe School
23705 Audrey
Warren, MI 48901

Kalamazoo Down Streamers
6820 Evergreen
Kalamazoo, MI 49002

Lansing Canoe Club
15480 S. Boichot Rd.
Lansing, MI 48906

Lower Michigan Paddling Council
8266 Patton
Detroit, MI 48228

Michigan Canoe Racing Association
Rt. 1, Box 1610
Roscommon, MI 48653

Michigan Trailfinders Club
2680 Rockhill N.E.
Grand Rapids, MI 49505

Niles-Buchanan Kayak Club
Rt. 1, Box 83
Buchanan, MI 49107

Raw Strength & Courage
1230 Asto Dr. #B2022
Ann Arbor, MI 48103

Sawyer Canoe Club
234 State St.
Oscoda, MI 48750

MINNESOTA

Big Water Associates
1905 River Hills Dr.
Burnsville, MN 55337

Boat Busters Anonymous
2961 Hemingway Ave.
St. Paul, MI 55119

Cascaders Canoe & Kayak Club
P.O. Box 61
Minneapolis, MN 55440

Minnesota Canoe Association
1091 Hawthorne Ave.
St. Paul, MN 55106

3M Canoe Club
224-4S-02, 3M Center
St. Paul, MN 55144

UMD Outdoor Program
Kirby Student Center, UMD
Duluth, MN 55812

MISSISSIPPI

Bayou Haystackers
112 Grossvenor
Waveland, MS 39576

Msubee Canoe Club
107 Freeman
Starkville, MS 39759

Paddle Pushers Canoe Club
All Saint's School
Vicksburg, MS 39180

Rapid Transit
113 Smith
Tupelo, MS 39801

MISSOURI

Arnold Whitewater Association
480 Pine Court
Arnold, MO 63010

CMS College Outing Club
c/o Biology Department
Warensburg, MO 64093

Maramec River Canoe Club
3636 Oxford Blvd.
Maplewood, MO 63143

Ozark Mountain Paddlers
P.O. Box 1581 SSS
Springfield, MO 65805

Ozark Wilderness Waterways
Box 16032
Kansas City, MO 64112

Wilderness Adventures
18 Read Hall
University of Missouri
Columbia, MO 65201

MONTANA

Adventures West
1401 1/2 5th Ave. S.
Great Falls, MT 59405

Montana Kayak Club
205 2nd Ave. S.E.
Cut Bank, MT 59427

Studies in Recreation
Dept. of HPER
University of Montana
Missoula, MT 59812

NEBRASKA

Fort Kearney Canoeists
2623 Ave. D.
Kearney, NE 68847

Midwest Canoe Association
First National Bank Bldg.
Lincoln, NE 68508

NEVADA

Basic High Canoe Club
751 Palo Verde Dr.
Henderson, NV 89015

Sierra Nevada Whitewater Club
7500 Gladstone Dr.
Reno, NV 89506

NEW HAMPSHIRE

Appalachian Mountain Club,
New Hampshire Chapter
75 Cathy St.
Merrimack, NH 03054

Coos County Cruisers
Weeks Memorial Library
Lancaster, NH 03584

Dublin School Outing Club
Dublin School
Dublin, NH 03444

Ledyard Canoe Club
Robinson Hall, Dartmouth College
Hanover, NH 03755

Merrimack Valley Paddlers
40 Dracut Rd.
Hudson, NH 03051

NEW JERSEY

Abnaki Canoe Club
Seneca Trail
Oak Ridge, NJ 07438

Appalachian Mountain Club
64 Lupine Way
Stirling, NJ 07980

Canoe Safety Club of New York
11 Overlook Dr.
Long Valley, NJ 07853

Garden State Canoe Club
142 Church Rd.
Willington, NJ 07946

Kayak & Canoe Club of New York
6 Winslow Ave.
E. Brunswick, NJ 08816

Knickerbocker Canoe Club
1263 River Rd.
Edgewater, NJ 07020

Monmouth County Canoe Club
Monmouth County Park System
Newman Springs Rd.
Lincroft, NJ 07738

Monoco Canoe Club
570 N. Lake Shore Dr.
Brick Town, NJ 08723

Murray Hill Canoe Club
52 W. Union Ave.
Bound Brook, NJ 08805

New Jersey Canoe & Kayak
20 Hastings Rd.
Lakehurst, NJ 08733

New York-New Jersey River Conference
52 W. Union Ave.
Bound Brook, NJ 08805

Outdoor Action Program
317 W. College, Princeton University
Princeton, NJ 08544

Passaic River Canoe Club
246 Madisonville Rd.
Basking Ridge, NJ 07920

Red Dragon Canoe Club
221 Edgewater Ave.
Edgewater Park, NJ 08010

Rutgers University Outdoor Club
P.O. Box 231
New Brunswick, NJ 08903

Sierra Club, New Jersey Chapter
360 Nassau St.
Princeton, NJ 08332

Sierra Club, North New Jersey Chapter
232 Elmwood Ave.
Maplewood, NJ 07040

Union Long Point Canoeing
1014 N. High St.
Millville, NJ 08332

Wanda Canoe Club
P.O. Box 723
Ridgefield Park, NJ 07660

NEW MEXICO

Adobe Whitewater Club
P.O. Box 926
Albuquerque, NM 87130

Albuquerque Whitewater Club
804 Warm Sands Dr. S.E.
Albuquerque, NM 87112

Explorer Post 20
758-47th
Los Alamos, NM 87544

Three Rivers Whitewater
P.O. Box 173
Farmington, NM 87499

NEW YORK

Adirondack Mountain Club Genesee
478 Hoffman Rd.
Rochester, NY 14622

Adirondack Mountain Club Schenectady
2917 Rosendale Rd.
Schenectady, NY 12309

Appalachian Mountain Club,
New York Chapter
56 Sandra Lane
Pearl River, NY 10965

ARC Syracuse Chapter
636 S. Warren St.
Syracuse, NY 13202

Boulder Bashers
353 Seneca Rd.
Hornell, NY 14843

Canoe Club of Niagara
College of Fine Art & Science
Niagara University
Niagara, NY 14109

Canoe & Kayak Club of Oneonta
9 Potter Ave. #2
Oneonta, NY 13820

Colgate University Outing Club
c/o Recreation Office
Colgate University
Hamilton, NY 13346

Cornell Outing Club
Cornell University
Box 28, Purcell Union
Ithaca, NY 14853

Ferry Slipp Canoe Club
39 Pier St.
Yonkers, NY 10705

Genesee Down River Paddlers
R.D. 2, Proctor Rd.
Wellsville, NY 14895

Green Mountain Club
Rt. 2, 6865 Bridge Lane
Cutchogue, NY 11935

Hibernia Canoe & Kayak
Masten Rd.
Pleasant Valley, NY 12538

Insignificant Boat Movement
R.D. 2, Echo Rd.
Vestal, NY 13850

Inwood Canoe Club
1454 Commonwealth Ave.
Bronx, NY 10460

Ka Na Wa Ke Canoe Club
238 Carbon St.
Syracuse, NY 13208

Kayak & Canoe Club
11 Main St., Box 351
Cooperstown, NY 13326

KCCNY
242 E. 50th St., Apt. 6-C
New York, NY 10022

KNIK Kanders and Kayakers
114 Pleasant Dr.
Syracuse, NY 13057

Long Island Club Kayaking
490 A Mastic Rd.
Mastic Beach, NY 11951

Metropolitan Canoe & Kayak
P.O. Box 1868
Brooklyn, NY 11202

New York Athletic Club
260 Centre Ave. #1D
New Rochelle, NY 10805

New York State Canoe Racing Association
18 Cheriton Dr.
Whitesboro, NY 13492

New York Whitewater Club
110 Bleecker St.
New York, NY 10012

Niagara Gorge Kayak Club
41 17th St.
Buffalo, NY 14213

Niagara University Canoe Club
2473 Parker Blvd.
Tonawanda, NY 14150

Nissequogue River Canoe Club
12 Hughes Lane
Babylon, NY 11703

Northern New York Paddler
P.O. Box 228
Schenectady, NY 12301

Otterkill Canoe Club
5 Yankee Main Lane
Goshen, NY 10924

Rockaway Olympic Canoe & Kayak
138 Beach 133 St.
Belle Harbor, NY 11694

Safety Service—ARC
150 Amsterdam Ave.
New York, NY 10023

Sebago Canoe Club
1751 67th St.
Brooklyn, NY 11204

Sierra Canoe Club
5 Lakeview Ave.
North Tarrytown, NY 10591

Sport Rites Club Inc.
Brayton Park
Ossining, NY 10562

Suffolk County Canoe Club
P.O. Box 114
Blue Point, NY 11715

Tasca Canoe Club
P.O. Box 41
Oakland Gardens, NY 11364

Tenandeho Canoe
711 Elizabeth St.
Mechanicville, NY 12118

The Outdoors Club
P.O. Box 227
Lenox Hill Station
New York, NY 10021

Touring Kayak Club
205 Beach St.
City Island, NY 10464

Wallkill River Rats
R.D. 3, Box 406
Pine Bush, NY 12566

Wellsville Downriver Paddlers
Proctor Rd.
Wellsville, NY 10701

Y's Men's Club of Cortland
9 Lincoln Ave.
Cortland, NY 13045

Yonkers Canoe Club
206 Sedgwick Ave.
Yonkers, NY 10705

NORTH CAROLINA

Asheville YMCA Kayak Club
30 Woodfin St.
Asheville, NC 28801

Atlantic Surf/Kayak Club
P.O. Box 2228
Greensboro, NC 27402

Camp Broadstone
Rt. 1, Box 447
Banner Elk, NC 28604

Carolina Canoe Club
Box 9011
Greensboro, NC 27408

High Adventure Outdoor
510 Larchmont Dr.
Wilmington, NC 28403

Hudson Bay Society
3324 Sunset Ave.
Rocky Mount, NC 27801

Lake Norman Canoe Club
401 Elwood St.
Kannapolis, NC 28081

Montreat-Anderson College
Montreat, NC 28757

Nantahala Outdoor Center
Star Rt. Box 68
Bryson City, NC 28713

Piedmont Paddlers Canoe Club
11724 Battery Place
Charlotte, NC 28210

Triad River Runners
P.O. Box 11283, Bethabara Station
Winston-Salem, NC 27116

Watauga Whitewater Club
State Farm Rd.
Boone, NC 28607

Western Piedmont College
Morgantown, NC 28655

The Wilderness Center
P.O. Box 2194
Greensboro, NC 27402

OHIO

Antioch Kayak Club
P.E. Dept, Antioch College
Yellow Springs, OH 45387

Cincinnati Inland Surf Team
7360 Aracoma Forest Dr.
Cincinnati, OH 45237

Columbus Council AYH
2832 Maryland Ave.
Columbus, OH 43223

Cuyahoga Canoe Club
Box T
Mantua, OH 44255

Dayton Canoe Club Inc.
1020 Riverside Dr.
Dayton, OH 45405

Keel Haulers Canoe Club
P.O. Box 30094
Middleburg Heights, OH 44130

Madhatter's Canoe Club
7690 Mary Lane
Mentor, OH 44060

Ohio Historical Canoe
P.O. Box 142039
Columbus, OH 43214

Outdoor Adventure Club
2845 Liberty Ellerton Rd.
Dayton, OH 45418

Valley Voyagers
7015 Salem Rd.
Cincinnati, OH 45230

OKLAHOMA

OK Canoers
3112 Chaucer Dr.
Village, OK 73120

Tulsa Canoeing & Camping Club
5810 E. 30 Place
Tulsa, OK 74114

OREGON

Lower Columbia Canoe Club
P.O. Box 40210
Portland, OR 97240

Oregon Kayak & Canoe Club
P.O. Box 692
Portland, OR 97207

Oregon Ocean Paddling Association
3000 S.E. 115th
Portland, OR 97266

Oregon Whitewater Enthusiasts
2909 Hilyard St.
Eugene, OR 97405

Outdoor Recreation Centre
Oregon State University
Corvallis, OR 97331

Southern Oregon Kayak Club
P.O. Box 49
Rogue River, OR 97537

Sundance Expeditions
14894 Galice Rd.
Merlin, OR 97532

Willamette Kayak & Canoe
P.O. Box 1062
Corvallis, OR 97330

PENNSYLVANIA

Allegheny Canoe Club
755 W. Spring St.
Titusville, PA 16354

Allentown Hiking Club
R.D. 3, Box 185, Hilltop Rd.
Orefield, PA 18069

Appalachian Mountain Club,
Delaware Valley Chapter
476 Kerr Lane
Springfield, PA 19064

Benscreek Canoe Club
P.O. Box 2
Johnstown, PA 15907

Bottoms Up Canoe Club
R.D. 2, Box 266
Pittsfield, PA 16340

Boy Scout Troop 30
Sunnyside Lane
Yardley, PA 19067

Boy Scout Troop 99
1400 Park Rd.
Lancaster, PA 17601

Bucknell Outing Club
Bucknell University
Lewisburg, PA 17837

Bucks County Whitewater Club
3241 Lower Mountain Rd.
Furlong, PA 18925

Canoe Club of Greater Harrisburg
R.D. 3, Box 332B
Andersontown Rd.
Dover, PA 17315

Conewago Canoe Club
113 Harrisburg Pike
Dillsburg, PA 17019

Delaware Canoe Club
610 Pardee St.
Easton, PA 18042

Delaware Valley AYH
35 S. 3rd St.
Philadelphia, PA 19106

Endless Mountain Voyageur
285 Shorthill Rd.
Clarks Green, PA 18411

Explorer Post 65
22 Caralpa Place
Pittsburgh, PA 15228

Fort Pitt Paddlers Inc.
1401 Maple Dr., Apt. #8
Pittsburgh, PA 15227

Fox Chapel Canoe Club
610 Squaw Run Rd.
Pittsburgh, PA 15238

Harrison Area Community College
Outdoor Club
3300 Cameron St.
Harrisburg, PA 17110

Keystone Canoe Club
202 Hancock Blvd.
Reading, PA 19601

Keystone River Runners
R.D. 6, Box 359
Indiana, PA 15701

Lancaster Canoe Club
442 S. Broad St.
Lititz, PA 17543

Lehigh Valley Canoe Club
Box 2726
Lehigh Valley, PA 18001

Mohawk Canoe Club
1035 Gravel Hill Rd.
Southampton, PA 18966

Mohawk Canoe Club
6 Canary Rd.
Levittown, PA 19057

Oil City Canoe Club
Rt. 62, Road 2
Oil City, PA 16301

Penn Hills Wildwater Canoe Club
12200 Garland Dr.
Pittsburgh, PA 15235

Penn State Outing Club, Canoe Division
4 Intramural Bldg.
University Park, PA 16802

Penn State Univ-Allentown
Campus Outdoors Club
Fogelsville, PA 18051

Pennsylvania Association Canoe & Kayak
113 Edward St.
Athens, PA 18810

Pennsylvania Paddle Packers
Box 346
Secane, PA 19018

Philadelphia Canoe Club
4900 Ridge Ave.
Philadelphia, PA 19128

Pittsburgh Council AYH
6300 Fifth Ave.
Pittsburgh, PA 15232

Post 42 BSA
Rt. 2
Palmerton, PA 19053

Raystown Canoe Club Inc.
Box 112
Everett, PA 15537

Slippery Rock State College Outing Club
Slippery Rock, PA 16057

Sylvan Canoe Club
132 Arch St.
Verona, PA 15213

Three Rivers Paddling Club
115 Delaney Dr.
Pittsburgh, PA 15235

Three Rivers Paddling Club
276 Thompsonville Rd.
McMurray, PA 15317

TUP Outing Club
Indiana University of Pennsylvania
Student Union Bldg.
Indiana, PA 15701

Wildwater Boating Club
R.D. 179
Bellefonte, PA 16823

Wildwater Rafting Club
326 W. Gay St.
York, PA 17404

Williamsport Outing Club
1005 W. 3rd St.
Williamsport, PA 17701

RHODE ISLAND

Appalachian Mountain Club
63 State St.
Westerly, RI 02891

Brown Outing Club
S.A.O. #3
Brown University
Providence, RI 02912

Rhode Island Canoe Association
20 Knowles St.
Lincoln, RI 02865

Rhode Island Whitewater Club
10 Pond St.
Wakefield, RI 02879

SOUTH CAROLINA

Carolina Paddlers
112 Pine St.
Walterboro, SC 29488

Carolina Wildwater Canoeing
3412 Harvard Ave.
Columbia, SC 29205

Pallmetto Paddlers
1920 Marley Dr.
Columbia, SC 29210

Savannah River Paddlers
Explorer Ship 211, Sea Scout 404
1211 Woodbine
Aiken, SC 29801

Sierra Club, Canoe Section
P.O. Box 463
Clemson, SC 29631

Sierra Club, Canoe Section
200 Saxum Way
Greenville, SC 29611

University of South Carolina
Whitewater Club
P.O. Box 80090
Columbia, SC 29225

TENNESSEE

Baylor Walkabout
P.O. Box 1337
Chattanooga, TN 37401

Bluff City Canoe Club
P.O. Box 40523
Memphis, TN 38104

Canoe & Hiking Club
2106 Andy Holt Ave.
Student Aquatic Center
Knoxville, TN 37916

Carbide Canoe Club
104 Ulena Lane
Oak Ridge, TN 37830

Chota Canoe Club
P.O. Box 8270
University Station
Knoxville, TN 37996

Knoxville Canoe & Kayak
530 S. Gay St., Suite 222
Knoxville, TN 37902

Sewanee Ski & Outing Club
University of the South
Sewanee, TN 37375

Tennessee Eastmen Recreation Club
P.O. Box 511
Kingsport, TN 37662

Tennessee Scenic Rivers Association
P.O. Box 159041
Nashville, TN 37215

Tennessee Valley Canoe Club
Box 11125
Chattanooga, TN 37401

Tenn-Tucky Lake Canoe-Camping Club
Rt. 1, Box 23-A
Tennessee Ridge, TN 37178

TEXAS

Austin Sierra Club
1002 Elm St.
Austin, TX 78703

Bayou City Whitewater Club
8323 Wilcrest #10002
Houston, TX 77072

Big Thicket Voyageurs
308 Pine
Port Neches, TX 77651

Down Hill Yacht Club
12802 La Quinta
San Antonio, TX 78233

Explorer Post 151
2008 Bedford
Midland, TX 79701

Explorer Post 425
708 Mercedes
Fort Worth, TX 76126

Goose Creek Canoe Club
P.O. Box 3128
Baytown, TX 77522

Greater Fort Worth Sierra, Touring Section
P.O. Box 1057
Fort Worth, TX 76101

Heart of Texas Canoe Club
Box 844
Temple, TX 76501

Houston Canoe Club
P.O. Box 61588
Houston, TX 77208

North Texas River Runners
5709 MacGregor Dr.
Fort Worth, TX 76117

Permian Basin Whitewater Association
501 E. 56th St.
Odessa, TX 79762

Texas Canoe Racing Association
102 Fawn Trail
Lake Jackson, TX 77566

Texas Explorers Club
Box 844
Temple, TX 76501

Texas Whitewater Association
P.O. Drawer 5429
Austin, TX 78763

TMI Canoe Club
800 College Blvd.
San Antonio, TX 78205

UTAH

VTE Alpine Club—River Trips
Union Bldg., University of Utah
Salt Lake City, UT 84112

Wasatch Mountain Canoe Club
904 Military Dr.
Salt Lake City, UT 84108

Wasatch Whitewater Association
161 S. 11 E.
Salt Lake City, UT 84102

VERMONT

Brattleboro Outing Club
P.O. Box 335
Brattleboro, VT 05301

Johnson Whitewater Club
Box 649
Johnson State College
Johnson, VT 05656

Marlboro College Outdoor
Marlboro, VT 05344

Northern Vermont Canoe
L-10 Stonehedge Dr.
S. Burlington, VT 05401

North Vermont Canoe Cruisers
R.D. 4
Enosburg Falls, VT 05450

West River Whitewater Association
R.D. 4, Box 661
W. Brattleboro, VT 05301

VIRGINIA

Blue Ridge River Runners
120 Kenwood Dr.
Lynchburg, VA 24502

Blue Ridge Voyageurs
1610 Woodmoor Lane
McLean, VA 22101

Canoe Cruisers Association
Box 572
Arlington, VA 22216

Coastal Canoeists
P.O. Box 566
Richmond, VA 23204

Collegiate Schools Canoe
Moreland Rd.
Richmond, VA 23229

Danville Canoe Club
P.O. Box 3300
Danville, VA 24541

Explorer Post 999
3509 W. Colonial Dr.
Hopewell, VA 23860

Greater Rappahannock Whitewater
1209 Powhatan St.
Fredericksburg, VA 22401

James River Basin Canoe
R.F.D. 4, Box 109-A
Lexington, VA 24450

Roanoke Valley ARC
352 Church St. S.W.
Roanoke, VA 24016

University of Virginia Outing Club
Box 101X
Charlottesville, VA 22903

WASHINGTON

Boeing Employees Whitewater &
Touring Club
15804 47th St. S.
Seattle, WA 98188

Desert Kayak & Canoe Club
450 Mateo Court
Richland, WA 99352

North Sound Sea Kayak Association
9018 10th Place S.E.
Everett, WA 98205

Pacific Water Sports
1273 S. 188th
Seattle, WA 98195

Paddle Trails Canoe Club
8909 27th Ave. N.E.
Seattle, WA 98115

Puget Sound Paddle Club
14603 29th Ave. Court
Tacoma, WA 98445

Seattle Washington Canoe Club
6019 51 N.E.
Seattle, WA 98115

Spokane Canoe & Kayak Club
W. 4625 Bonnie Dr.
Spokane, WA 99204

Tacoma Mountaineers
Kayak & Canoe Committee
3512 Crystal Spring
Tacoma, WA 98466

Takoma Kayak & Canoe Club
3512 Crystal Spring
Tacoma, WA 98466

University of Washington Canoe Club,
Intramural Activity
University of Washington Bldg. 6D-10
Seattle, WA 98195

Washington Kayak Club
P.O. Box 2527
Seattle, WA 98111

Washington Paddle Trails Canoe Club
9510 20th N.E.
Seattle, WA 98115

Western Trek Canoe Club
5037 S. Maniton Way
Tacoma, WA 98409

Whatcomb Association
P.O. Box 1952
Bellingham, WA 98227

WEST VIRGINIA

Canoe Association of West Virginia
111-18th St. E.
Wheeling, WV 26003

Shepherd Outing Club
Shepherd College
Shepherdstown, WV 25443

West Virginia Wildwater Association
P.O. Box 8413
S. Charlestown, WV 25303

Whitewater Canoe Club
Mt. Lair Recreation Center
West Virginia University
Morgantown, WV 26506

WISCONSIN

American Outdoor Learning Center
Box 133, Star Rt.
Athelstane, WI 54104

Madison Canoe & Kayak
4945 Black Oak Dr.
Madison, WI 53711

Northeast Wisconsin Paddling Society
Rt. 4, Box 657-E
Shawano, WI 54166

Pack & Paddles Outing Club
331 10th St. N.
Wisconsin Rapids, WI 54494

Piers Gorge Wildwater Ltd.
P.O. Box 84
Niagara, WI 54151

Rock River Canoe Association
P.O. Box 691
Janesville, WI 53547

Sierra Club, John Muir Chapter
2372 Kimberly Lane
Green Bay, WI 54303

Trippers Outing Club
University of Wisconsin
Stevens Pt., WI 54481

University of Wisconsin
Lacrosse Recreation Dept.
Michell Hall, University of Wisconsin
Lacrosse, WI 54601

Wausau Whitewater Kayak Club
909 Ethel St.
Wausau, WI 54401

Wisconsin Canoe Association
100 West Lane
Mosinee, WI 54455

Wisconsin Hoofers Outing Club
800 Langdon St.
Madison, WI 53706

Wisconsin Whitewater River Runners
5530 W. Coldspring Rd.
Milwaukee, WI 53220

Wolf River Canoe Club
Wolf River Lodge
Yellow Brick Rd.
White Lake, WI 54491

WYOMING

Snake River Yacht Club
P.O. Box 290
Teton Village, WY 83025

Outside the United States

ARGENTINA

Federacion Argentina de Canoas
Ave. Pte Roque Saenz Pena 615, 9°,
Officina 905
1393 Buenos Aires, Argentina

AUSTRALIA

Australian Canoe Federation
157 Gloucester St., Room 510, Sports House
Sydney, N.S.W. 2000, Australia

Indooroopilly Canoe Club
Box 36, Indooroopilly
Queensland, Australia

Tasmanian Sea Canoeing Club
P.O. Box 599F
Habart, Tasmania 7001 Australia

AUSTRIA

Osterreichischer Kanu Verband
Berggasse 16
1090 Wien, Austria

BELGIUM

Royal Belgian Canoe Fédération
2800 Mechelen, Belgium

BRAZIL

Carioca Canoeing Association
Ave. Grande Canal 285, Barra de Tijuca
Rio de Janeiro, Brazil

BULGARIA

Bulgarian Canoe Federation
Bulevar Tolbuhina 18
Sofia, Bulgaria

CANADA

Alberta Recreational Canoeing Association
Box 10, Site 20
R.R. #2
Calgary, Alta., Canada T2P 2G5

B.C. Ocean Kayaking Association
Box 1574
Victoria, B.C., Canada V8W 2X7

B.C. Sea Kayakers
16064 80th Ave.
Surrey, B.C., Canada V3S 2J7

British Columbia Recreational
Canoeing Association
Canoe Sport British Columbia
1200 Hornby St.
Vancouver, B.C., Canada V6Z 1Z2

Canadian Canoe Association
333 River Rd., Tower C, 10th Floor
Ottawa, Ont., Canada K1L 81-19

Canoe Nova Scotia
P.O. Box 3010 S.
5516 Spring Garden Rd.
Halifax, N.S., Canada B3J 3G6

Dean MacLeod
28A 380 Assinaboine Ave.
Winnipeg, Man., Canada R3C 0Y1

Fédération Québecoise de Canoe Camping
4545 Ave. Pierre de Coubertin
C.P. 1000
Succursale M
Montreal, Que., Canada H1V 3R2

New Brunswick Recreational
Canoeing Association
C.P. 220
Kedgwick, N.B., Canada E0K 1C0

Newfoundland Canoe Association
P.O. Box 5961
St. John's, Newfoundland, Canada A1C 5X4

N.W.T. Recreational Canoeing Association
P.O. Box 2763
Yellowknife, N.W.T., Canada X1A 2R1

Ontario Recreational Canoeing Association
1220 Sheppard Ave. E.
Willowdale, Ont., Canada M2K 2X1

Prince Edward Island
Recreational Canoeing Association
P.O. Box 2000
Charlottetown, P.E.I., Canada C1A 7N8

Saskatchewan Canoe Association
P.O. Box 6064
Saskatoon, Sask., Canada S7K 4E5

Yukon Recreational Canoeing Association
5131 5th Ave.
Whitehorse, Yukon, Canada Y1A 1L8

CHILE

Federacion Chilena de Canotaje
Compania 2982, Casilla 154
Santiago, Chile

PEOPLE'S REPUBLIC OF CHINA

Chinese Canoe Association
9, Tiyukuan Rd.
Peking, People's Republic of China

COSTA RICA

Costa Rica Canoe Federation
Apartado 472-1200
Pavas, Costa Rica

CUBA

Federacion Cubana de Canotaje
Via Blanca y Boyeros, Suidad Deportiva
La Habana, Cuba

CYPRUS

Cyprus Canoe Association
P.O. Box 4222
Nicosia, Cyprus

CZECHOSLOVAKIA

Československy Svaz Kanoistiky
Na Poriči 12
11530 Praha 1 Č.S.S.R.

DENMARK

Dans Kano of Kajak Forbund
Id raettens Hus
DK-2605 Brøndby, Denmark

FINLAND

Suomen Kanoottiliitto ry
Radiokatu 12
00240 Helsinki 25 Finland

FRANCE

Connaissance du Kayak de Mer
BP 67B
22500 Paimpol, France

Fédération Française de Canoe-Kayak
17 Route de Vienne
69007 Lyon, France

GERMANY (EAST)

Deutscher Kanu-Sport Verband der DDR
Storkower Strasse 118
1055 Berlin, German Democratic Republic

GERMANY (WEST)

Deutscher Kanu-Verband
Berta-Allee 8
4100 Duisburg 1 Federal Republic of Germany

Salz-Wasser Union
Reinhauser Landstr. 44
D-3400 Gottingen
Federal Republic of Germany

GREAT BRITAIN

British Canoe Union
Flexel House, 45/47 High St.
Addlestone-Weybridge,
Surrey KT15 1JV Great Britain

International Long River Canoeist Club
238 Birmingham Rd.
Redditch, Worcs., England B97 6EL

The Advanced Sea Kayak Club
4 Wavell Garth
Sandal, Wakefield, W. Yorkshire
England WF2 6JP

GREECE

Athletic Club of Neo Petritsi
24 Mikinon St. 24
54643 Thessaloniki, Greece

HONG KONG

Hong Kong Canoe Union
Queen Elisabeth Stadium, Room 1010
18 Oi Kwan Rd., Wan Chai
Hong Kong, Hong Kong ˙

HUNGARY

Magyar Kajak-Kenu Szövetseg
Dòzsa György Ut. 1–3
1143 Budapest, Hungary

INDIA

Indian Kayaking & Canoeing Association
606, Akash Deep, 6th Floor–Barakhambra Rd.
New Delhi–110001 India

INDONESIA

Indonesian Canoe Association
Jalan Prapatan 38
Jakarta 10410 Indonesia

IRAN

Canoe-Kayak & Water Ski Federation
10, Ave. Varzandeh, Mejab
Teheran-Amjadieh, Islamic Republic of Iran

IRELAND

Irish Canoe Union
4/5 Eustace St.
Dublin 2 Ireland

ISRAEL

Israel Canoe Association
4 Marmorek St., P.O.B. 4575
6104 Tel Aviv, Israel

ITALY

Federazione Italiana Canoa Kayak
Viale Tiziano 70
00196 Roma, Italia

IVORY COAST

Fédération Ivorienne de Pirogue
01 B.P. 4733
Abidjan, Ivory Coast

JAPAN

Japan Canoe Federation
Kishi Memorial, 1–1–1 Jinnan, Shibuya-ku
Tokyo, Japan

KOREA (NORTH)

Canoe Association of the DPR Korea
Munsin-Dong 2, Dongdawon District
Pyongyang, DPR of Korea

KOREA (SOUTH)

Korean Canoe Federation
19, Mookyodong, Jung-gu
KASSA Bldg., Rm. 605
Seoul 100 Korea

LUXEMBOURG

Fédération Luxembourgeoise
de Canoe-Kayak
6, Rue du Pulvermühle
2356 Luxembourg, Luxembourg

MALAYSIA

Malaysia Canoe Association
13, Jalan Bungah Orchid
Hillside Tanjong Bungah
Penang, Malaysia

MALTA

Canoeing Association of Malta
Dipartiment ta`1–Edukazzjoni Lascaris
Valletta, Malta

MEXICO

Federacion Mexicana de Canotaje
Xola 1301–41
Mexico 03020, D.F., Mexico

NETHERLANDS

Nederlandse Kano Bond
Ut rechtseweg 17, Postbus 434
1380 Ak Weesp, Netherlands

NEW ZEALAND

New Zealand Canoeing Association Inc.
P.O. Box 3768
Wellington, New Zealand

NORWAY

Norges Kajak og Kanoforbund
Hauger Skolovei 1
1351 R.U.D., Norway

PANAMA

Union Panamena de Canotaje
Apartado 2927, Panolimpic
Panama 3 Republic de Panama

POLAND

Polski Zwiazek Kajakowy
Ul. Sienkiewicza 12, Pok. 433
00-010 Warszawa, Poland

PORTUGAL

Federacao Portuguesa de Canoagem
Rua Antonio Pinto Machado 60
4100 Porto, Portugal

ROMANIA

Federatia Romana de Caiac-Canoe
Str. Vasile Conta 16
70139 Bucarest, Rumania

SENEGAL

Fédération Sénégalaise de Régates
B.P. 517 (Mr. Bouna Gaye)
Dakar, Senegal

SINGAPORE

Singapore Canoe Association
585 N. Bridge Rd., 10-03 Blanco Court
Singapour 0718 Singapore

SOUTH AFRICA

South African Canoe Federation
P.O.B. 889
7130 Somer Set W., South Africa

SPAIN

Federacion Espagnola de Piraguismo
Cea Bermudez 14, 1°
Madrid 3 Spain

SWEDEN

Svenska Kanotförrbundet
Idrottens Hua
123 87 Farsta, Sweden

SWITZERLAND

Schweizerischer Kanu Verband
Obere Rebgasse 570
CH 4314, Zeiningen, Switzerland

URUGUAY

Federacion Uruguaya de Canotaje
Canelones 978/982, Casa de los Deportes
Montevideo, Uruguay

U.S.S.R.

Canoe Federation of the U.S.S.R.
Loujnetzkaya Nab. 8
Moskow, U.S.S.R.

VENEZUELA

Federacion Venezolana de Canotaje
Apartado de Coreos Nr 75224
Caracas 10701 Venezuela

YUGOSLAVIA

Kajakaški savez Jugoslavije
Bulevar revolucije 44
11000 Beograd, Yugoslavia

Index